Henry Playford

Wit and Mirth

Or, pills to purge melancholy; being a collection of the best merry ballads and songs, old and new

Henry Playford

Wit and Mirth

Or, pills to purge melancholy; being a collection of the best merry ballads and songs, old and new

ISBN/EAN: 9783744781701

Printed in Europe, USA, Canada, Australia, Japan

Cover: Foto ©Thomas Meinert / pixelio.de

More available books at **www.hansebooks.com**

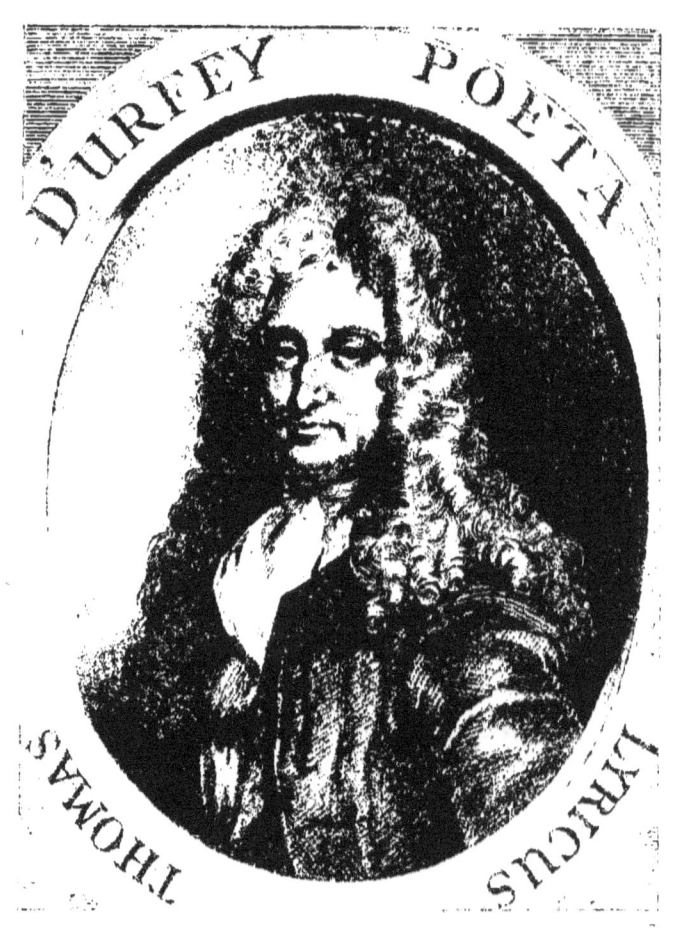

Whilst D'urfey's voice his verse do's ruise,
When Durfey sings his Tunefull Layes,
Give Durfeys Lyrick-Muse the Bayes

F. G.

SONGS Compleat,

Pleasant and Divertive;

SET TO

MUSICK

By Dr. JOHN BLOW, Mr. HENRY PURCELL, and other Excellent Masters of the Town.

Ending with some ORATIONS, made and spoken by me several times upon the PUBLICK STAGE in the THEATER. Together with some Copies of VERSES, PROLOGUES, and EPILOGUES, as well for my own PLAYS as those of other Poets, being all Humerous and Comical.

Written by Mr. D'URFEY.

Omne tulit punctum qui miscuit utile dulci.
Hor.

L O N D O N:
Printed by *W. Pearson*, for *J. Tonson*, at SHAKESPEAR'S Head, against *Catherine* Street in the *Strand*, 1719.

To the Right Honourable the Lords *and* Ladies, *and also to the Honoured* Gentry *of both kinds, that have been so Generous to be* Subscribers *to these Volumes of SONGS; which end with some* Orations, *Copys of Verses,* Prologues *and* Epilogues.

My Lords, Ladies and Gentry,

I Once thought to have been particular in my *Dedication,* and have assign'd it to one or two of the Nobility or Gentry; but considering that it would

lessen

Dedication.

lessen the Value I have for the rest of my Noble *Subscribers*, I have desisted in that particular; and hope this General Address will more exert my Duty, and increase your Favour.

I am oblig'd first then to acknowledge my Obligations for your ready and willing Compliance: And also secondly to declare, that to oblige ye, and compleat your Diversion, I have added above a Hundred new Pieces to the *Publick Stock*, and hope, as the rest have generally had Applause above others of this kind, they will happily be receiv'd by you when read or perform'd in your merry and vacant Hours.

I have (with a great deal of Trouble and Pains) made some part of this Collection, and render'd ye many of the Old Pieces which were thought well of in former Days, and consider'd for their Pleasure and

Dedication.

and Hardness of their Composition; being written, and difficultly made apt, and proper to wonderful and uncommon Tunes, which the best Masters of Musick were then famous for: And I must presume to say, scarce any other Man could have perform'd the like, my double Genius for *Poetry* and *Musick* giving me still that Ability which others perhaps might want; nor was the Encouragement inconsiderable; for as well as obliging the Nobility, Gentry, and Commonalty, I had the Satisfaction of diverting Royalty likewise with my Lyrical Performances: And when I have perform'd some of my own Things before their Majesties King *CHARLES* the IId, King *JAMES*, King *WILLIAM*, Queen *MARY*, Queen *ANNE*, and Prince *GEORGE*, I never went off without happy and commendable Approbation. The Remembrance of my Success at that time, makes me hope the present Affair,

Dedication.

My Noble Lords, Ladies and Gentry, will add to your Pleasure, and divert your Hours, when your Thoughts are unbended from the Times, Troubles, and Fatigues; to be assur'd of which, will be a perpetual Satisfaction to

Your most Humble,

Oblig'd, and

Devoted Servant,

T. D'URFEY.

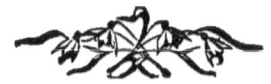

AN

AN
Alphabetical TABLE
OF THE
SONGS and POEMS
Contain'd in this
BOOK.

A
	Page
A Tory, *a Whigg, and a moderate Man*,	8
As far as the glittering God of Day,	61
Arise my Muse, and to thy tuneful Lyre,	62
As the Delian God to fam'd Halcyon,	104
All the World's in Strife and Hurry,	110
All you that either hear or read,	129
Ah, how sweet are the cooling Breez,	138
As soon as the Chaos,	145
At Winchester *was a Wedding*,	276
Ah! Phillis *why are you less tender*,	279
And in each Track of Glory since,	285
Amynta *one Night had occasion to p——*	336

B
B Ritains *now let Joys increase*,	26
Behold, behold the Man that with,	73
Blow, blow Boreas *blow, and let thy*	96

Behold

An Alphabetical TABLE.

Behold how all the Stars give way,	111
Blowzabella *my bouncing Doxy*,	194
Bright was the Morning, cool was,	261
Beat the Drum, beat, beat the,	269

C

*C*Hurch Scruples and Jars plunge all,	87
Come all, great, small, short, tall,	91
Celemene, *pray tell me*,	109
Celadon, *when Spring came on*,	179
Come Jug, *my Hony, let's to bed*,	293
Chloe *found* Amyntas *lying*,	329

D

*D*Raw, draw the Curtain, fye,	108
Damon *turn your Eyes to me*,	256
Dear Pinckaninny, if half a Guinea,	283
De'l take the War that hurry'd,	295

F

*F*Rom rosie Bowers where sleeps the God,	1
Fame and Isis *joyn'd in one*,	17
From glorious Toyls of War,	50
From azure Plains, blest with eternal,	113
Flow the flow'ry Rain,	122
Farewel the Towns ungrateful Noise,	126
Fame loudly thro' Europe *passes*,	146
For too many past Years with,	175
Fill every Glass, and recommend 'em,	182
From Dunkirk *one Night they stole*,	225
Fly, fly from my Sight, fly far away,	236
Fate had design'd this worst of all,	243
Fareweel my bonny, bonny witty,	252

G

*G*Iovani amanti voi chi Sapete,	12
Great Lord Frog *to Lady Mouse*,	14
Grand Lewis *let Pride be abated*,	78
Great Cæsar *is crown'd*,	120
Groves and Woods, high Rocks and,	172
Genius *of* England, *from thy*,	219
Grand Louis *falls headlong down*,	223
Great Jove *once made Love like*,	280

Hark

An Alphabetical TABLE.

H

H<i>Ark</i>, Lewis *groans, good Fader*, 244
How vile are the sordid Intrigues, 297
Hark the thundring Cannons roar, 300
Hark, the Cock crow'd, 'tis Day all abroad, 311

I

J<i>Olly</i> Roger *twangdillo of*, 19
In Kent *so fam'd of old*, 45
I burn, I burn, I burn, I burn, 76
Jug, jug, jug, jug, jug, jug, 85
In old Italian *Tales we read*, 125
In Kent *I hear there lately did dwell*, 127
If you will love me, be free in 164
I hate a Fop that at his Glass, 177
If a woful sad Ditty to know thou, 203
Jockey *was a dawdy Lad*, 289
In January *last, on* Munnonday, 306
Joy to the Bridegroom, 323

L

L<i>ET</i> the dreadful *Engines*, 48
Lord! what's come to my Mother, 157
Le printems, r'apelle aux Armes, 189
Life's short Hours too fast are hasting, 221
Lads and Lasses blith and Gay, 305

M

M<i>Aiden fresh as a Rose</i>, 57
Mad Loons of Albany, 149
Monsieur looks pale, 161
Madam je vous prie *you will right me*, 201
Monsieur grown too mighty, 208
Musing of late on Windsor, 232
My dear Cock adoodle, 308

N

N<i>OW, now comes on the glorious</i>, 27
Now Cannon smoke Clouds all, 59
Now over England *Joy to express*, 116
Now some Years are gone, 118
Near famous Covent-Garden, 143
Now is the Sun, 187

One

An Alphabetical TABLE.

O

O NE Sunday at St. James's Prayers, 10
One long Whitson Holiday, 39
Old Lewis must thy frantick Riot, 66
One April Morn, when from the Sea, 69
Oh Love, if a God thou wilt be, 101
Of old, when Heroes thought it base, 114
Opening Budds began to shew, 121
Of all noble Sports, 150
One Morn as lately Musing, 153
Oh Jenny, Jenny, where hast thou been, 169
Of all the simple things we do, 250
Of all the World's Enjoyments, 269
On the Brow of Richmond Hill, 303

P

P Ray, now John let Jug prevail, 141
Pastorella inspire the Morning, 195

Q

Q UE chacun remplisse son verre, 180

R

R Ide all England o'er, 123
Raptures attending Dwellers divine, 241
Remember ye Whigs what was formerly, 248
Rise bonny Kate, 313
Royal and fair, 315

S

S Ing mighty Marlborough's Story, 40
Since Times are so bad, I must tell, 88
Sleep, sleep, poor Youth, 151
Sing, sing all ye Muses, 158
Spring invites, the Troops are going, 189
Sound Fame thy golden Trumpet, sound, 196
Since long o'er the Town, 197
Since now the World's turn'd upside down, 213
Snug of late the Barons sate, 226
Says Roger to Will, both our Teams, 231
Sylvander royal by his Birth, 234
Sawney was tall, and of noble Race, 317

The

An Alphabetical TABLE.

T

THE Glorious Day is come,	70
The old Wife she sent to the,	186
The Valiant Eugene to Vienna,	206
The infant blooming Spring appears,	220
To shew Tunbridge Wells,	221
'Twas early one Morning the Cock,	229
'Then welcome from Vigo,	253
Twanty Years and mear at Edinborough,	254
The Clock had struck, faith I cannot,	262
'Twas when the Sheep were shearing,	319
The Sun had loos'd his weary Team,	321
The Night her blackest Sable wore,	324
'Twas within a Furlong of,	327
To Horse brave Boys of New-Market,	333

V

Victumnus Flora, you that bless,	72

W

Where Oxen do low,	4
Welfare Trumpets, Drums and,	22
When Love fair Psyche made,	43
What Beauty do I see,	46
Woe is me, what mun I do,	54
What are these Ideots doing,	81
Within an Arbor of Delight,	98
We Prophets of the Modern Race,	106
Would you have a Young Virgin,	134
When Innocence and Beauty meet,	136
Well may'st thou prate with,	159
When Phœbus does rise,	167
We London Valets all are Creatures,	173
When the Spring in Glory,	183
Who in Old Sodom would live,	210
Whilst favour'd Bishops new Sleeves,	258
Whilst wretched Fools sneak up,	272
Where divine Gloriana her Palace,	299
When Phillida with Jockey play'd,	331
When first Amyntas su'd for a Kiss,	335

An Alphabetical TABLE.

Y

YE Beaus of Pleasure, 12
Ye Jacks of the Town, 28
Ye Peers that in State, 32
Ye Britons aw that, 36
You love, and yet when I ask you, 165
You Nymphs and Sylvian Gods, 238
Young Philander woo'd me long, 266
Young Collin, cleaving of a Beam, 291

POEMS.

A Mongst all Characters divine, 356
As in Intrigues of Love we find it, 354
As when some mighty Monarch, 345
As when repentant Israel once distrest, 346
As when Hiperion with victorious 357
Brave is that Poet that dares draw, 351
Come Spouse, to talk in Mode now, 353
If this strange Vice in all good, 342
In this wise Town two Games precedence, 337
In hopes the coming Scenes your, 348
In sweet Retirement, freed from, 359
'Mongst our Forefathers, that pure, 350
When the New World all Laws, 339

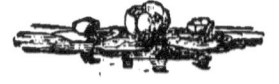

SONGS

Songs Compleat,
Pleasant and Divertive, &c.

A Mad Song.

By a Lady distracted with LOVE. *Sung in one of my Comedies of Don* QUIXOTE: *The Notes to it done by the late famous Mr.* HENRY PURCELL; *which, by reason of their great Length, are not Printed in this Book, but may be found at the Musick Booksellers singly, or in his* Orpheus Brittannicus; *performing in the Tune all the Degrees of Madness.*

[*Sullenly Mad.*]

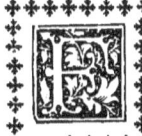Rom rosie Bowers, where sleeps the
God of Love,
Hither, ye little waiting Cupids, fly,
fly, fly,
Hither, ye little waiting Cupids, fly.

Teach me in soft melodious Strains to move
In tender Passion my Heart's darling Joy.
Ah, let the Soul of Musick tune my Voice,
To win dear *Strephon*, who my soul enjoys.

Mirth.

SONGS *Compleat*,

[*Mirthfully Mad. A Swift Movement.*]
Or if more influencing,
 Is to be Brisk and Airy ;
With a Step and a Bound,
And a Frisk from the Ground,
 I'll trip like any Fairy.
As once an *Ida* dancing
 Were three Cœlestial Bodies,
With an Air, and a Face,
And a Shape, and a Grace,
 I'll charm, like Beauties Goddess,
 With an Air, &c.

[*Melancholly Madness.*]
Ah, 'tis in vain, 'tis all, 'tis all in vain ;
Death and Despair must end the fatal Pain :
Cold, cold Despair, disguis'd like Snow and Rain,
Falls on my Breast, bleak Winds in Tempests blow,
My Veins all shiver, and my Fingers glow ;
My Pulse beats a dead March, for lost Repose,
And to a solid lump of Ice my poor fond Heart is froze.

[*Fantastically Mad.*]
Or, say ye Powers, my Peace to crown,
Shall I thaw my self, and drown
 Amongst the foaming Billows ;
Increasing, all with Tears I shed
 On Beds of Ooze, and Chrystal Pillows.
Lay down, lay down my lovesick Head.
Say, say, ye Powers, my Peace to crown,
Shall I, shall I thaw myself, and drown ?

[*Stark Mad.*]
No, no, no, no, I'll straight run mad,
 Mad, mad, mad, mad, that soon my Heart will warm ;
Whene'er the Sense is fled, is fled,
 Love has no Power, no Power to charm.
                                                      Wild

Pleasant and Divertive. 3

Wild, thro' the Woods I'll fly, I'll fly,
Robes, Locks—shall thus—be tore;
A thousand, thousand Deaths I'll Dye,
E'er thus, thus, in vain—e'er thus in vain adore.

A Country Dialogue. *Set by Mr.*
DANIEL PURCELL.

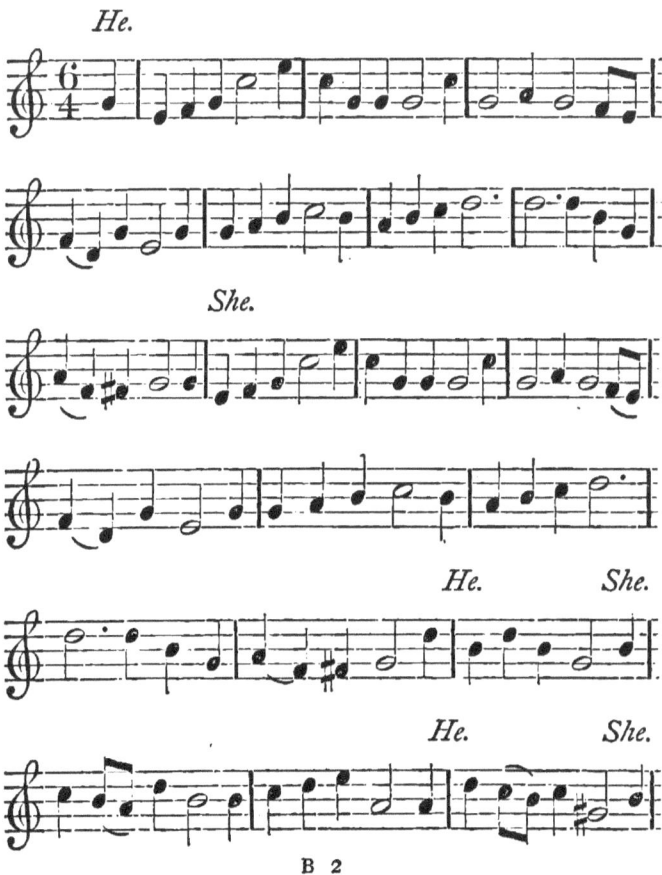

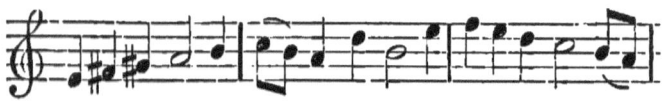

He.

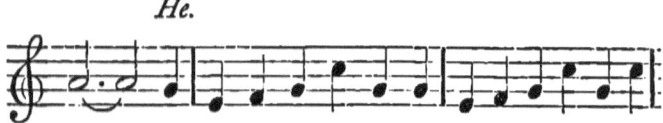

She.

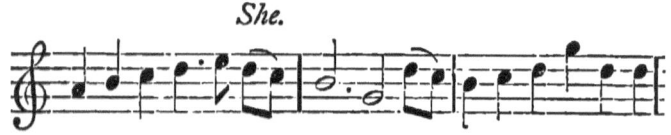

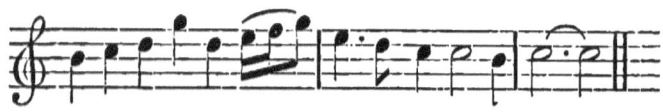

He WHere Oxen do Low,
And Apples do grow,
Where Corn is sown,
And Grass is mown;
Where Pigeons do fly,
And Rooks Nestle high;
Fae give me for Life a Place:
She Where Hay is well Cock'd,
And Udders are Strok'd !
Where Duck and Drake,
Cry quack, quack, quack;
Where Turkeys lay eggs,
And Sows suckle Pigs,
Oh! there I would pass my Days.
He On nought we will feed,
She But what we do breed;
And wear on our backs,
He The wool of our flocks

She

Pleasant and Divertive.

She　And tho' Linnen feel
　　　Rough, Spun from the wheel,
　'Tis cleanly tho' course it comes.
He　Town follies and Cullies,
　　　And Molleys and Dolleys,
　　For ever adieu, and for ever;
She　And Beaus that in Boxes
　　　Lie smuggling their Doxies,
　　With Wigs that hang down to their Bums.

He　Good b'uye to the Mall,
　　　The Park and Canal;
　　St. *James's* Square,
　　　And Flaunters there:
　　The Gaming house too,
　　　Where high Dice and low,
　Are manag'd by all degrees:
She　Adieu to the Knight,
　　　Was bubled last Night,
　　　That keeps a Blowz,
　　　And beats his spouse;
　　　And now in great haste,
　　　To pay what he's lost,
　Sends home to cut down his Trees:
He　And well fare the Lad,
She　Improves e'ry Clad,
He　That ne'er set his hand,
　　　To Bill or to Bond.
She　Nor barters his Flocks,
　　　For Wine or the Pox,
　To chouse him of half his Days:
He　But Fishing and Fowling,
　　　And Hunting and Bowling,
　　His Pastime is ever, and ever;
She　Whose Lips when you buss 'em,
　　　Smell like the Bean-blossom,
　　Oh, he 'tis shall have my praise!

He   To Tavern where goes,
     Sow'r Apples and Sloes,
    A long adieu !
    And farewel too,
     The House of the Great,
     Whose Cook has no Meat,
  And Butler can't quench my Thirst.
She Good b'uye to the Change,
     Where Rantepoles range ;
    Farewel cold Tea,
    And Rattafee,
     Hide-Park too, where Pride
     In Coaches do ride,
  Altho' they be choak'd with Dust.
He   Farewel the Law-Gown,
She The plague of the Town,
He   And Foes of the Crown,
     That should be run down,
She With City-Jack-daws ;
     That make Staple Laws,
  To Measure by Yards and Ells.
He   Stock-Jobbers and Swobbers,
    And Packers and Tackers,
    For ever adieu, and for ever ;

CHORUS.

We know what you're doing,
And home we're both going,
And so you may ring the Bells.

The

Pleasant and Divertive.

The Moderate MAN.

To a pretty Tune.   By the famous Signior Corelli.

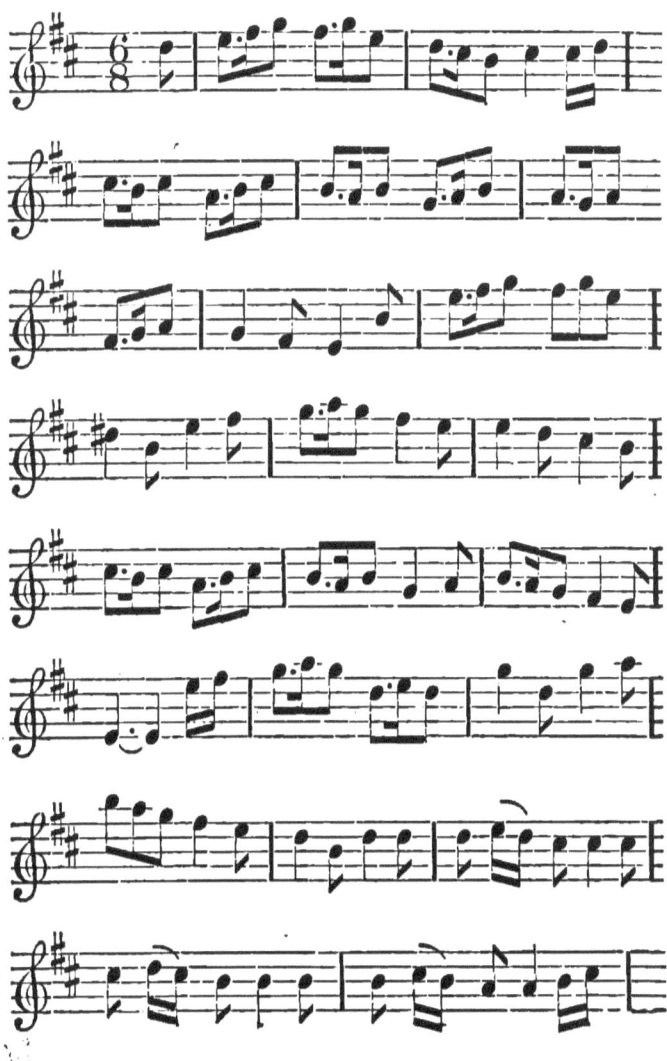

8   SONGS *Compleat,*

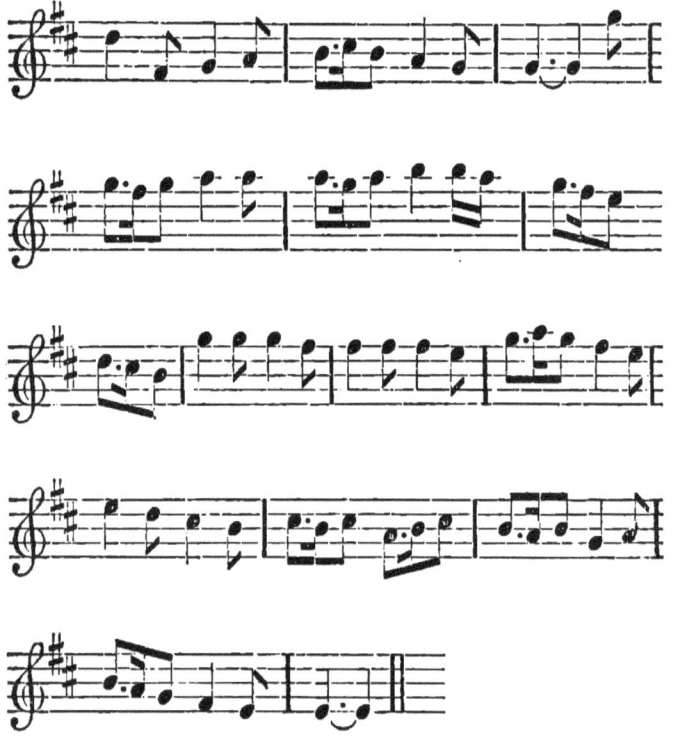

A Tory, a Whig, and a Moderate Man,
   O'er a Tub of strong Ale
   Met, in *Ailesbury* Vale,
Where there liv'd a plump Lass they call'd buxom *Nan*:
   The Tory a *Londoner* proud and high,
   The Whig was a Tradesman plaguy sly;
   The Trimmer a Farmer, but merry and dry,
      And thus they their Suit began:
Pretty *Nancy* we're come to put in our Claim,
Resolv'd upon Wedlocks pleasing Game;
      Here's *Jacob* the Big,
      And *William* the Whig,
      And *Roger* the Grigg,
                                        Jolly

Pleasant and Divertive.

Jolly Lads, as e'er were buckled in Girdle fast;
    Say which you will chuse,
    To tye with a Noose,
For a Wife we must carry what e'er comes on't,
    Then think upon't,
You'll never be sorry when y'have don't,
Nor like us the worse for our Wooing so blunt,
    Then tell us who pleases best.

The Lass who was not of the motion shy,
    The ripe Years of her Life
    Being Twenty and Five :
To the Words of her Lover straight made reply,
I find you believe me a Girl worth Gold,
And I know too you like my Coppy-hold ;
And since Fortune favours the brisk and the bold,
    One of ye I mean to try.
But I am not for you nor *S———'s* Cause,
Nor you with your *H———y's* Hums and Hawes ;
    No *Jacob* the Bigg,
    Nor *William* the Whigg,
    But *Roger* the Grigg,
With his Mirth and mildness happily please me can ;
    'Tis him I will choose,
    For th' Conjugal Noose ;
So that you the Church Bully may rave and rant,
    And you may Cant,
'Till both are Impeacht in Parliament ;
'Tis Union and Peace that the Nation does want,
    So I'm for the Moderate Man.

The Saint at St. James's Chappel.
A New Song.

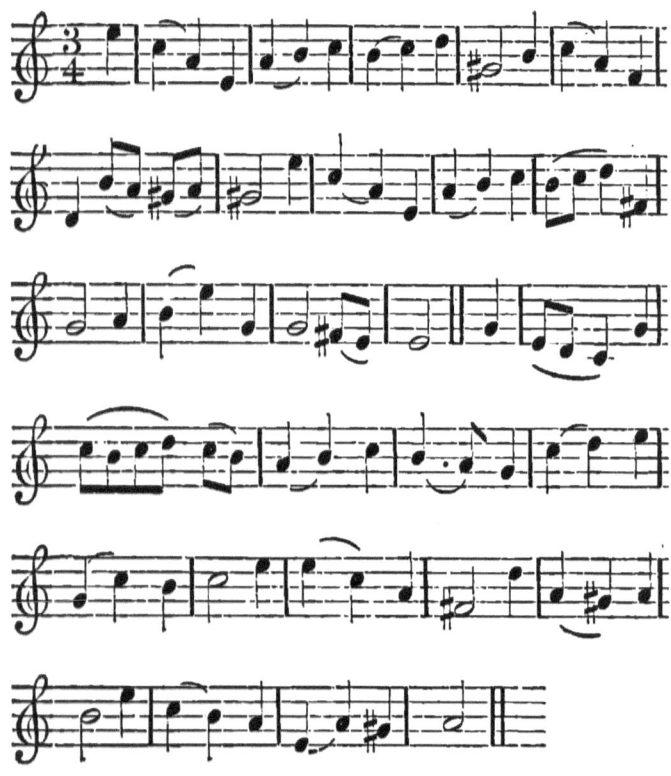

O Ne Sunday at St. *James's* Prayers,
    The *Prince* and *Princess* by,
I dress'd with all my Whalebone Airs,
    Sate in the Closet nigh.
I bent my Knees, I held my Book,
    I read the Answers o'er,
But was perverted by a Look,
    That pierc'd me from the Door.

High

Pleasant and Divertive. 11

High thoughts of Heaven I came to use,
  And blest Devotion there,
Which gay young *Strephon* made me loose,
  And other Raptures share.
He watch'd to lead me to my Chair,
  And bow'd with courtly grace,
But whisper'd Love into my Ear,
  Too warm for that grave place.

Love, Love, cry'd he, by all Ador'd,
  My fervent Heart has won ;
But I grown peevish at that Word,
  Desir'd he would be gone :
He went, whilst I, that lookt his way,
  A kinder Answer meant,
And did for all my sins that day,
  Not half so much repent.

A New Song. *Translated from the* Italian.

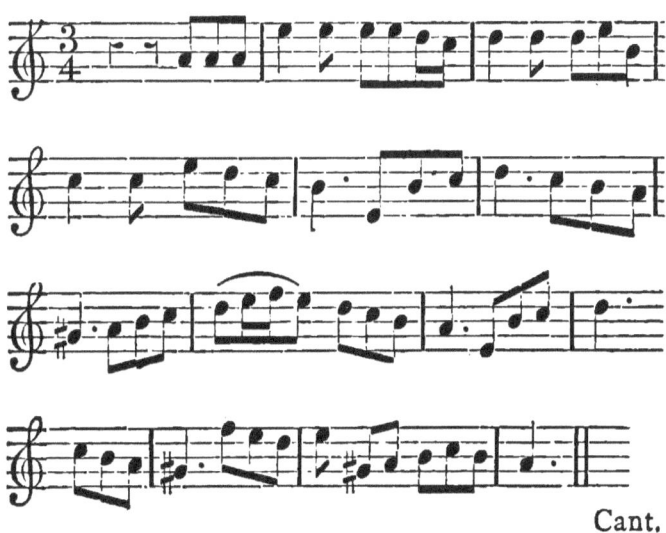

Cant.

Cant. Italian.

GIOVANI *amanti voi chi Sapete,*
L'Arte secreti d'un crudo Amor;
In Cortesia scoltato un puoro,
L'Ardente fuoco chi marde il Cor.

Egia tre mesì ch' una sitella,
Le giadra Bella ch'ogni lo sa;
Quel sua bel chilio cosci Gallante,
Mi feci amanti di sua bella.

In English.

YE Beaus of Pleasure,
    Whose Wit at Leasure,
Can Count Loves Treasure,
    It's Joy and Smart;
At my desire,
With me retire,
To know what fire,
    Consumes my Heart:
At my desire,
With me retire,
To know what fire,
    Consumes my Heart.

Three Moons that hasted,
Are hardly wasted,
Since I was blasted,
    With Beauty's Ray:
Aurora shows ye,
No Face so Rosie,
No *July's* Posie,
So fresh and gay,
    Aurora, &c.

Pleasant and Divertive.

Her Skin by Nature,
No *Ermin* better,
Tho' that fine Creature,
   Is white as Snow;
With blooming Graces,
Adorn'd her Face is,
Her flowing Tresses,
   As black as Sloe.
With, &c.

She's Tall and Slender,
She's Soft and Tender,
Some God commend her,
   My Wit's too low:
'Twere Joyful plunder,
To bring her under,
She's all a wonder,
   From Top to Toe.
'Twere joyful, &c.

Then cease, ye Sages,
To quote dull Pages,
That in all Ages,
   Our Minds are free:
Tho' great your Skill is,
So strong the Will is,
My Love for *Phillis*,
   Must ever be.
Tho' great, &c.

*A Ditty on a high Amour at St. James's.
Set to a Comical Tune.*

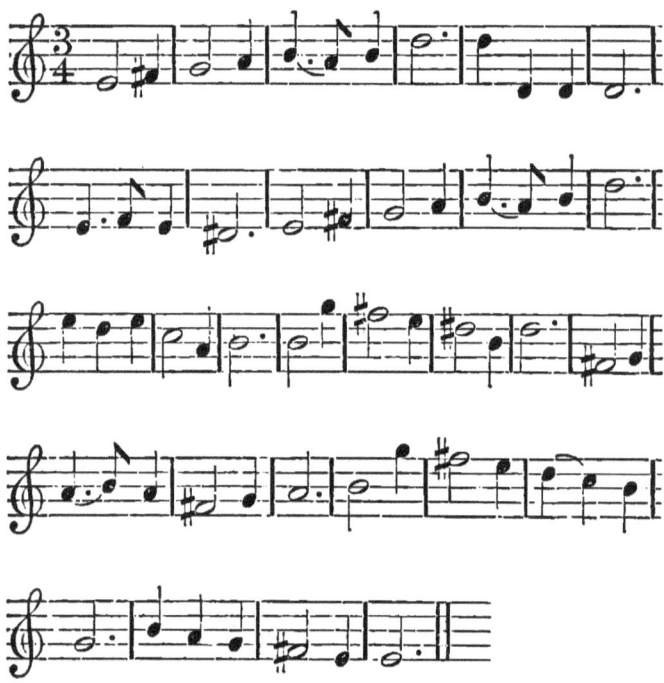

  GReat Lord Frog to Lady Mouse,
   Croakledom hee Croakledom ho;
 Dwelling near St. *James's* house,
  Cocky mi Chari she;
 Rode to make his Court one day,
 In the merry Month of *May*,
 When the Sun Shon bright and gay,
  Twiddle come Tweedle twee.

Lord

Pleasant and Divertive.

Lord Frog.
Countess, y'have three Daughters fine,
Croakledom hee Croakledom ho ;
I'd fain make the youngest mine,
　Cocky mi Chari she :
I'm well made as ever was Male,
Only bating one simple aile ;
Pox upon't, I've never a Taile,
　Twiddle come Tweedle twee.

Lady Mouse.
Welcome Noble Peer to Town,
Croakledom hee Croakledom ho ;
I'll strait call my darling down,
　Cocky mi Cari she :
So much wealth will sure prevail,
Yet I wish that you might not fail ;
Your fine Lordship had a Tail,
　Twiddle come Tweedle twee.

Lord Frog.
Here She comes shall be my Spouse,
Croakledom hee Croakledom ho ;
If she'll design to grace my house,
　Cocky mi Cari she ;
I've a head where Love can plant ;
Tho' a trifling Tail I want ;
Will you fair one liking grant,
　Twiddle come Tweedle twee.

Miss Mouse.
I can ne'er to one consent,
Croakledom hee Croakledom ho ;
Wants that needful ornament,
　Cocky my Cari me :
Uncle Rat too so well known,
That a swinger has on's own ;
Ne'er will let me wed to none,
　Twiddle come Tweedle twee.

　　　　　　　　　　　Lord

16 SONGS *Compleat,*

Lord Frog.
Sing I can't, my Voice is low
Croakledom hee Croakledom ho ;
But for Dancing dare *Santlow*,
　　Cocky mi Chari she :
Than altho' my Bum be bare,
All must own 'tis smooth and fair ;
I've no Scars of *Venus* there,
　　Twiddle come Tweedle twee.

Miss Mouse.
When we treat you at our Cheese,
Croakledom hee Croakledom ho ;
All that naked part one sees,
　　Cocky mi Chari me :
Cover'd close we creep and crawl,
When you swim or diving fall :
Fy for shame, you shew us all,
　　Twiddle come Tweedle twee.

Lord Frog.
Since y'are on these lofty strains,
Croakledom hee Croakledom ho ;
I'll get one shall value brains,
　　Cocky mi Chari she :

Miss Mouse.
Now your Lordship idle prates,
Those that will have constant mates,
Must have Tails as well as Pates,
　　Twiddle come Tweedle twee.

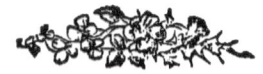

OCEAN'S

OCEAN'S GLORY:

Or, A Parley of the Rivers. A Royal ODE or CANTATA; made in Honour of King GEORGE'S Coronation. Set to Musick by Dr. PEPUSCH, after the Italian manner.

[*Recitative.*]

Fame and *Isis* joyn'd in one,
    Flowing with Cenubial Pride,
Late by fam'd *Augusta* ran ;
    Posting to the Ocean they
    To great *Neptune* seem'd to pray
      To send in the happy Tide.

    Haughty grown, they seem'd to slight
Ancient *Humber*, *Sabrine* fair,
    Boasting, now they were to bear
      Such a blest, and glorious Weight,
As never prest their Waves before :
And thus their Joy resounded to the Shore.

[*Aire.*]

Let your Streams be clearly waving,
GEORGE is come, Great *Britain* saving ;
    Dance, ye Fish, both great and small ;
Pretty Birds in Groves be singing,
Active Deer in Lawns be springing ;
    Joyn in Pleasure with us all.

[*Recitative.*]

Humber renown'd, and bright *Sabrine* reply'd,
The *Ocean* sends the Loyal Tide,
    And Fate does you the greatest Honour shew :
                  We'll

We'll make our firm Allegiance good,
With you, or any other Flood,
    To shame the Parties High and Low:
Unite large Rivers with each strugling Spring,
And shew great *GEORGE* the way to make
    a Glorious King.

[*Aire.*]

Plants and Flowers, the Sweets of Nature,
Cheering now each mortal Creature,
    Blest with bright *Apollo's* Beams;
Spring and *Summer* fair and lasting,
All forget the *Winter's* blasting,
    Mounts of Snow, and frozen Streams.

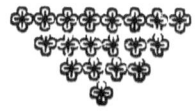

TWANG-

Pleasant and Divertive. 19

TWANGDILLO.

A New Ballad. *The Words made to the Tune of a pretty Country Dance, call'd the* Hobby-horse.

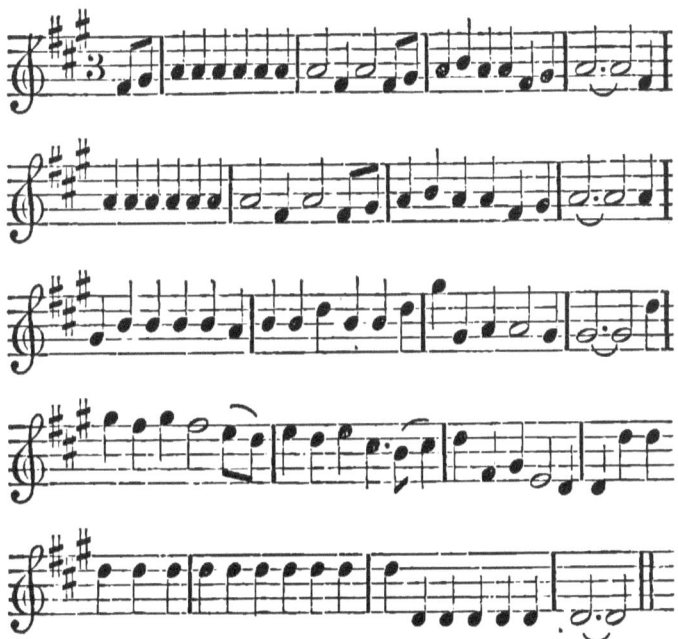

Jolly *Roger Twangdillo* of *Plouden* Hill,
   In his Chest had two thousand good Pounds,
Fat Oxen and Sheep, and a Barn well fill'd,
   And a hundred good Acres of Ground ;
Which made ev'ry Maiden with Maiden-heads laden,
   And Widows, tho' just set free,
To wrangle and fret, and pump up their Wit,
   To train to the Net, *Twangdillow, Twangdillo,*
Twangdillo, Twangdillo, young lusty *Twangdillo, Twangdee.*

The first that brake Ice was a Lass had been
    Born of a good House, but decay'd;
Her Gown was new Dy'd, and her Night-trail clean,
    And to sing and talk French had been breed;
      She'd dance *Northern Nancy*,
      Ask'd *Parler vous Fransay*,
    That *Hodge* might her breeding see,
      She'd rowl her black Eye,
      Breath short with a sigh,
When e'er she came nigh *Twangdillo, Twang*, &c.

The next was a Sempstress of Stature Low,
    That fancy'd she wanted a Male,
Her Hair as black as an *Autumn* Sloe,
    And hard as a Coach-horses Tail:
      She'd Oagle and Wheedle,
      And prick with her Needle;
    What d' lack, what d' buy, cry'd she?
      But now the brisk Tone,
      Is chang'd to a Groan,
Ah! pity my moan, *Twangdillo, Twang*, &c.

A musty old Chamber-maid lean and tall,
    The next as a Suitor appears,
With a Tongue loud and shrill, but no Teeth at all,
    For time had drawn them many Years:
      Cast Gowns and such Lumber,
      Old Smocks without number,
    She bragg'd should her Dowry be,
      Forty pair of Lac'd Shoes,
      Ribbons Green, Red and Blews,
But all would not Noose *Twangdillo, Twang*, &c.

The next was a Lass of a Popish strain,
    That *Jesuite* Whims had been taught,
She bragg'd they shou'd soon have King *J——s* again,
    Tho' her Spouse was late hang'd for the Plot;
      The *French* would come over,
      And land here at *Dover*,

                        And

Pleasant and Divertive.

And all as they wish'd, would be;
  The *Jacobite* Jade,
  Talk'd as if she was mad,
In hopes to have had *Twangdillo, Twang*, &c.

A Vintner's fat Widow then straight was view'd,
  Whose Cuckold had pick'd up some Pelf:
He had kill'd half his Neighbours with Wine he'd brew'd,
  And lately had Poyson'd himself.
  With Bumpers of Claret,
  No Souse paying for it,
She'd *Roger's* Companion be;
  Strike Fist on the Board,
  Huzza was the Word,
Come Kiss me ador'd *Twangdillo, Twang*, &c.

But *Roger* resolv'd not to be her Man,
  And so gave a loose to the next,
The Niece of a Canting Bleer-Ey'd *Non Con*,
  That stifly could canvass a Text.
  A Dame in *Cheapside* too,
  Would fain be his Bride too,
And make him of *London* free;
  But no Lass wou'd down
  In Country or Town,
So purse-proud was grown, *Twangdillo, Twang*, &c.

Till at last pretty *Nancy*, a Farmer's Joy,
  That newly a Milking had been,
Round-fac'd, Cherry-cheek'd, with a smirking Eye,
  Came tripping it over the Green:
  She mov'd like a Goddess,
  And in her lac'd Bodice,
  A Span she could hardly be;
  Her Hips were plump grown,
  And her Hair a dark Brown;
'Twas she that brought down *Twangdillo, Twangdillo,
Twangdillo, Twangdillo,* young lusty *Twangdillo,
Twangdee.*

                                                                                   A

A DIALOGUE *in the Opera for Mr.* Leveridge *and Mr.* Edwards; *representing two Country Boors arguing about the War.*

Coridon.

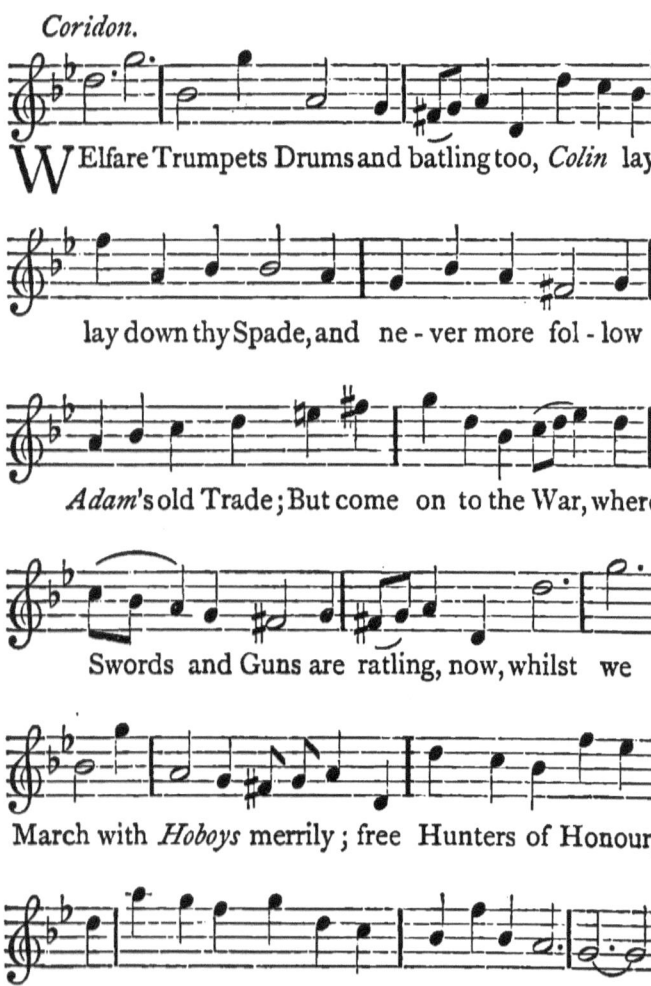

Welfare Trumpets Drums and batling too, *Colin* lay,

lay down thy Spade, and ne-ver more fol-low

Adam's old Trade; But come on to the War, where

Swords and Guns are ratling, now, whilst we

March with *Hoboys* merrily; free Hunters of Honour,

Thou'rt slave to the Pride of some Boar of a Man-nor;
Colin.

Pleasant and Divertive. 23

Colin.

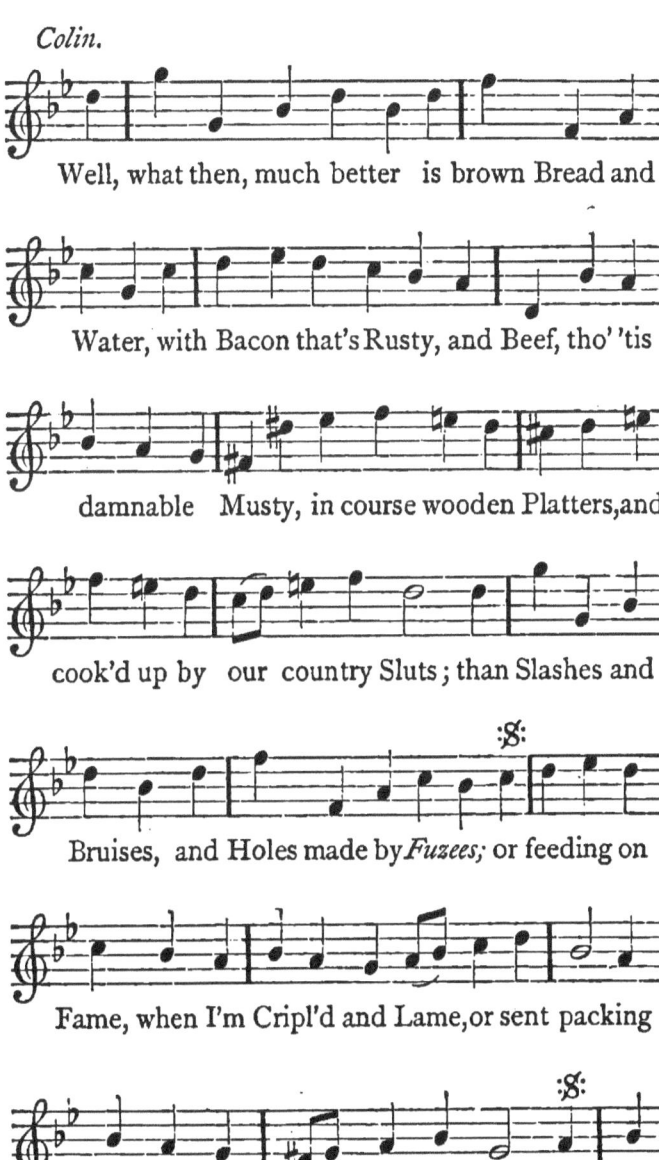

Well, what then, much better is brown Bread and

Water, with Bacon that's Rusty, and Beef, tho' 'tis

damnable Musty, in course wooden Platters, and

cook'd up by our country Sluts; than Slashes and

Bruises, and Holes made by *Fuzees;* or feeding on

Fame, when I'm Cripl'd and Lame, or sent packing

with a broad Sword thro' my Guts, Z—ns, with

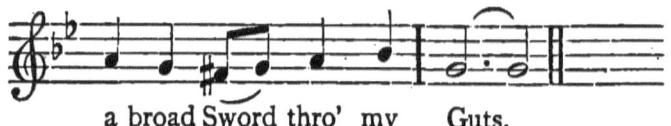

a broad Sword thro' my Guts.

Coridon.

Dull Fool rail no more at Cavaleering,
What a damn'd Scandal it is,
To sneak here at home,
Grow mouldy with peace,
When loud Fame calls thee out;
Where bold Dragoons are Domineering,
Thou'lt see fortune ready to befriend thee,
    If thou art wounded,
    For Honour and Valour,
    Preferment's propounded.

Colin.

I fear my Commission,
Will prove but a Vision,
For when I am posted,
On Mines, where I'm like to be roasted,
'Tis forty to one but I'm puff'd from my future
    Command,
    Or if with much Toyling,
    I chance to scape Broyling,
    A damn'd bit of Lead,
    Drills me quite thro' the Head,
How the Devil then shall I kiss the King's Hand,
Zoons, how shall I kiss the King's Hand.

To the Second Part of the Tune.

Coridon.

From Bullets and Fire,
Tho' oft we retire,
                                    Our

Pleasant and Divertive. 25

Our wishes we Crown,
When we enter a Town
That is Rich, where the Lasses are kind,
And the Plunder's refreshing and Cool.

Colin.

But what if foul weather
Won't let us come thither,
The Trench full of Water,
Then is it not better,
Lye safe at home, and our Plowjobbers rule.

Coridon.

Gad zooks you're a Cowardly Fool.

A New SONG. *On the happy Accession to the Crown, and coming in of our Gracious Sovereign, King* GEORGE.

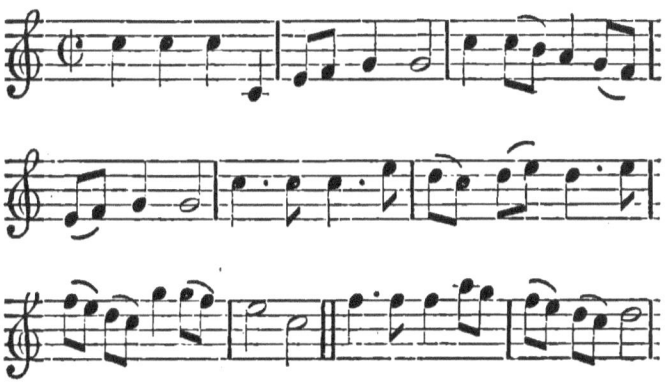

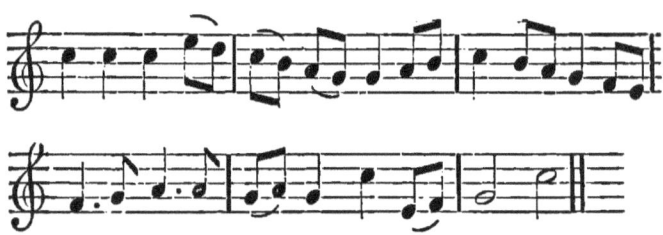

B*Ritains* now let Joys increase,
  Revel all in happy days,
Royal *George* has crost the Seas,
    Ye Natives homage tender;
Fate to save us made him hast,
Britains Genius doubly Blest,
And renown'd as was e'er in Ages past,
The Saint our Isles defender.

Halcyon Peace that all must grant,
Has been so long the Nations want,
Glorious and brave some people vaunt,
    Has lately fill'd our story;
But kind Stars so well provide,
And this grand truth will soon be try'd,
For a *Monarch* is Reigning that will decide
What is for *Britains* glory.

By our late most Zealous Aid
The *French* a lucky game have play'd,
'Tis now high time to help our Trade,
    And mend our bad condition;
You the scoundrels charm'd with hope,
To gain by *Mounsieur*, or the *Pope*,
At this Juncture much sooner may find a Rope,
Reward for vile Ambition.

Gentle winds have swell'd his Sails,
Blest the *King* with happy gales,
And the darling Prince of *Wales*,
    Our second Faiths defender;

Now

Now let jarring discords cease,
Now we're sure of lasting Peace,
Since the Right must set all our minds at ease,
And baulk the false *Pretender*.

A Song. *Design'd to be Sung between the Acts in the* Modern Prophets. *To the foregoing Tune.*

NOw, now comes on, the Glorious Year,
    Britain has hope, and *France* has fear;
Lewis the War has cost so dear,
    He slyly Peace does tender:
But our two *Heroes* so well know
The breach of his Word some years ago,
They resolve, they will give him another blow,
    Unless he *Spain* Surrenders.

Health to the *Queen* then straight begin,
To *Marlborough* the great, and to brave *Eugene*
With them let Valiant *Webb* come in,
    Who late perform'd a wonder:
Then to the Ocean an offering make,
And boldly Carouze to brave Sir *John Leak;*
Who with Mortar and Cannon *Mahon* did take,
    And made the *Pope* knock under.

Beat up the Drum a new Alarm,
The foe is cold, and we are warm;
The *Mounsieur's* Troops can do no harm,
    Tho' they abound in Numbers:
Push then once more and the War is done,
Old Men and Boys will surely run;
And we know we can beat 'em if four to one;
    Which he too well remembers.

The

SONGS Compleat,

The FART;

Famous for its Satyrical Humour in the Reign of Queen ANNE.

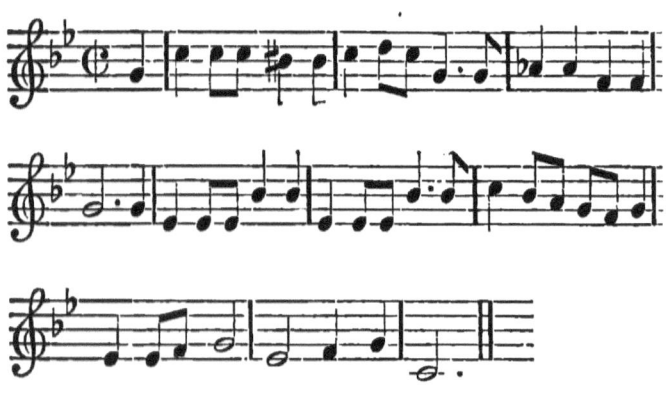

YE *Jacks* of the Town,
    And *Whiggs* of renown,
Leave off your Jarrs and Spleen,
    And hast to your Arms
    All thronging in swarms
Be ready to guard the *Queen;*
    With a *hum, hum, hum, hum.*

For last LORD'S-day,
    at St. *James's* they say,
A strange odd thing did chance,
    Which put into the News,
    All *Holland* would amuse,
But would make 'em rejoyce in *France;*
    With a *hum,* &c.

Each Commoner and Peer,
    Of both Houses were there,
                  And

Pleasant and Divertive.

And folks of each rank and Station,
    Had thither free recourse,
    From the Keeper of the Purse,
To the Mayor of a Corporation;
    With a hum, &c.

When at Noon as in State
    The *Queen* was at Meat,
And the Princely *Dane* sat by Her,
    A *Fart* there was hear'd,
    That the Company scar'd,
As a Gun at their Ears had been fir'd;
    With a hum, &c.

Which Irreverent Sound
    Made 'em stare all around,
And in each Countenance lower,
    Whilst judgment thereupon
    Said, it needs must be done,
As afronting the Soveraign pow'r;
    With a hum, &c.

The Chaplain in place
    Had but just said Grace,
And then cringing behind withdrawn,
    When they call'd back,
    To examine if the Crack,
Came from him or the Lords in Lawn,
    With a hum, &c.

For just by the Chair,
    Some fat *Bishops* were there,
Whom the *Whigg* boys fain would bespatter,
    Who with a Sober look,
    Declar'd upon the Book,
That the Clergy knew nought of the matter;
    Of the hum, &c.

                              But

But they would not swear,
    For the Parties were there,
Of the High *Church* and the Low,
    Who from a mighty Zeal,
    For good o' th' commonweal
Might let some of their Bagpipes blow ;
With a hum, &c.

At this when heard,
    Late Comptroler strokt his Beard,
And declar'd with an Antique bow,
    He tho' of some nothing knew,
    Yet he would vouch for two,
Himself, and his Brother *John How ;*
For the hum, &c.

For the Squire was well bred,
    And his Key might have had,
But refus'd for an old State Trick,
    And that he that had made Sport,
    With Places of the Court,
Now resolv'd upon *Wharton's* white stick ;
With a hum, &c.

When this was done,
    And the Crime not yet known,
Came a Law Peer to plead the Case,
    How they had no intent,
    To affront the Government
Nor had he to regain the Mace ;
With a hum, &c.

A Garter and Star,
    Next censure did bear,
Who for all he lookt so high,
    And carry'd it so great,
    In Intrigues of the State,
Yet might condescend to let fly
A hum, &c.

Pleasant and Divertive.

But he, in a heat,
    Said the thing in debate,
Impos'd on Each sex might be,
    And would have made it clear,
    That some Dutchesses there,
Were as likely to do't as he;
    With a hum, &c.

The Colour then rose,
    'Mongst the noble Furbelows,
Of Honour, and most too, Wives,
    Who declar'd upon their rep,
    They ne'er made such a 'scape,
Nor e'er did such a thing in their lives
    As a hum, &c.

But the Gigling rout,
    That were waiting round about,
'Twas likely were heedless Jades,
    So that saving their own fame
    They agreed upon the sham,
To have turn'd it upon the poor Maids;
    With a hum, &c.

Who all drown'd in Tears,
    Charg'd the Ladys there in years,
To tell truth if that hideous rore,
    So Thunder-like sent,
    From Audacious Fundament,
Could consist with their Virgin bore;
    With a hum, &c.

Who answering no,
    All disputes fell too,
For now they believ'd it was reason,
    To pass the matter of,
    As a Joke, and in a Laugh,
Since they ne'er could make it High Treason;
    With a hum, &c.

                      So

So that turning the Jest,
    They agreed it at last,
That nought from the Presence did come,
    But the noise that they heard,
    Was some Yeoman o' the Guard,
That brought Dishes into the next Room;
    With a hum, &c.

But the truth of the sound
    Not at all could be found,
Since none but the doer could tell,
    So that hushing up the Shame,
    The Beef-eater bore the blame,
And the *Queen,* God be prais'd, din'd well;
    With a hum, hum, hum, hum.

The Second Part of the FART;
Or the Beef-eaters *Appeal to Mr. D'*URFEY.
[To the same Tune.]

YE *Peers* that in State,
    Now with *Commons* are met,
To right both the Weak and the Strong,
    Prepare to redress
    A poor *Beef-eater's* Case,
Who has had a most damnable wrong;
    By a hum, &c.

Strange Jarring I know,
    'Twixt the *High-Church* and *Low,*
Does your dear valu'd hours ingross,
    Yet mine is such a case,
    That I beg it may take place,
As soon as the *Speaker* is chose,
    With a hum, &c.

For

Pleasant and Divertive.

For tho' I'm no Lord,
    Nor to *Senate* preferr'd,
Yet my Priviledge I'll maintain,
    And as free-born of the Land,
    You my wrong shall understand,
Which I here will undaunted explain;
    Of a hum, &c.

The *Fart* you late heard,
    Laid to one of the Guard,
That of late did the *Court* Surprise,
    'Tis prov'd was not his,
    As Informers did guess,
But a *Females* of his Jolly size;
    With a hum, &c.

The thing came out thus,
    Near to *Buckingham* House,
And the *Motto* all Fancies excelling,
    Near the Ancient *Pall-mall*,
    The *Park*, and *Canal*,
Two Buxom young *Ladies* were dwelling;
    With a hum, &c.

Related so near,
    It does plainly appear,
That they both from one Bottom did come,
    The one thin and lean,
    As a Garden French Bean,
And the tother as round as a Drum;
    With a hum, &c.

The Elder when dress'd,
    And her Belly straight lac'd,
If she stoop'd from behind must Roar,
    The Younger as frail,
    If she laugh'd at any Tale,
Could not keep in the *Juices* before;
    With a whisse, hum, &c.

Strange quarrels had past,
    'Twixt the first and the last,
And many Tongue combats had been,
    For the Youngest well knew,
    'Twas her Sister that *Blew*,
The late *Blast* as she stood by the *Queen;*
    With a hum, &c.

But letting that go,
    Since Winds pass too and fro,
As Fate soon the Case made plain,
    By a Visit they made,
    To a haughty *Court* Jade,
Who a Page had to hold up her Train;
    With a hum, &c.

Who when at her Gate,
    She the Sisters had met,
Bowing low with her back-bone crump,
    As she gave a Salute,
    Tother stooping to do't,
Gave a proof she was loose in her Rump;
    By a hum, &c.

Which unfortunate noise,
    Made her Sister rejoyce,
And as nothing more pleasing could come,
    With a laugh screw'd so high,
    She was ready to die,
As she follow'd her into the Room;
    With a hum, &c.

But oh, dismal lot,
    Her own Case she forgot,
For just as a filly Foal pisses,
    When she romping does pass,
    O'er the gay springing grass,
So the Room was Embroyder'd with S S.
    And a whisse, hum, &c.

Pleasant and Divertive.

The Dame of the House,
   That perceiv'd this abuse,
From Passion could not refrain,
   As knowing what was dropp'd,
   Could not easily be mopp'd,
Being mixt with a Stercus humain;
   And a hum, &c.

And strongly perfum'd,
   To Inform her presum'd,
How the Nymphs in the days of Yore,
   Who were cleanly inclin'd,
   Us'd a *Cork* for behind,
And a *Spung* for the Cranny before;
   With a whisse, &c.

Come *Ractcliff,* come *Hans,*
   From the *Vine,* or from *Manns,*
Come *Morley,* to mend this matter,
   And if these prove vain,
   Come Occult *Chamberlain,*
Deep learn'd in the Secrets of Nature;
   And a hum, &c.

Come *Blackmore,* come *Mead,*
   Come Sir William *Read,*
Of late by the *Soveraign* grac'd,
   And peeping in their Tails,
   Quickly cure these Sisters ails,
Some five Inches under the wast,
   Of a whisse, hum, &c.

And the Secret to trace,
   Manage both private ways,
Tho' I mean not the ways of a Sinner,
   That she who does Trump,
   Through defect in her rump,
Never more may Perfume the *Q———ns* dinner;
   With a hum, &c.

And she that is found,
  To be Juicy and sound,
And each Night fills her two white Pots,
  May no more by a gush,
  That has oft made her blush,
Deck the Room with her true Lovers knots;
  And a Whisse hum, whisse hum.

The Northern Resenter.

A Song, *made to a* Scotch *Tune call'd* Robin *the Highlander.*

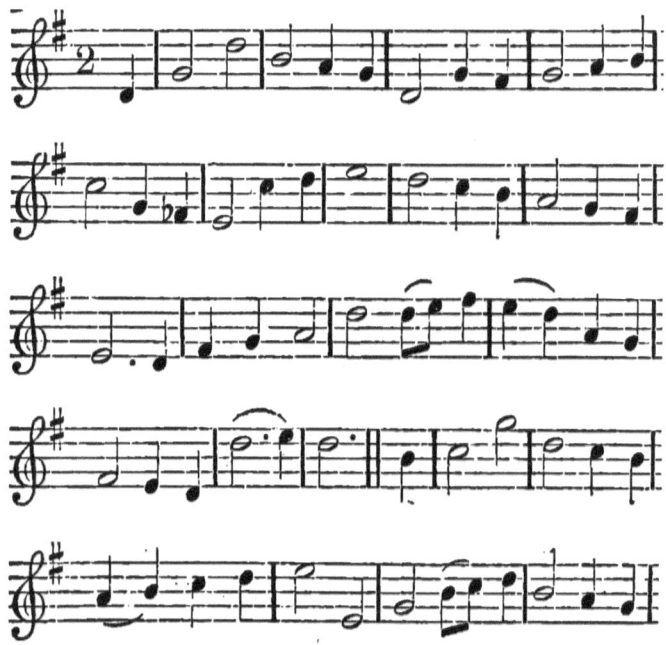

Pleasant and Divertive. 37

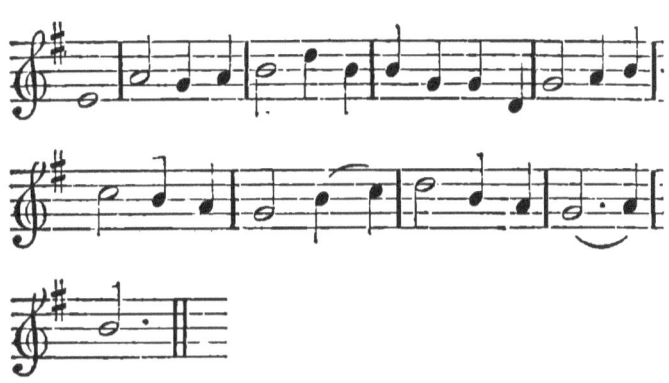

YE *Brittons* aw,
  Who are moulding the Law,
For your use as occasion is fitting;
  What a Deel did you gain,
  By late muckle pain,
When our Peers were outvoted from Sitting:
  Woons, dant we know,
  That a few Years ago,
Ere ye twin'd the Rose with the Thistle;
  Yead a gin any Flower,
  That ye had in your pow'r,
Tho' we now are scarce worth a Whistle.

  Gud feth we see,
  Like a Lass that too free,
Has bin bob'd of her Maidenly treasure;
  That instead of regard,
  For a bargain so hard,
You think you may Slight us at pleasure:
  But woons, take heed,
  Say our Loons near the *Tweed*,
For if no brave *Calledonian;*
  Made a Lord by the Queen,
  Mayn't do like the Sixteen,
Deel awa with the rest of the U——n.

The

The Parson *among the* Peas. *A New* Song.

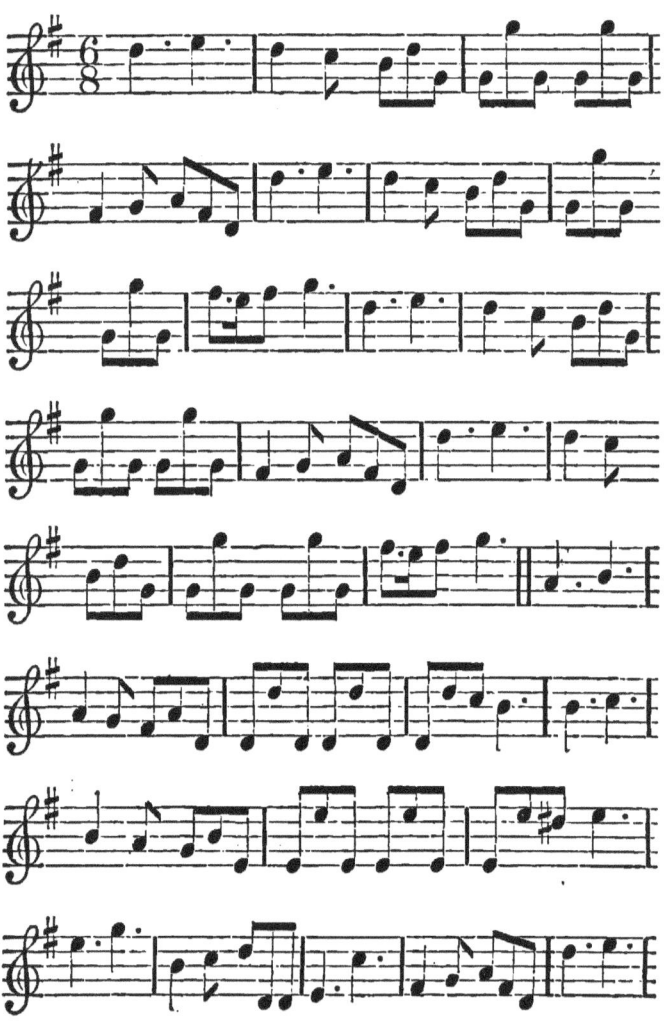

Pleasant and Divertive. 39

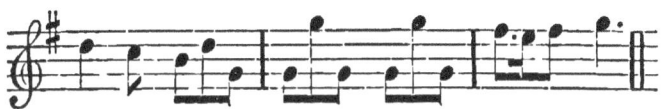

ONe long *Whitson* Holliday,
    Holliday, Holliday, 'twas a Jolly day;
Young *Ralph*, Buxom *Phillida, Phillida*, a welladay,
    Met in the *Peas:*
They long had community,
He lov'd her, she lov'd him,
Joyful Unity, nought but Opportunity,
    scanting was wanting their bosoms to Ease:
But now Fortunes Cruelty, Cruelty,
You will see, for as they lye,
In close Hugg, Sir *Domine Gemini, Gomini*,
    chanc'd to come by;
He read Prayers i' th' Family,
No way now to frame a Lie,
They scar'd at old Homily, Homily, Homily,
    both away fly.

Home, soon as he saw the Sight, full of Spight,
As a Kite runs the Recubite,
Like a noisy *Hypocrite, Hypocrite, Hypocrite*,
    mischief to say;
Save he, wou'd fair *Phillida, Phillida, Phillida:*
Drest that Holy day,
But poor *Ralph*, Ah welladay, welladay, welladay,
    turn'd was away,
Ads niggs crys Sir *Domini, Gemini, Gomini*,
Shall a Rogue stay,
To baulk me as commonly, commonly, commonly,
    has been his way,
No I serve the Family,
They no nought to blame me by,
I'll read Prayers and Homily, Homily, Homily,
    three times a day.

A

A New HEALTH *to the Duke of* Marlborough, *with three Glasses; ending with a Stanza in Honour of the Prince of* Hanover, *and Prince* Eugene; *made on the occasion of the late Glorious Victory at* Audenard.

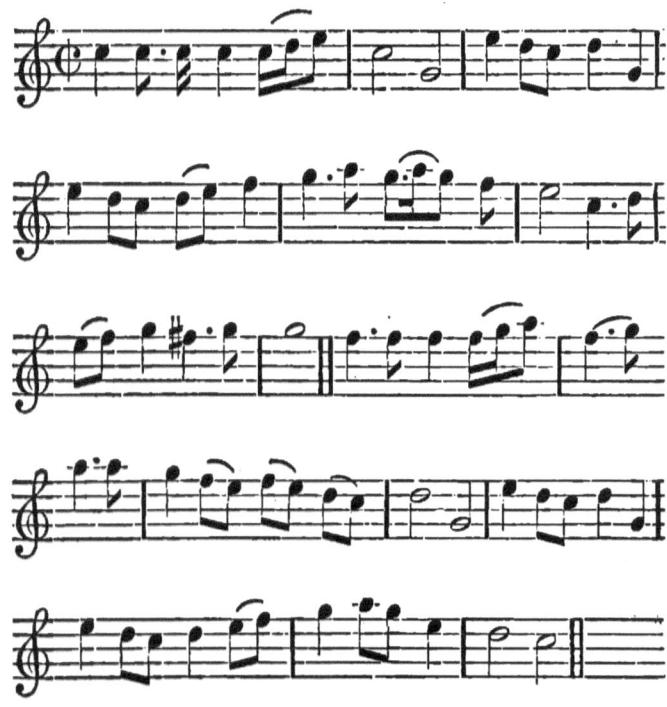

SIng mighty *Marlborough's* Story,
   Mars of the Field,
He passes the *Scheld;*
And to increase his Glory,
The *French* all fly or yield:

                Vendosme

Pleasant and Divertive. 41

               Vendosme drew out to spite him,
               Th' Houshold Troops to fright him,
               Princes o' th' Blood,
               Got off as they cou'd,
               But ne'er durst return to Fight him.

               This is the year of Wonders,
               The Gen d'arms Gor'd,
               With Bullet and Sword,
               Quake when the General Thunders:
               Almanza was the Word;
               Sound the Trumpet Sound Boys,
Take the first This to his Health be crown'd Boys,
   Glass   Circle his Brows
               With fresh *Oaken* boughs,
               And thus let the Glass go round Boys.

Take the 2*nd* Now we made a Motion,
Glass and put *Eugene* the Brave
into the first. A Second shall have,
               And could we tope an Ocean,
               His due we hardly give:
               Still there's one more must be Boys,
               Hannover makes 'em up three Boys,
               Three in a hand,
Drink the 3*rd* I'll drink to my Friend,
.   *Glass.*   And so let us all agree Boys.

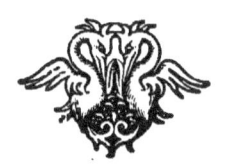

A

A New SONG *in Honour of the Glorious Assembly at Court, on the Queens Birthday; made to a pretty* Scotch *Tune.*

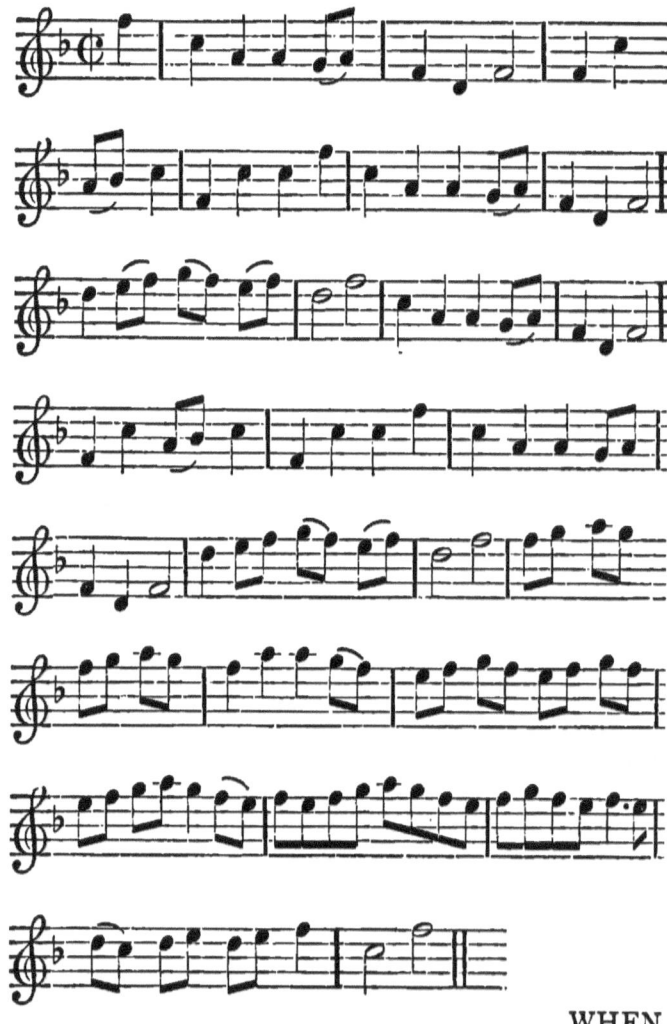

WHEN

Pleasant and Divertive. 43

WHen Love fair *Psyche* made his Choice,
    Jove sent *Mercury* from the Skies;
    To summon all the Deities,
        To a Divine Collation:
    Sol with sweet *Aurora* came,
    Vulcan with his charming Dame,
    And *Iris* put on a Robe of Flame,
        Streakt with a fresh Carnation:
Juno had a Mantle full of Moons and Stars,
And *Venus* had a Trophy Gown a present made by *Mars*,
Embroyder'd o'er with Swords and Guns and Implements of Wars,
        With Triumphs of many a Nation.

    Yet tho' adorn'd in their bright Aray,
    Shining Glorious, fresh and Gay,
    'Twas a trifle all to Queen *Anns* Birth-day,
        Should they compare in Splender:
    Every Duke and Dutchess here,
    Sham'd each God and Goddess there,
    Nor could their Joy with ours compare,
        Shewn to our Faiths Defender:
The States-man that talks on the Wool-sack big,
Could bustle to the Opera, as merry as a Grig,
To Oagle there a Tory tall, or a pretty little Whig,
        Defying the Pretender.

    The great *Eugene*, whose renown does soar,
    Well deserving the * Sword he wore,
    Were Diamonds valu'd at ten times more,
        Thought he beheld a wonder;
    Senates Jars he late has seen,

---

* *A Sword presented him by the Queen of great Value.*
High

44 SONGS *Compleat,*

High and Low exalt their Spleen,
But here in Reverence to the Queen,
Both sides truckle under:
Joy, from this Minute shall each hour increase,
And *Europe* find the Benefit of Honourable Peace,
And he like *Jove* the dire effect of bloody War must cease,
And lay aside his Thunder.

CONJUGAL LOVE.

Made on a Man of Quality and his Lady, to an Air in Pyrrhus.

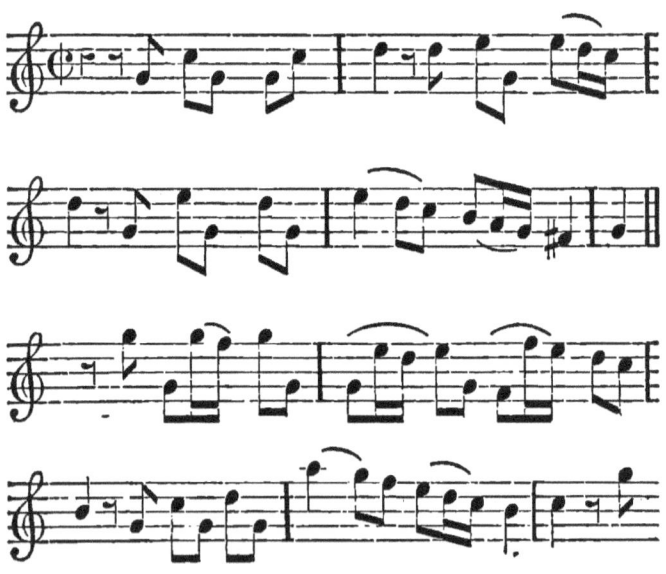

Pleasant and Divertive. 45

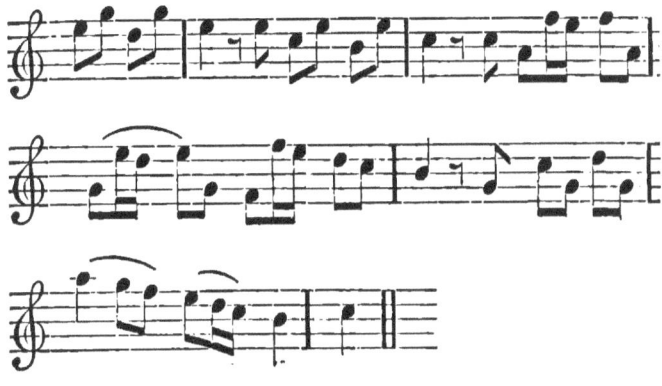

IN *Kent* so fam'd of Old,
  Close by the famous *Knoll*,
A Swain a Goddess told,
  An Am'rous story :
In *Kent* so fam'd of Old,
Close by the famous *Knoll*,
A Swain a Goddess told,
  An Am'rous story :
Cry'd he, these Jarring Days,
When Kings contend for Bays,
Your Love my Soul does raise,
  Beyond their Glory ;
Cry'd he these Jarring Days,
When Kings contend for Bays,
Cry'd he these Jarring Days,
When Kings contend for Bays,
Your Love my Soul, &c.

My Life my Lovely dear,
Whil'st you are Smiling here,
The Plants and Flow'rs appear,
  More Sweetly charming :
The Sun may cease to Shine,
And may his pow'r resign,
Your Eyes give rays Divine,
  All nature warming :

The

The Sun may cease to Shine,
And may his pow'r resign,
The Sun may cease to Shine,
And may his pow'r resign,
Your eyes give, &c.

She made a kind return,
That nothing had of scorn,
This Youth, thought I, does burn,
  To bring her under:
But as they homeward mov'd,
And walk'd, and talk'd and Lov'd,
I found his Spouse she prov'd,
  That was his wonder;
But as they homeward mov'd,
And walk'd, and talk'd, and Lov'd,
But as they homeward mov'd,
And walk'd, and talk'd, and Lov'd,
I found his Spouse, &c.

A Dialogue *in the Comedy of the* Bath, *or the* Western *Lass: Sung by Mr.* Burdon *and Mrs.* Lucas. *The Tune by Mr.* Akeroyde.

He. **W**Hat Beauty do I see,
    That Heart and Soul commands,
Sweet Madam, honour me,
  with leave to kiss your Hand.
                                        She

She. Oh good, a Man, I swear!
    and begs my Hand to kiss,
Methinks I'm pleas'd to hear
    he does not call me Miss.

He. Your Eyes, sweet Lady shine so bright,
And I'm so wounded at first Sight,
My Heart does throb,
I sigh and sob,
    And am like one just slain,
Unless you Pity show,
    And Life restore again.

She. Nay, pray Sir, good Sir go,
    I know not what you mean.
You may talk of a Wound
By my Eyes you have found;
But I cannot believe
Any Hurt they can give:
For I look in your Face,
And it is as it was,
    And your Body is sound and whole.

He. Loves Wounds are all within,
    whose Pangs the Breast controuls,
Like Lightning pass the Skin,
    and blast the very Soul.

She. Why sure, this Love, this dreadful Word,
Is then some sharp and pointed Sword:
Or is't a Snake, Or is't a Bird,
    That will pick out my Eyes.

He. Go with me, you'll perceive
    in Love a Treasure lies,
She. I'll ask my Mother leave,
    and follow in a Trice.

48 SONGS *Compleat*,

He. No, no, no not a Word,
I can better afford
You the Love, if you'll go
Where your Mother don't know;
For if she should be crost,
All the Treasure is lost,
  And I conjure for Love in vain;
The Circle you embrace
 Is where it must be done.
She. Oh Lard, the Devil you'll raise,
 But catch me if you can.

Let the dreadful Engines. *In Orph. Britt.*
A SONG. *Set by Mr.* Henry Purcell.

LET the dreadful Engines of eternal Will,
 The Thunder roar, and crooked Lightning kill,
My Rage is hot, is hot, is hot as theirs, as fatal to,
And dares as horrid, and dares as horrid, horrid
  Execution do.
Or let the frozen North its Rancour show,
Within my Breast far, far greater Tempests grow,
Despair's more cold, more cold than all the
  Winds can blow:

Can nothing, can nothing warm me,
Can nothing, can nothing warm me,
  yes, yes, yes, yes *Lucinda's* Eyes,
  yes, yes, yes, yes, yes, yes, *Lucinda's* Eyes;
  yes, yes, yes, yes, yes *Lucinda's* Eyes,
  there, there, there, there, there *Etna*,
   there, there, there, there, there *Vessuvio* lies,
To furnish Hell with Flames, that mounting,
  Mounting reach the Skies.
            Can

Pleasant and Divertive.

Can nothing, can nothing warm me,
Can nothing, can nothing warm me,
    yes, yes, yes, yes *Lucinda*'s Eyes,
    yes, yes, yes, yes, yes, yes *Lucinda*'s Eyes,
    yes, yes, yes, yes, yes *Lucinda*'s Eyes.
Ye Pow'rs, I did but use her Name,
And see how all the Meteors flame ;
Blue Lightning flashes round the Court of *Sol*,
And now the Globe more fiercely burns,
Than once at *Phaetons* Fall.

Ah, ah, where, where are now,
Where are now those flow'ry Groves,
Where Zephirs fragrant Winds did play ;
Ah, where are now, where are now,
Where are now those flow'ry Groves,
Where Zephirs fragrant Winds did play,
Where guarded by a Troop of Loves,
The fair, the fair *Lucinda* sleeping lay,
There sung the Nightingale and Lark,
Around us all was sweet and Gay,
We ne'er grew sad 'till it grew dark,
Nor nothing fear'd but shortning Day.

I glow, I glow, I glow, but 'tis with hate,
Why must I burn, why must I burn,
Why must I burn for this ingrate,
Why, why must I burn for this ingrate ;
Cool, cool it then, cool it then, and rail,
Since nothing, nothing will prevail,
When a Woman Love pretends,
'Tis but till she gains her Ends,
And for better and for worse,
Is for Marrow of the Purse,
Where she jilts you o'er and o'er,
Proves a Slattern or a Whore,
This Hour will tease, will tease and vex,
And will cuckold you the next ;

SONGS Compleat,

They were all contriv'd in Spight,
To torment us, not delight,
But to scold, to scold, to scratch and bite,
And not one of them proves right,
But all, all are Witches by this Light,
And so I fairly bid 'em and the World good night,
Good night, good night, good night,
Good night, good night.

A New Ode, *or* Dialogue, *between* Mars *the God of War and* Plutus, *or* Mammon *God of Riches ; made for the Entertainment of his Grace the Duke of* MARLBOROUGH, *and General Officers, by the Right Honourable Sir* Robert Bedingfield, *then Lord-Mayor, and the Honourable the Court of Aldermen in the City: Set to Musick by Mr.* Weldon, *and perform'd by Mr.* Elford *and Mr.* Leveridge, Decemb. —, 1706.

Mars.
First Movement with Violins.

FRom Glorious Toyls of War,
With dazling Banners brought from far,
Behold, behold,
Thou potent God of Gold,
My Hero by the Warriours follow'd, comes;
Prepare a Royal Feast
To treat the Noble Guest;
Thy gorgeous Purse unty,
Let shining Medals fly,
To give 'em joyful Welcome to their Homes.

If

Pleasant and Divertive.

If *Mammon* e'er unlocks the Store,   *Mammon.*
And deals to mortal Hands the sacred Ore,
The Soul of all things here below;
   That baffles Crowns,   2d *Move-*
   And raises Towns,   *ment.*
The Will controuls, and makes a Friend a Foe.

He first must know for what he pays,
Since for Desert alone he turns the Keys;
Let Merit then inspire each Voice and Tongue,
Prepare to hear, for charming is the Song,   *Mars.*
Prepare to hear, &c.
[*Here both sing the two last Lines.*]

   The Power of *Gallia* shaken,   *Mars.*
   Ramillies Trophies taken,
   Proud *Flanders* too subjected,   3d *Move-*
   And *Belgian* States protected,   *ment with*
With daily Wonders still more strange and   *Trumpets.*
   great,
Too high for Praise, too numerous to repeat.

   As Noble Merit claims Regard,   *Mammon.*
   To prove I always am prepar'd;
Remember the renown'd *Eugene;*
   I do,   *Mars.*
How speedy Bounty did your Wish pursue, *Mammon.*
And golden Seraphs to his Succour flew,
That sav'd the sinking Cause;
   I do, I do,   *Mars.*
All this ador'd, Divinity is true.

   Beyond the *Alpine* Mounts of Snow,   *Mammon.*
   Far as the Banks of ancient *Po,*
The Cordial Coyn was sent, O happy Chance,
To heal their fainting Troops, and send a
   Plague to *France;*
                                Mars.

SONGS *Compleat*,

Mars. Blest be the happy Hour the News was brought,
Mammon. Blest be the Great *Eugene* that bravely fought,
Mars.   The happy Hour,
Mammon.   The Great *Eugene*,
Mars.   The happy Hour,
Mammon.   The Great *Eugene;*
        Blest be the happy Hour, &c.
        [*Both sing the two last Lines.*]

Mammon Now Sons of Art, ye tuneful Muses call,
  and   And sing the *Gallick* Tyrant's Fall,
Mars In soaring Alts his Grand Ambition shew,
together. Then let your Bases sink him down as low :
        In Consort next Celestial Voices raise,
        And be the *Chorus* still, our God-like Generals Praise ;
        In Consort next, &c.
        [*Here's a General* Chorus *of Voices and Instruments.*]

Mars. By him, to my Prophetick Soul appears
        A lasting Joy, that crowns succeeding Years,
        The valiant, the successful Deeds
        Of him, and the Renown'd he leads
        Will be eterniz'd, to the utmost Shore,
Mammon. Then to regale the Chiefs, take all my Store,
        All, all my Wealth, is a Reward too poor.

Another Sweet Peace like Paradice is blooming,
Movement And *Halcyon* Days in Prospect coming ;
with The rural Swains, with War affrighted,
Flutes With rosie Nymphs shall sing delighted ;
        And whilst their harmless Flocks are bleating,
        Soft Tales of Love be still repeating.

Mars.   But first bring *Gallia* down,
Mammon.   And fix the *Spanish* Crown :
Mars.   From *Bourbon* keep the *Swede*,
Mammon.   Drive *Philip* from *Madrid :*
                            Mars.

Pleasant and Divertive. 53

Let *Scotland* banish Spleen,   *Mars.*
And *Albion* guard their Queen :   *Mammon.*
These Joys, that as a Vision now appear,
All, all shall come to pass, and crown
    Th' approaching Glorious Year.
    [*Here's a Grand* Chorus *of Voices and
    Instruments.*]

The Scotch LOVER *at* Epsom.

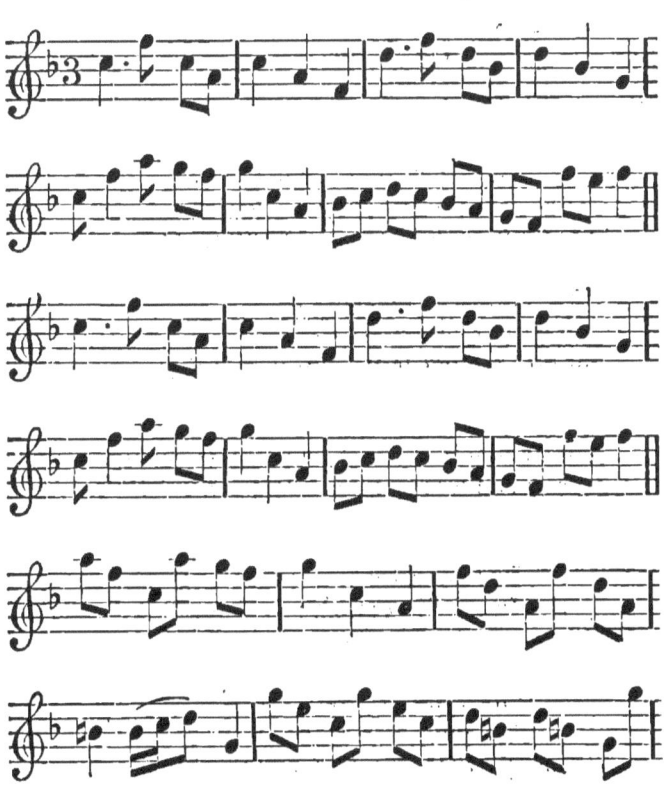

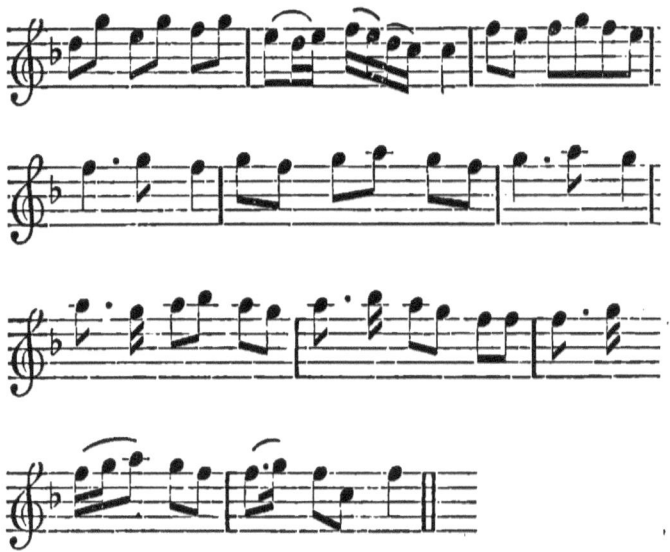

Woe is me, what mun I doe,
　　Drinking waters I may rue;
Since my heart soe muckle harm befel,
Wounded by a bonny Lass at Epsom well.
　'Ise ha bin at *Dalkeith* Fair,
　　Seen the Charming Faces there,
But all *Scotland* now geud feth defye,
Sike a lipp to shew, and lovely rowling Eye.

Jennys skin was white, her fingers small,
Moggy she was slender straight and tall,
But my Love here bears away the Bell from all;
　　For her I Sigh,
　　For her I dye,
　　In a Wild dispair:
Never Man in Woman took such joy,
Never Woman was to man so coy,
　　She'll not be my hony,
　　For my Love or mony,
Welladay, what Torment I mun bear.

　　　　　　　　　　　　　　When

Pleasant and Divertive.

When Ise to the Lottery gang,
Where the Ladds and Lasses throng;
What I lose alas, I never care,
All my heart, and soul, were won before by her:
 Or when Raffling is her choice,
 For the pretty Silver Toyes;
Then I wish, the Dice may all run low,
Glad of losing that I may oblige her so:
Ah, what muckle difference is there found
In the pliant Girles of *London* Toon,
 Besse, and *Pegg*, and *Moll*,
 And *Kate*, and *Sue*, and *Doll*,
  The fair and small,
  The Brown and tall;
   Will aw come too:
Nean will boggle at five hundred Pound,
Nean refuse a fine embroyder'd Goon,
  Aw will shew their nature,
  But this Cross grain'd creature,
Deel en take her, friend—what mun I do.

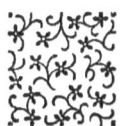

A Song *in my Play call'd the* Richmond Heiress : *Sung by Mr.* Pack.

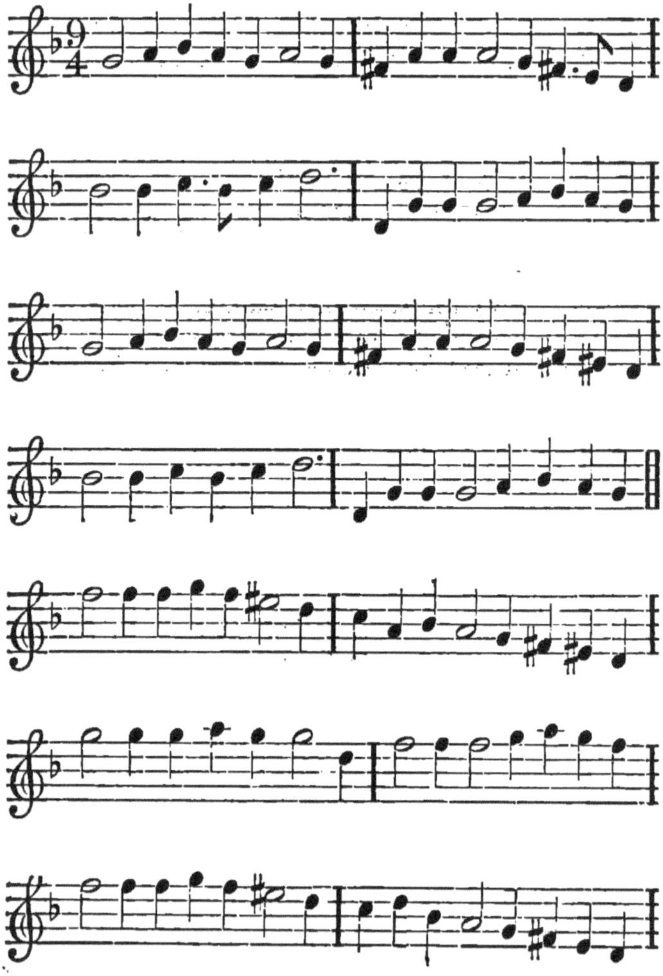

Pleasant and Divertive.

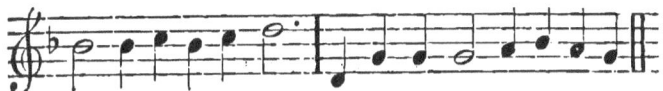

MAiden fresh as a Rose,
  Young buxome and full of jollity,
Take no Spouse among Beaux,
  Fond of their Raking quality;
He who wears a long bush,
  All powder'd down from his Pericrane,
And with Nose full of Snush,
  Snuffles out Love in a merry vein.

Who to Dames of high place,
  Do's prattle like any Parrot too,
Yet with Doxies a brace,
  At Night, piggs in a Garret too;
Patrimony out-run,
  To make a fine shew to carry thee,
Plainly Friend thou'rt undone,
  If such a Creature Marry thee.

Then for fear of a bribe,
  Of flattering noise and vanity,
Yoak a Lad of our Tribe,
  He'll shew thee best humanity;
Flashy, thou wilt find Love,
  In civil as well as secular,
But when Spirit doth move,
  We have a gift particular.

Tho' our graveness is pride,
  That boobys the more may venerate,
He that gets a Rich Bride,
  Can jump when he's to Generate;
Off then goes the disguise,
  To bed in his Arms he'll carry thee,
Then to be happy and wise,
  Take *Yea* and *Nay* to Marry thee.

58   SONGS *Compleat,*

A New SONG.

Made on the late Glorious Battle and Victory gain'd over the French *by the Duke of* Marlborough *and Prince* Eugene; *and also the taking of* Mons.

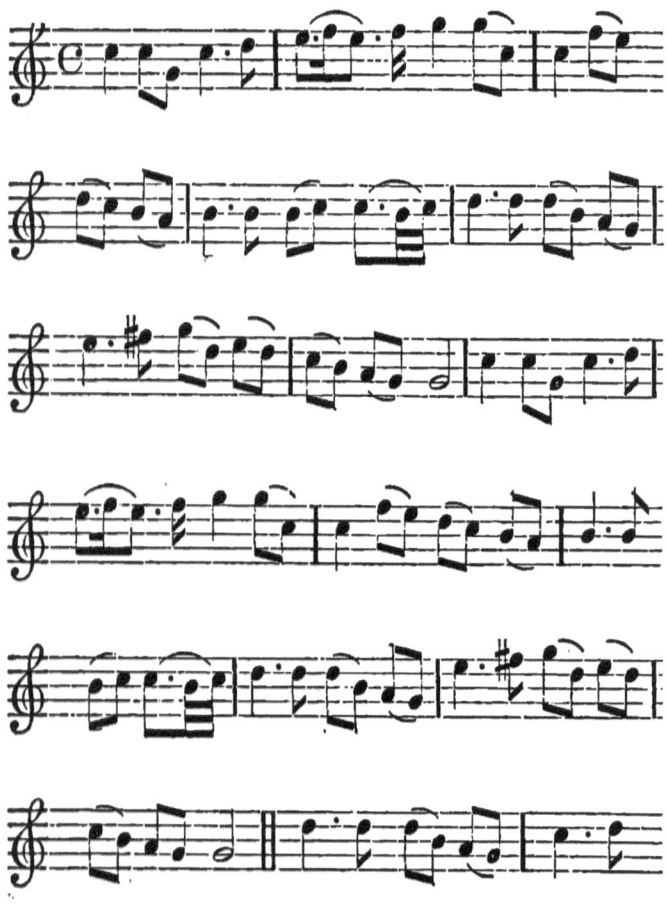

Pleasant and Divertive.

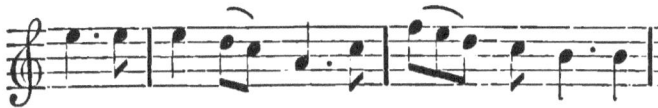

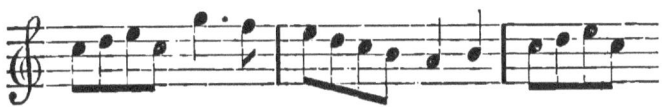

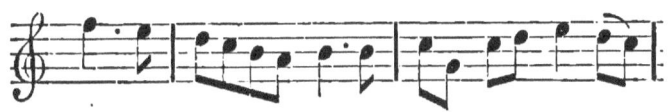

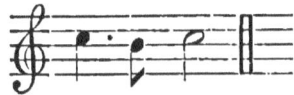

NOw Cannon smoke clouds all the sky,
And through the gloomy wood;
From ev'ry Trench the bougers fly,
Besmeer'd with dust and Blood:
Whilst valour's palm, is ours in fight,
And *Mons* to terms we bring;
Let Bragging *Boufflers* vainly write,
False wonders to the *King*:
Fate resolves to end the war,
And *Lewis* like a falling star,
Though late he sate on high,
A meteor of the sky,
Shall from his place remove,
Whilst *Europe* o'er does rove
With welcome olive branch, the Peaceful Dove.

Hail

Hail mighty *Marlborough*, great *Eugene*,
Thanks for your glorious toile ;
And 'mongst the best of Marshal men,
Nassau and brave *Argyle:*
Warriours in honours bed who lye,
Whose fame shall ever spring,
Take for reward perpetual joy ;
Whose great renown we sing :
Mounsieur, Mounsieur, leave off *Spain*,
To think to hold it is in vain,
Thy Warriours are too few ;
Thy Martials must be new,
Worse losses will ensue :
Then without more ado
Be wise, and strait call home, Petite *Anjou.*

Forty long years thou hast in gore
Been dabling up and down ;
Seek now Imperial Crowns no more,
But plot to save thy own :
Sweden the buckler to thy arm,
Fomenter of the war ;
Who kept thy blind Ambition warm,
Flyes from the frozen Czar :
Fill then a glass each *Brittish* heart,
From this great Health let no one start;
Here's to our happy Queen,
To *Marlborough* and *Eugene:*
And those that shortly mean,
To wade the River Sein,
'Tis, 'tis a Cordial rare to cure the Spleen.

Lyrical

Lyrical VERSES;

Made in honour of the Nobility and Gentry Assembling on the first day of March 17$\frac{14}{15}$. *Being the Anniversary of St.* DAVID : *Also the Birth-day of Her Royal Highness the* PRINCESS ; *Written, Set to Musick, and humbly Address'd by* T. D'URFEY.

As far as the glittering God of day
    Extends his radiant light ;
Old *Britain* her Glory will display,
    In every Action bright :
The *Fleur de lise*, and English *Rose*,
    May boast of their Antique tales ;
But the *Leek* with the greatest honour grows,
    For the lasting renown of *Wales*.

In vain all our Musical Bards did seek,
    To know whence this glory sprung ;
For time out of mind has the famous *Leek*
    In Tuneful Verse been sung :
By the *Tentons* allow'd, and victorious Rome,
    And the brave *Black Prince* ne'er fails ;
The Battle of old by this *Signal* o'recome,
    To exalt the renown of *Wales*.

The brave British Heroes did often appear,
    Recorded in Golden lines,
Cadwallader first led the van without fear,
    With whom *Conan* and *Griffieth* joyns :
    We'll give them their due,
    But must now find out new,
And our valiant young *Prince* bring in play ;
    Who by pow'r divine,
    Proves, he's fated to shine,
In a sphere, as serene as they.

Let

Let *Cinthia* give up her Reign of the Night,
    And abscond in the foamy seas;
The *Princess* that power must claim as her right,
    If Beauty has power to please:
        The Goddess confest,
        All our hearts has possest;
And will more every Age o'ercome,
        By her temper that charms,
        And adorably warms,
And her brace of young Angels at home.

Shine out then bright Star, and whilst Nations from far,
    All unite to applaud thy worth;
        We sounding our joys,
        With a general voice,
Bless the *Day* that first gave the *Birth*:
        To *George* and his race,
        Let Pretenders give place,
Wheresoe'er they are known or seen,
And when he soars on high, twill to them be some joy;
    Who survive to see thee a *Queen*.

An ODE *on the Anniversary of the* Queens-Birth. *Set to Musick by Mr.* Henry Purcel, *April* 30*th*, 1690.

ARise my Muse, and to thy tuneful Lyre,
    Compose a mighty Ode:
Whose Charming Nature may Inspire
The Bosom of some listning God
To Consecrate, thy bold Advent'rous Verse,
And *Gloriana's* Fame disperse
O're the Wide Confines of the Universe;
Ye Sons of Musick raise your Voices high:
And like your Theme be your blest Harmony:
                      Sound

Pleasant and Divertive.

Sound all your Instruments & charm the earth;
Upon this Sacred day of *Gloriana's* Birth.

[*Second Movement.*]

See how the Glittering Ruler of the Day,
From the cool Bosom of the Sea,
Drives, Drives with speed away,
And does attending Planets all
To wanton Revels Call.
Who from the Starry East and West;
To Celebrate this day make hast,
And in new Robes of Glory drest
Dance in a Solemn Ball,
Chorus. Hail gracious *Gloriana* Hail;
May every future year
Rowl on, unknown to Care;
May each propitious Morn arise
Bright as your vertue, charming as your Eyes,
And each succeeding hour new pleasures bring,
To make the Muses yearly sing:
All Hail, All Hail,
Brightest and best of Queens, *all Hail.*
And though the times distress, to Wars alarms
Calls the lov'd Monarch from your Arms;
Your *Phœbus* does to lower Spheres decline,
Only to Rise again, and with more Lustre shine.

[*Third Movement.*]

To quell his Countries Foes
Behold, the God-like Hero goes,
Fated and born to Conquer all,
Both the great, vulgar and the small,
To hunt the Savages from Dens:
To teach 'em Loyalty and Sence:
And sordid Souls of the true Faith Convince.
*. *The* But ah, I see *Eusebia drown'd in Tears;
Church. The sad *Eusebia* mourning Wears,
And

And in dejected State
Thus moans her hapless Fate;
Ah wretched me, must *Cæsar* for my sake,
These fatal dangers undertake.
No, no, ye awful Powers, no, no,
Fate must some meaner force Employ.
  Fate must not let him go;
But Glory cryes go on;
  On, on, Illustrious Man;
Leave not the Work undone,
Thou hast so well begun.
Go on, great Prince go on.
*Chorus.*See, See, all *Europe* bend their eyes
  On thy great enterprize:
Advance thy dazling Shield,
  And hast then to the Field;
Hast, hast, to Honour and Renown,
Honour, that on a Heroe's brow shines brighter
  than a Crown.

Chorus *of All.*

Exalt, exalt, your Voices high,
  And with your skilful melody:
Raise Gloriana's *grief to Joy:*
Bring warbling Lutes to hush her Cares,
Bring moving Flutes to Charm her ears.
  Ah! may their softning Influence
  Each passion Calm, please every sence:
And never, never, let her Mourn;
Great Cæsar's *Absence short will be, and Glorious*
  His Return.

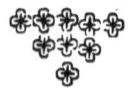

A

Pleasant and Divertive. 65

A Mock Address to the French KING.

A SONG. *Occasioned by the two Glorious Victorys at* Donawert, *and* Hochstet, *by his Grace the Duke of* MARLBOROUGH *and Prince* EUGENE. *The Tune by Mr.* Corbet.

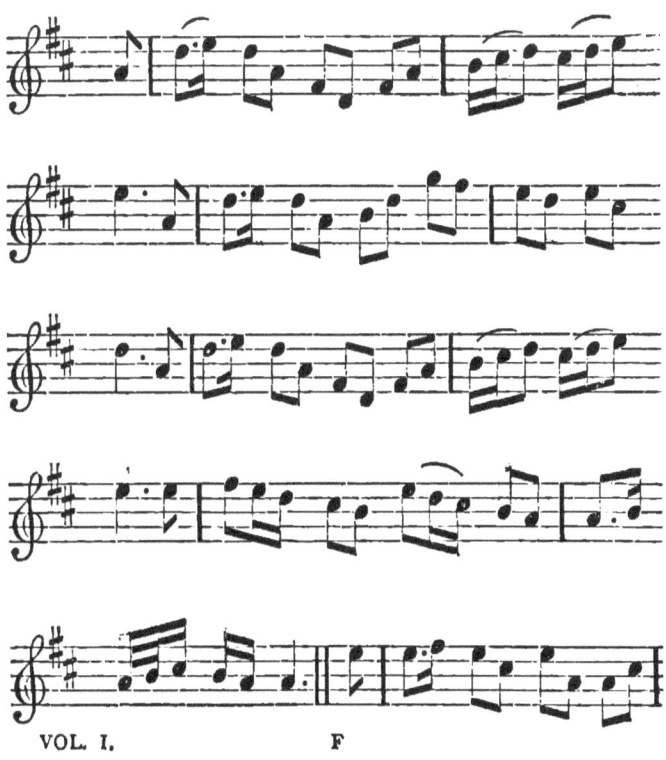

SONGS *Compleat,*

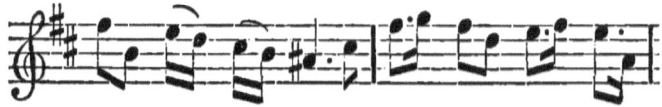
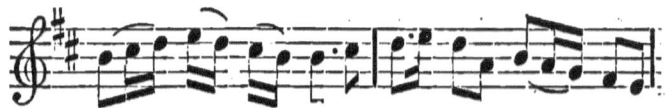
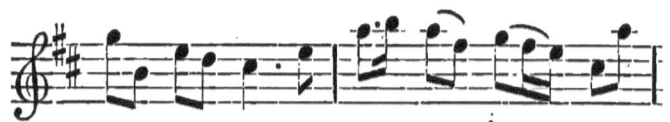

OLd *Lewis* must thy Frantick Riot
    Still all *Europe* vex ?
Methinks 'tis high time to be quiet,
    Now at Sixty Six :
Thou late hast Acted, as Distracted,
    Placing *Phillips* Crown,
And faith if that I, can Prophecy,
    Thy own is tumbling down :
For now thy Flower of Arms are lost,
    Of Empire dream no more,
Thy trembling *Gensd'arms* off will post,
    When English Cannons roar :
And whilst *Tallard* and others frown,
    To play their captive Scene,
The fates with Oaken Garlands crown
    Great *Marlborough* and *Eugene.*
                        Rebellious

Rebellious, vile, and abject state,
  In lost *Bavaria* see,
From Princely station forc'd of late,
  To serve now basely thee :
His scatter'd Race to corners fled,
  Scarce having means for Life,
And he for their poor distressful bread,
  Beholding to his Wife :
The Bann inrag'd, his Country gon,
  Thy Plots too all unhing'd,
The baseness to our Kingdom shewn,
  In proper time reveng'd ;
And all by Wars renown'd alarms,
  Made by our Glorious Queen,
For who can e're oppose in arms,
  Brave *Marlborough* and *Eugene.*

Pharsalia, where fames golden book,
  Shews *Cæsar's* glorious Theme,
Must yield to her, whose *Hero* took,
  An Army at *Blenheim :*
Landau retriev'd, and *Traerbach* gain'd,
  Do's next years fate presage,
And end the most Renown'd Campaign,
  E're known in any Age ;
Yet *Lewis*, pray be sure for this,
  Te-Deums loud you roar,
And let your Cousin the Arch-Bish,
  Appoint 'em as before :
Whilst we that with good Reason think,
  Our Joys are now serene,
Extol when flowing Bowls we drink,
  Great *Marlborough* and *Eugene.*

Love *of no* Party : *A New* Song.

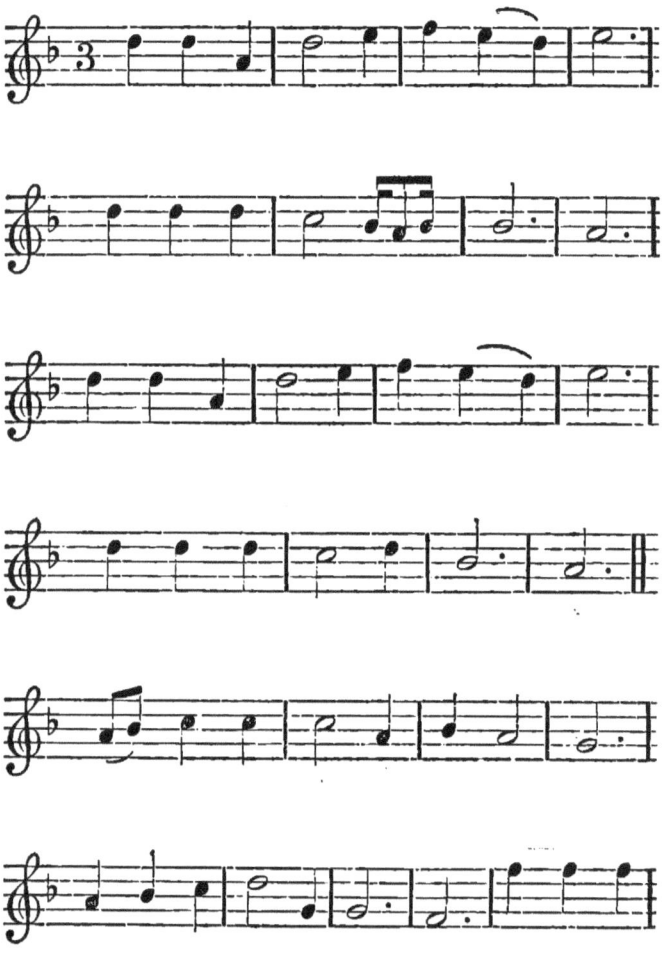

Pleasant and Divertive. 69

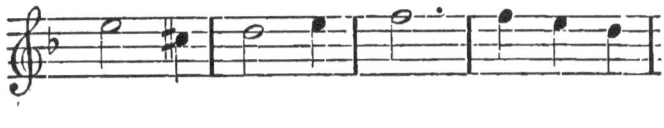

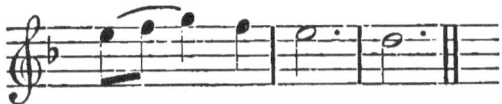

ONe *April* Morn, when from the Sea,
   Phœbus was just appearing;
Damon and *Celia* young and gay,
   Long settled Love indearing:
Met in a Grove to vent their spleen,
   On Parents unrelenting;
He bred of *Tory* race had been,
   She of the Tribe *Dissenting*.

Celia, whose Eyes outshone the God,
   Newly the hills adorning;
Told him Mamma wou'd be stark mad,
   She missing Pray'rs that morning:
Damon, his Arm around her wast,
   Swore tho' nought shou'd 'em sunder;
Shou'd my rough Dad know how I'm blest,
   Twou'd make him roar like Thunder.

Great ones whom proud Ambition blinds,
   By Faction still support it;
Or where vile money taints the mind,
   They for convenience court it:
But mighty Love, that scorns to shew,
   Party shou'd raise his glory;
Swears he'll Exalt a Vassal true,
   Let it be *Whigg*, or *Tory*.

An

An ODE

For the Anniversary Feast of ST. CÆCILIA,
On the 23d Day of *November*, 1691.
Set to Music by Dr. *John Blow.*

THE *Glorious Day* is come, that will for ever be
Renown'd as MUSIC'S greatest *Jubilee:*
The Spheres, those Instruments Divine,
    Tun'd to *Apollo's* Charming Lyre;
The Sons of all the Learned Nine,
    With soft Harmonious Souls Inspire;
Behold, around *Pernassus* Top they sit,
And Heavenly Music now, vies with Immortal Wit.
Warm'd by the *Nectar* from the *Thespian* Spring,
Of bright *Cæcilia* they sing;
Admir'd *Cæcilia* that informs their Brains:
Their awful Goddess, that their Cause maintains;
    And with her sacred Pow'r supplies,
        The Artful Hand and tuneful Voice,
And gives a taste of Paradice, in more than mortal Strains.

        And first the Trumpets Part
        Inflames the Heroe's Heart;
        The Martial Noise compleats his Joys,
        And Soul Inspires by Art:
        And now he thinks he's in the Field,
        And now he makes the foe to yield;
Now Victory does eagerly pursue,
And Music's warlike Notes make every fancy true.

The Battle done, all loud alarms do cease,
Hark how the charming Flutes conclude the Peace;
Whose softening Notes make fiercest Rage obey:
If *Pan*, beneath the famous Mirtle's shade,
    To *Midas* half so well had Play'd,
The *Delphian* God himself had lost the Day.

                      Ex-

Pleasant and Divertive.

Excesses of Pleasure now crowd on apace;
How sweetly the Violins sound to each Bass:
The ravishing Trebles delight ev'ry Ear,
And Mirth in a Scene of true Joy does appear:
No Lover of *Phillis*'s rigour complains;
None mourn for their losses, or laugh for their gains;
But lost in an Extasie publish their Joy,
Whilst the Name of *Cæcilia* resounds to the Sky.
   Ah Heaven! what is't I hear?
The Warbling Lute Inchants my Ear:
Now Beauty's Pow'r Inflames my Breast again;
I Sigh, and Languish with a pleasing Pain.
   The Notes so soft, so sweet the Air,
   The Soul of Love must sure be there,
That mine in Rapture charms, and drives away Despair.
Musick! Celestial Musick! what can be,
   On this side Heaven, compar'd to thee?
   Thou only Treat, fit for a Deity:
Monarchs by Flattery or Fame,
   May Arrogate a Glorious Name,
But in each Soul Delighting Symphony,
   Address'd to bright *Cæcilia*'s Royalty,
Are Sacred Honours fit for none, but for Divine degree.
This that blest King, and God-like Prophet knew,
   That oft from Worldly Joys withdrew;
From Glittering Pomp, and all the Courtly Throng;
   And to th' Eternal King of Kings,
   To the sweet Harp's well govern'd Strings,
Paid best Devotion in Seraphick Song.

CHORUS.

And thus by Musicks Pow'r,
Above dull Earth we soar;
Exalt our Chorus *to the Skie,*
And in Transporting Melody
Cæcilia's *Name Adore.*
Divine Cæcilia, *whom we all confess*
Our Arts Inspire; Musick's Patroness.

A

A SONG *in* Don Quixote.

Sung by one representing Joy. Set to Musick by Mr. Ralph Courtivill.

VIctumnus *Flora* you that bless the fields,
    Where warbling *Philomel,*
Warbling *Philomel* in safety builds;
And to the Nymphs, to the Nymphs and Swains,
That Revel, Revel, Revel o're these plains,
    That Revel o're these plains:
Dispose the Joy, dispose the Joy,
Dispose the Joys that Heav'n and Nature yields.

Call *Hymen*, call *Hymen*, call, call, call, call;
Call *Hymen* from his merry, merry, merry, merry,
    merry, merry home;
From his merry, merry, merry, merry home;
From his merry, merry, merry, merry home:
Call *Hymen*, call, call *Hymen* from his merry, merry,
    merry, merry, merry home;
Bid him prepare, prepare, bid him prepare,
Bid him prepare, prepare, prepare his Torch,
And come to Sing and Drink, to Sing and Drink,
To Sing and Drink full Bowls;
Call, call, call loud, call, call, call loud, loud,
Call loud, and say, 'tis Beauty's feast, 'tis Beauty's
    feast,
'Tis Beauty's feast, *Quitera's* Wedding Day;
'Tis Beauty's feast, *Quitera's* Wedding Day,
    Quitera's Wedding Day.

A Mad DIALOGUE.

Sung in my Play, call'd the Richmond Heiress, *by Mr.* Leveridge *and Mrs.* Lynsey; *Set to Musick by Mr.* Henry Purcell. *In* Orph. Britan.

He. Behold, behold the Man that with Gigantick Might,
Dares, dares, dares Combat Heav'n again;
Storm *Joves* bright Palace, put the Gods to flight;
Chaos renew, and make perpetual Night;
Come on, come on, come on ye Fighting, Fighting Fools,
Come on, come on, come on ye Fighting, Fighting Fools,

That petty, petty Jars maintain,
That petty, petty Jars maintain;
I've all, all the Wars of Europe,
All the Wars of Europe in my Brain,
I've all, all, all the Wars of Europe in my Brain.

She. Who's he that talks of War?
When charming, charming Beauty comes,
Whose sweet, sweet, sweet Face divinely Fair,
Eternal pleasure, eternal pleasure, eternal pleasure blooms;
When I appear, the Martial, Martial God a conquer'd Victim lyes;
Obeys each glance, each awful Nod,
And dreads the lightning of my killing Eyes;
More, more than the fiercest, the fiercest,
The fiercest Thunder in the Skies.

He. Ha! ha! now, now, now, now we mount up high,
Now, now we mount up high,
The Sun's bright God and I,
Charge, charge, charge on the *Azure*,
Charge on the *Azure* downs of ample Sky.

See, see, see, see, see, see, see, see,
See, see, see, see, see, see, see, see,
How th' immortal Spirits run,
See, see, see, see, see, see, see, see
How th' immortal Spirits run ;
Pursue, pursue, pursue, pursue, pursue,
Pursue, pursue, pursue, pursue, pursue,
Drive 'em o'er the burning Zone ;
Drive 'em o'er the burning Zone,
From thence come rowling down,
Come rowling down, and search the Globe below,
With all the Gulphy Main, to find my lost,
My wandring Sense, my wandring Sense again.

She. By this disjoynted matter,
    That crouds thy Pericranium,
        I nicely have found
        That thy Brain is not sound,
        And thou shalt be,
        And thou shalt be my Companion.

    Come, come, come, come, come, come,
He. Let us plague the World then,
    I embrace the blest Occasion ;
        For by instinct I find
        Thou art one of the Kind,
        Thou art one of the Kind,
        That first brought in,
        That first brought in Damnation.

She. My Face has Heaven inchanted
    With all the sky born Fellows,
Jove press'd to my Breast, and my Bosom he kiss'd,
    Which made Old *Juno* Jealous.

He. I challeng'd grisly *Pluto*,
    But the God of Fire did shun me,
Witty *Hermes* I drubb'd, round the Pole with my Club,
    For breaking Jokes upon me.
                              Chorus

Pleasant and Divertive.

[*Chorus* of both.]
Then mad, very mad, very mad let us be,
For Europe *does now with our Frenzy agree,*
And all Things in Nature are made too as we.

She. I found *Apollo* singing,
　　The Tune my Rage increases,
　I made him so blind with a Look that was kind,
　　That he broke his Lyre to pieces.

He. I drank a Health to *Venus*,
　　And the Mole on her white shoulder;
　Mars flinch'd at the Glass, and I threw't in his Face,
　　Was ever Hero bolder?

She. 'Tis true, my dear *Alcides*,
　　Things tend to Dissolution;
　The charms of a Crown, and the crafts of the Gown,
　　Have brought all to Confusion.

He. The haughty *French* begun it,
　　The *English* Wits pursue it.
She. The *German* and *Turk* still go on with the Work,
He. And all in Time will rue it.

CHORUS.
Then mad, very mad let us be,
Very mad, very mad let us be,
For Europe *does now with our Frenzy agree,*
And all Things in Nature are mad too as we.

A

A Song by a Mad Lady in Don Quixote. Set by Mr. John Eccles.

I Burn, I burn, I burn, I burn, I burn,
I burn, I burn, I burn, I burn, I burn,
   My Brain consumes to Ashes,
   Each Eye-ball too like Lightning flashes,
   Like Lightning flashes;
Within my Breast there glows a solid Fire,
Which in a thousand, thousand Ages can't expire.

   Blow, blow, blow,
   Blow the Winds, great Ruler blow,
   Bring the *Po* and the *Ganges* hither,
   'Tis sultry, sultry, sultry Weather;
Pour 'em all on my Soul, it will hiss,
   It will hiss like a Coal,
   But never, never be the cooler.

'Twas pride, hot as Hell, that first made me rebel,
From Love's awful Throne a curst Angel I fell;
   And mourn now the Fate,
   Which my self did create,
Fool, Fool, that consider'd not when I was well;
   And mourn now the Fate,
   Which my self did create,
Fool, Fool, that consider'd not when I was well.

   Adieu, adieu transporting Joys,
   Adieu, adieu transporting Joys;
   Off, off, off, ye vain fantastick Toys,
   Off, off ye vain fantastick Toys,
That drep'd this Face and Body to allure,
   Bring, bring me Daggers,
   Poyson, Fire, Fire, Daggers, Poyson, Fire,
   For Scorn is turn'd into Desire;
   All Hell, all Hell feels not the Rage,
Which I, poor I, which I, poor I endure.

Pleasant and Divertive. 77

Remarks for the French KING.

A Song *Occasioned by the taking of* Lisle *and that Glorious Campaign.*

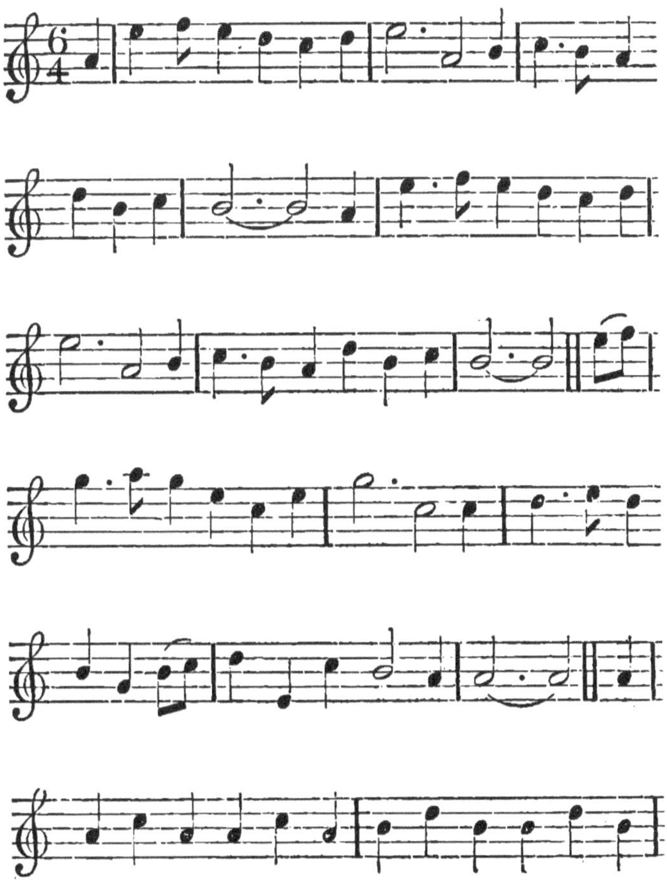

SONGS Compleat,

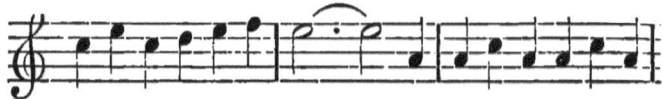

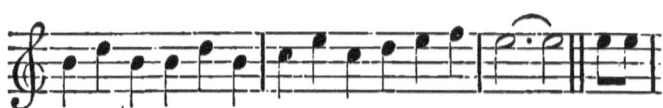

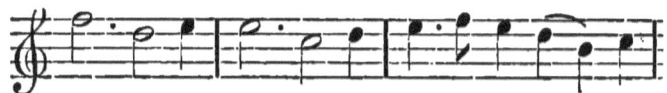

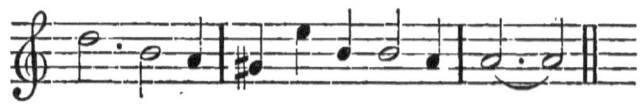

GRand *Lewis* let pride be abated,
Thy Marshals have all had a foyle;
Boufflers like *Tallard* is ill Fated,
And *Vendosme* remembers the *Dyle.*
Thy hand is quite out at Invasions,
And spite of thy Fortifications,
Brave *Eugene* has taken *Lisle :*
Tho' one day *Burgundy,*
Was merry with *Berry,*
And bragg'd the Queens Troops he would scourge,
Make *Britains,* and great ones,
This Summer run from her,
And own *Chevalier de* St. *George ;*
Tho' the Crump too that Season,
Got *Bruges* and *Ghent* by Treason,
We'll make him e'er long disgorge.

A

Pleasant and Divertive.

A Pox of your race of high Flyers,
That late on the Battlements stood ;
Who shew'd to get out of the Bryers,
What Princes you had of the Blood ;
And welfare the Gallant *Hanover*,
Who late his high Birth to discover ;
Charg'd as a young Hero shou'd :
'Tis said too, who fled too,
Were snapt so, and cropt so,
They never could face us again ;
That cunning, or running,
Won't better the matter,
They shun mighty *Marlborough* in vain,
And *Monsieur* t'alarm ye,
If once more he *Hockstets* your Army,
We'll give ye no thanks for *Spain*.

Thy Troops can do nothing but rattle,
Brave *Webb* the discovery begun ;
Who prov'd at the *Wynendale* Battle,
How fast thy Mob Army could run :
His valour shall flourish in Story,
And thus while he adds to our Glory,
His own will out-Post the Sun.
Forgetting that beating,
A hearty bold party,
Late Marcht towards *Brussels* fair Town,
There bouncing and clattring,
With Cannon for battring,
The *Electoral* Hotspur sate down ;
But when some time after,
Our Generals cross'd o're the water,
Away the wild Goose was flown.

Bavaria this shameful disaster,
Not half yet repays thy past ill,
For first being base to thy Master,
And afterwards false to King *Will*;

And

80   SONGS *Compleat*,

And if 'tis thy simple Opinion,
Le Roy can restore thy Dominion,
Parblew thou art frantick still :
Pursuing his Ruin,
We're Marching and Charging,
Resolv'd on a winter's Campaign,
Cold Snowing, and Blowing,
In Terrour are shewing,
Great *Marlborough* and Glorious *Eugene*.
We'll Storm too like Thunder,
Vile Towns that are Fated for Plunder,
And take 'em *L'Espee a la main*.

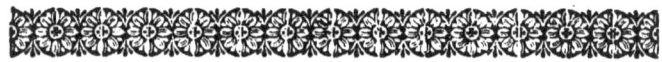

A SONG.

Sung by Mr. Pack *in the* OPERA *call'd the* Kingdom *of the* Birds, *to the Dance between the High and Low Flyers.*

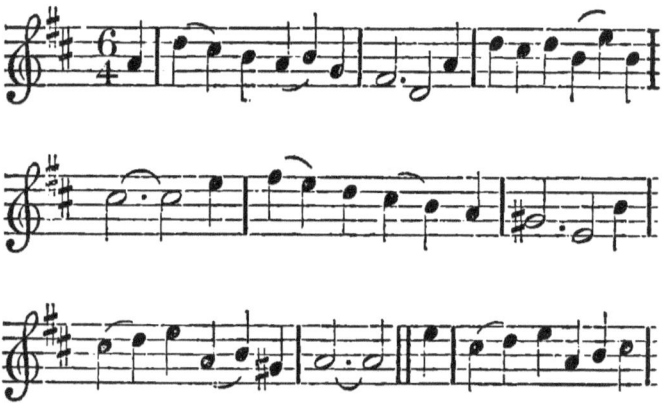

Pleasant and Divertive. 81

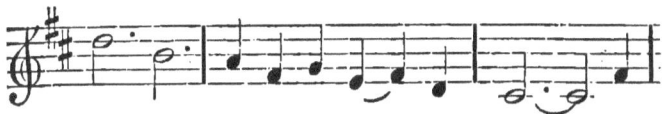

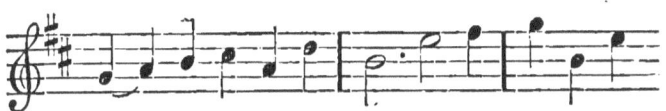

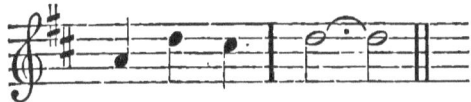

W Hat are these Ideots doing,
That daily their Feuds advance ;
As if they were pursuing,
New ways to favour *France?*
For shame give over your Dance ;
Your National danger see ;
No longer forfeit your sense,
But agree, ye rash *Britains*, agree.

Whilst strange and trivial Reasons,
The whimsical Brain allures ;
You lose the happy Season,
That shou'd encourage your Powers.
The *Monsieur* is at your Doors,
And if he received must be ;
The Shame and the Scandal is Yours :
Then agree, ye Rash *Britains* agree.

Ye Soaring High-flown People,
In Politicks so profound,
You climb so high on your Steeple,
It makes your Brain turn round.

Consider how you lose Ground,
   If Foreigners Master be,
Whilst you with Maggots abound;
   Then agree, silly *Britains*, agree.

And you, whose senseless Jargon,
   Contentious Night and Morn,
Declaims against an Organ,
   As 'twere a Sow-gelder's Horn:
Let Concord's Power adorn
   Your Hearts, if wise you'll be,
Nor longer merit a Scorn;
   But agree, silly *Britains*, agree.

'Tis known you are richly landed,
   And you have a place at Court;
And you the *Bank* have commanded,
   And you have two Ships in Port,
Yet still ye Reason retort;
   And if ye ruin'd must be,
'Tis all rank Folly in short;
   Then agree, silly *Britains*, agree.

Religious Safety doubted
   Still makes the Nation groan,
You make such Stirs about it,
   Some Wise Heads think you have none;
But all is for Interest done,
   As faith it likely may be,
Let that Point stated be known,
   And agree, ye rash *Britains*, agree.

Pleasant and Divertive. 83

The NIGHTINGALE.
Sung by Mrs. Balwin, *in the* Kingdom *of the* Birds.

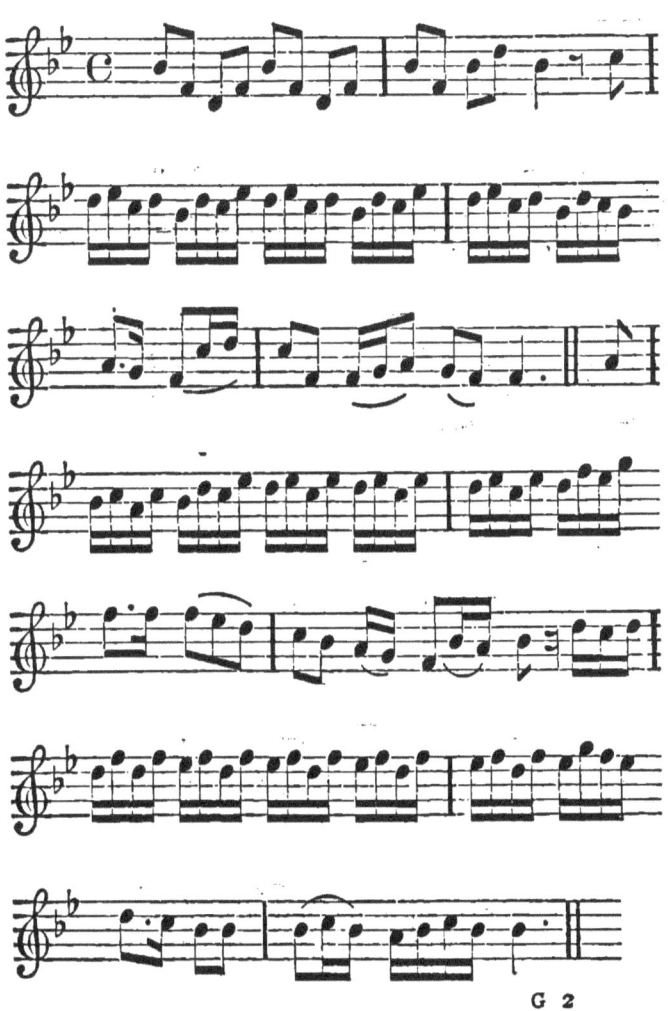

84 Songs *Compleat*,

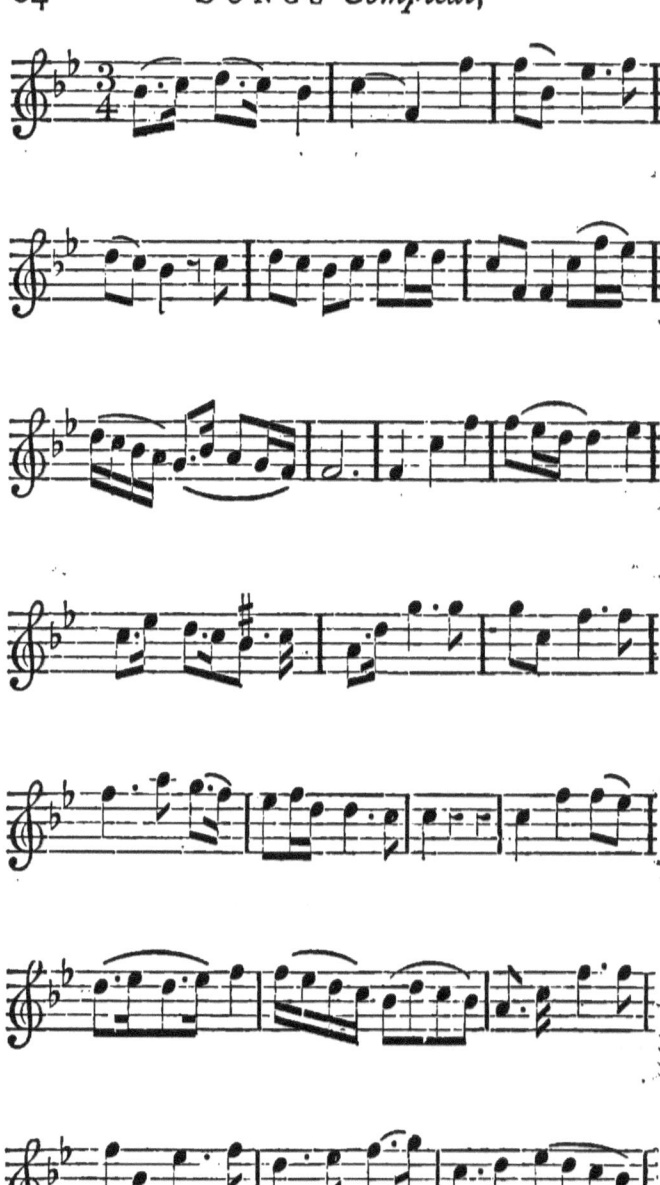

Pleasant and Divertive. 85

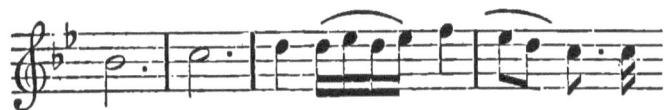

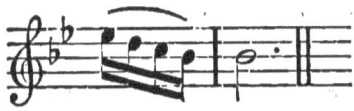

JUG, jug, jug, jug, jug, jug, jug,
    jug, jug, jug, jug, jug, jug,
The jolly Philomel upon the Hawthorn sings,
The jolly Philomel upon the Hawthorn sings,
    sings, upon the Hawthorn sings.

    Happy we, that all, all excel
In what true Pleasures, true Pleasures bring;
Yet one Island, one Island lyes below,
Who, did they but the Blessing know,
    They reap by Glorious Means,
Wou'd raise their tuneful Voices high,
And never cease this Song of Joy,
    Long live the best of Queens,
    Long live the best of Queens.

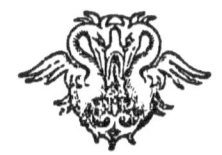

86   SONGS *Compleat,*

On the Affairs Abroad, and King
WILLIAM'S *Expedition.*

Set by Dr. Blow.

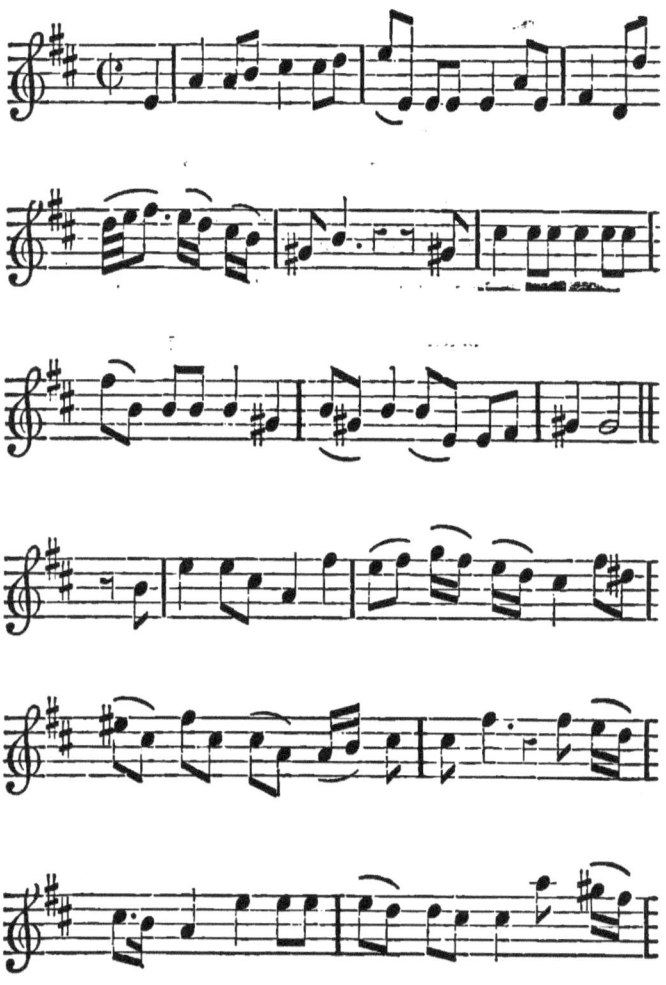

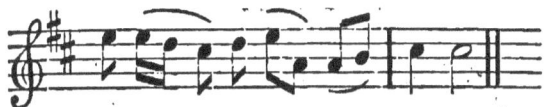

CHurch Scruples and Jars plunge all *Europe* in
  Wars,
English Cæsar espouses our Quarrel,
Predestin'd to stand against *Lewis* le Grand,
  And wear his now flourishing Laurel.

The Cause that is best, now comes to the Test,
  For Heaven will no longer stand Neuter,
But pronounce the great Doom for old *Luther* or
  Rome,
  And prevent all our Doubts for the future:

'Twould turn a wise Brain, to consider what Pain
  Fools take to become Politicians,
Fops, Bullies, and Cits, all set up for Wits,
  And ingeniously hatch New Divisions.

Some shew their hot Zeal for a New Common-weal,
  And some for a New Restauration,
Thus cavil and brawl, 'till the Mounsieur gets all,
  And best proves the Wit of the Nation.

Tho' we Med'cines apply, yet the Feaver swells high,
  First caus'd by a Catholick Riot,
Which no Cure can gain, 'till the breathing a Vein
  Corrects the mad Pulse into Quiet;

Yet whate'er Disease on our Country may chance,
  Let's drink to its healing Condition,
And rather wish *William* were Victor in *France*,
  Than *Lewis* were *England*'s Physician.

A DIALOGUE.

Highly diverting Queen Mary, *in the* 4th *Act of the second Part of* DON QUIXOTE; *for a Clown and his Wife. Sung by Mr.* Reading *and Mrs.* Ayliff. *Set by Mr.* Henry Purcell

In Orph. Britan.

He. Since Times are so bad, I must tell you Sweet-Heart,
I'm thinking to leave off my Plough and my Cart;
And to the fair City a Journey will go,
To better my Fortune as other folk do :
Since some have from Ditches,
And course Leather Breeches,
Been rais'd, been rais'd to be Rulers,
And wallow'd in Riches;
Prithee come, come, come, come from thy Wheel,
Prithee come, come, come, come from thy Wheel,
For if Gypsies don't lye,
I shall, I shall be a Governor too, e're I dye.

She. Ah! *Collin* ah! *Collin*, by all, by all thy late doings I find,
With sorrow and trouble, with sorrow and trouble the pride of thy Mind :
Our Sheep now at random disorderly run,
And now, and now Sundays Jacket goes every day on;
Ah! what dost thou, what dost thou, what dost thou mean?

He. To make my Shooes clean,
And foot it, and foot it to the Court,
To the King and the Queen,
Where shewing my Parts I Preferment shall win.
She

Pleasant and Divertive. 89

She. Fye, fye, fye, fye, fye, fye, fye, fye, fye, fye, 'tis better,
  'Tis better for us to Plough and to Spin:
  For as to the Court when thou happen'st to try,
  Thou'lt find nothing got there, unless thou can'st Buy;
  For Money, the Devil, the Devil and all's to be found,
  But no good Parts minded, no, no, no, no good Parts minded without the good Pound.

He. Why then I'le take Arms, why then I'le take Arms, I'le take Arms,
  And follow, and follow Alarms,
  Hunt Honour, that now a-days plaguily charms:

She. And so lose a Limb, by a Shot or a Blow,
  And curse thy self after, for leaving, for leaving the Plough.

He. Suppose I turn Gamester?

She. So Cheat and be Bang'd:

He. What think'st of the Road then?

She. The High-way to be Hang'd;

He. Nice Pimping however yields Profit for Life,
  I'le help some fine Lord to another's fine Wife:

She. That's dangerous too, amongst the Town Crew,
  For some of 'em will do the same thing by you;
  And then I to Cuckold ye may be drawn in,
  Faith, *Collin*, 'tis better I sit here and Spin,
  Faith, *Collin*, 'tis better I sit here and Spin.

He. Will nothing Prefer me, what think'st of the Law?

She. Oh! while you live, *Collin*, keep out of that Paw:

He

He. I'le Cant and I'le Pray.

She. Ah! there's nought got, ah! there's nought got that way,
There's no one minds now what those black Cattle say;
Let all our whole care, be our Farming Affair,
To make our Corn grow, and our Apple-Trees bear.

[*Verse for Two Voices.*]
Ambition, Ambition's a Trade, a Trade no Contentment can show,

She. So I'le to my Distaff;

He. And I to my Plough;

Ambition, Ambition's a Trade, a Trade no Contentment can show,
No, no, no, no, no, no, no, no, no, no, no, no, no, no, no, no, no, no, no, no, no, no, no, no, no Contentment can show,
no, no, no Contentment can show.

CHORUS.

She. *Let all our whole care, be our Farming Affair;*
To make our Corn grow and our Apple-Trees Bear:
Ambition, Ambition's a Trade, a Trade no Contentment can show.

She. *So I'le to my Distaff;*

He. *And I'le to my Plough;*

Ambition, Ambition's a Trade, a Trade no Contentment can show,
No, no, no, no, no, no, no, no, no, no, no, no, no, no, no,
no, no, no, no, no, no, no, no, no, no, no, no Contentment can show,
No, no, no Contentment can show.

Pleasant and Divertive. 91

A Humerous Song, *Sung at* Mary *the* Buxom's *Wedding, in my Play of* Don Quixote.

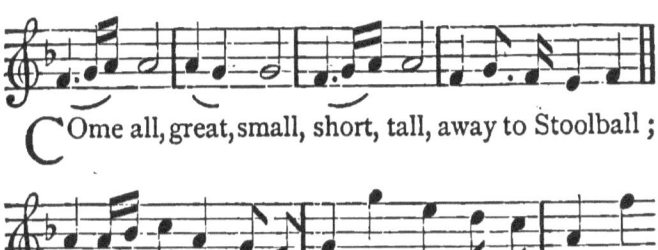
COme all, great, small, short, tall, away to Stoolball;

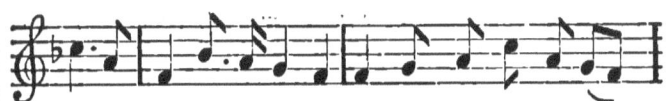
Down in a Vale on a Summers day, all the Lads and

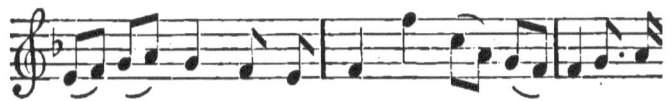
Lasses met to be Merry, a match for Kisses at

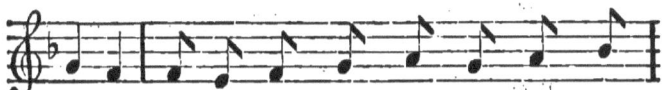
Stoolball play, and for Cakes and Ale, and Sider and

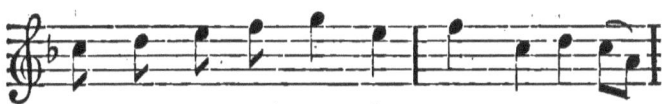
Perry. *Will* and *Tom*, *Hall*, *Dick* and *Hugh*, *Kate*,

Doll, Sue, Bess and Moll, with Hodge, and Briget,
and

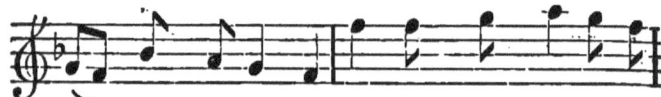
and *James*, and *Nancy*; but when plump *Siss* got the

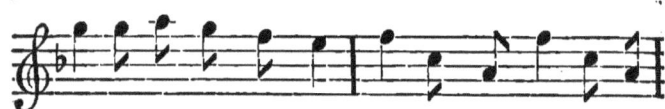
Ball in her Mutton Fist, once fretted, she'd hit it

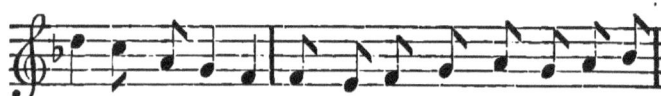
farther than any; Running, Haring, Gaping, Staring

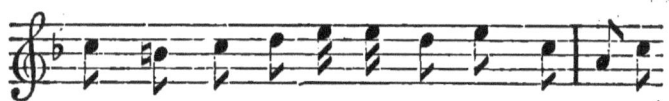
Reaching, Stooping, Hollowing, Whooping; Sun a

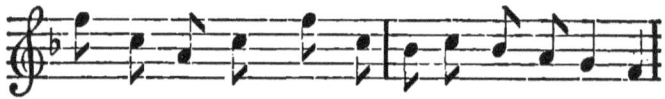
setting, all thought fitting, by consent to rest 'em;

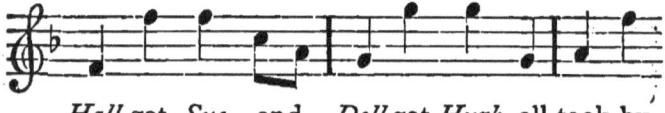
Hall got *Sue*, and *Doll* got *Hugh*, all took by
turns

Pleasant and Divertive.

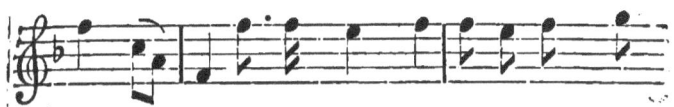

turns their Lasses and Buss'd 'em. Jolly *Ralph* was

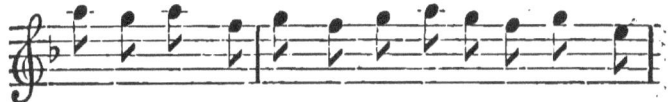

in with *Peg*, tho' freckl'd like a *Turkey* Egg, and

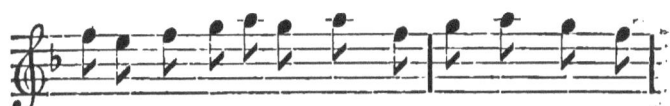

she as right as is my Leg, still gave him leave to

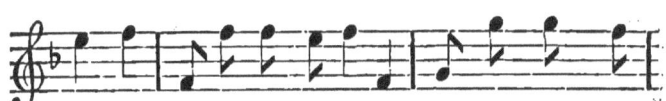

towze her. *Harry* then to *Katy*, swore, her Duggs were

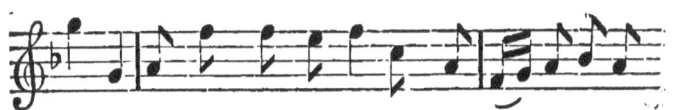

pretty, tho' they were all sweaty, and large as any

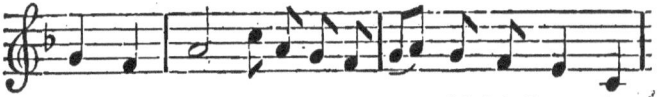

Cows are. *Tom* Melancholy was with his Lass ; for

Sue

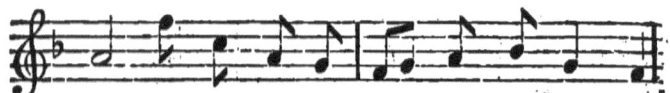
Sue do what e'er he cou'd, wou'd not note him.

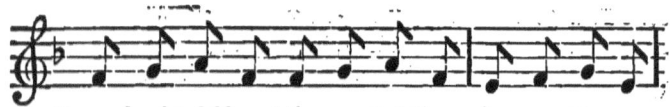
Some had told her, b'ing a Soldier in a Party,

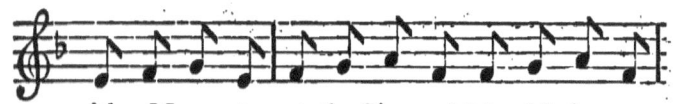
with *Mac-carty* at the Siege of *Limrick*, he was

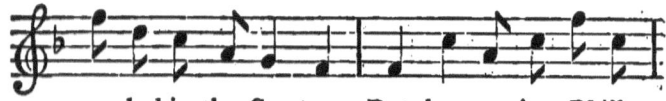
wounded in the *Scrotum*. But the cunning *Philly*

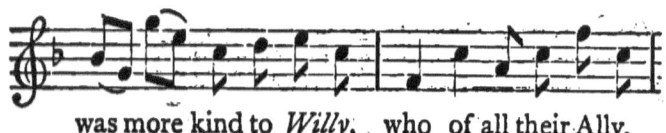
was more kind to *Willy*, who of all their Ally,

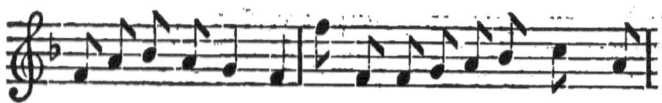
was the ablest Ringer; He to carry on the Jest, be-
gins

Pleasant and Divertive. 95

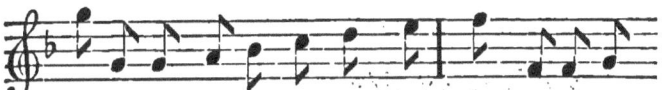

—gins a Bumper to the best, and winks at her of

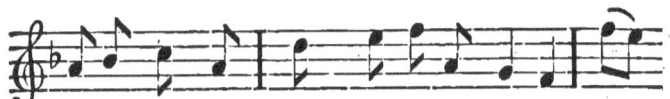

all the rest, and squeez'd her by the Finger. Then

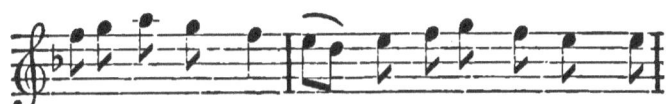

went the Glasses round, then went the Lasses down, each

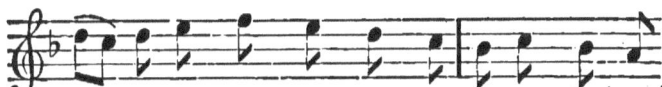

Lad did his Sweet-heart own, and on the Grass did

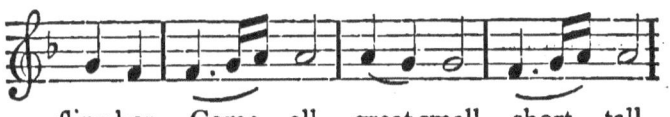

fling her. Come all, great small, short, tall,

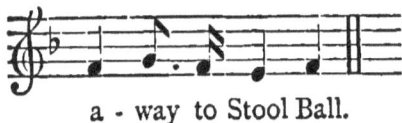

a - way to Stool Ball.

The

The STORM:

Set to Music by Mr. Henry Purcell. *To be found in his* Orph. Britt.

Blow, blow *Boreas*, blow, and let thy surly Winds
    Make the Billows foam and roar;
Thou can'st no Terror breed in valiant Minds,
But spight of thee we'll live, but spight of thee we'll live and find a Shoar.

Then cheer my Hearts, and be not aw'd,
    but keep the Gun-Room cleer;
Tho' Hell's broke loose, and the Devils roar abroad,
    Whilst we have Sea-room here:
    Boys, never fear, never, never fear.

Hey! how she tosses up! how far,
The mounting Top-mast touch'd a Star;
The Meteors blaz'd, as thro' the Clouds we came,
And *Salamander*-like, we live in Flame;
But now, now we sink, now, now we go
Down to the deepest Shades below.

Alas! alas! where are we now! who, who can tell!
Sure 'tis the lowest Room of Hell,
Or where the Sea-Gods dwell:
With them we'll live, with them we'll live and reign,
With them we'll laugh, and sing, and drink amain,
With them we'll laugh, and sing, and drink amain,
But see we mount, see, see we rise again.

[*Second Movement.*]

Tho' flashes of Lightning, and Tempests of Rain,
Do fiercely contend which shall conquer the Main;
Tho' the Captain does swear, instead of a Pray'r,
And the Sea is all Fire by the Damons *o' th' Air;*
We'll drink and defie, we'll drink and defie
The mad Spirits that fly from the Deep to the Sky,

That

Pleasant and Divertive. 97

*That fly, fly, from the Deep to the Sky,
And sing whilst loud Thunder, and sing whilst loud
   Thunder does bellow;
For Fate will still have, a kind Fate for the Brave,
And ne're make his Grave of a Salt-water Wave,
To drown, to drown, no, never to drown a good Fellow;
No, never, no, never to drown a good Fellow;
No, never, never to drown, no, never, never to drown a
   good Fellow,
No, never, no, never to drown a good Fellow.*

A Poole at Piquette. *The Words made, and set to a Tune by Mr.* D'Urfey; *made at* Ramsbury *Mannor.*

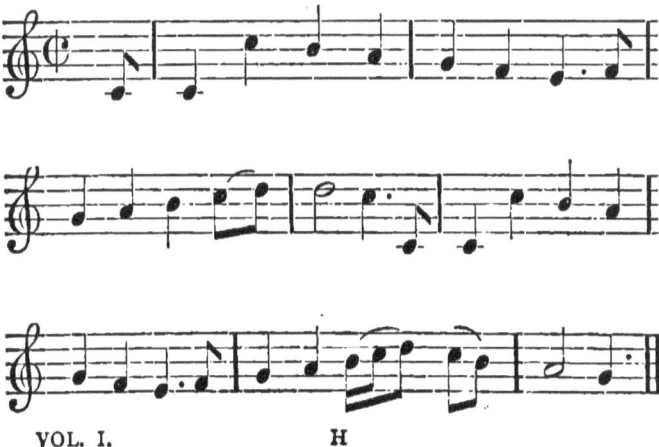

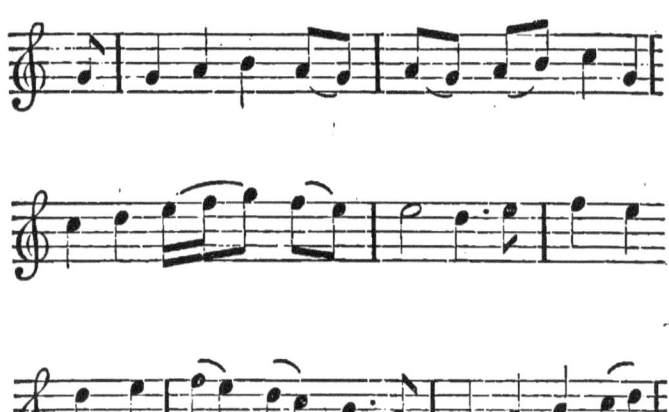

Within an Arbour of Delight,
　　As sweet as Bowers Elisian,
Where famous *Sidney* us'd to write,
　　I lately had a Vision;
Methought beneath a Golden State,
　　The Turns of Chance obeying,
Six of the World's most noted great,
　　At *Piquette* were a playing.

The first two were the brave *Eugene*,
　　With *Vendosme* Battle waging,
The next a Nymph, who to be Queen,
　　Her *Mounsieur* was engaging:
The *Fleur de-lis*, old *Maintenon*,
　　With sanctified *Carero;*
And next above the scarlet *Don*,
　　Queen *Anne*, and *Gallick Nero*.

　　　　　　　　　　　　The

Pleasant and Divertive.

The Game between the Martial braves
    Was held in diff'rent Cases,
The Frenchman got Quatorze of Knaves,
    But Prince *Eugene* four Aces :
And tho' the 'tothers eldest Hand
    Gave Hopes to make a Jest on't,
Yet now the Point who soonest gain'd,
    Could only get the best on't.

From them I turn'd mine Eyes to see
    The Churchman and the Lady,
And found her pleas'd to high degree,
    Her fortune had been steady ;
The Saints that cram'd the *Spanish* Purse,
    She hop'd would all oblige her,
For he had but a little *Terse*,
    When she produc'd *Quint-Major*.

But now betwixt the *King* and *Queen*
    An Empire was depending,
Within whose mighty Game was seen
    The Art of State-contending :
The *Mounsieur* had three Kings to win't,
    And was o'er *Europe* roaming,
But her full Point, *Quatorze* and *Quint*,
    Won all, and left him foaming.

A Dialogue *between Mr.* Pack *and Mrs.* Bradshaw, *in the* Opera *call'd,* The Kingdom of the Birds.

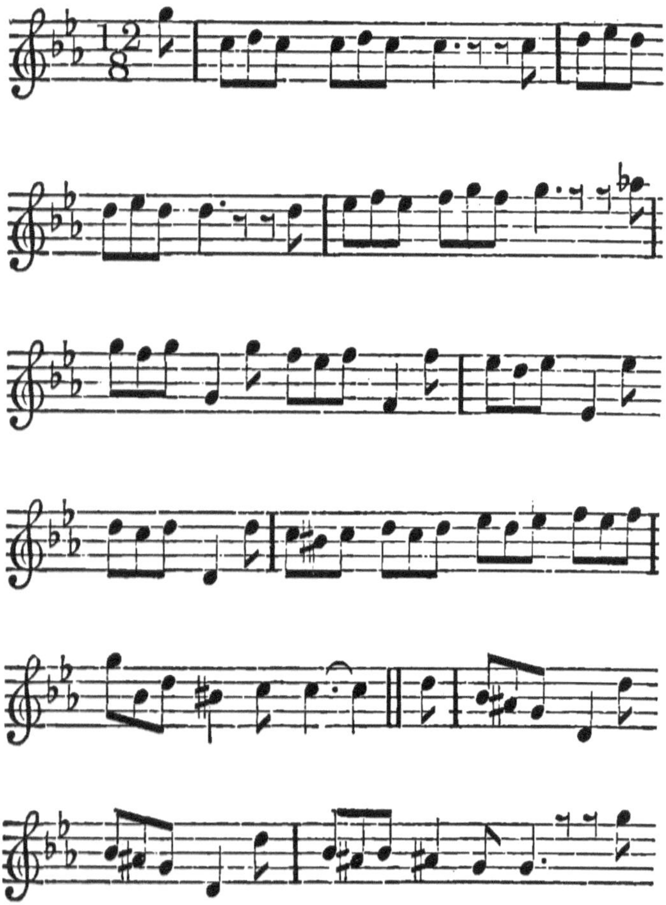

Pleasant and Divertive. 101

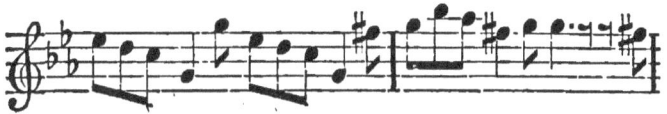

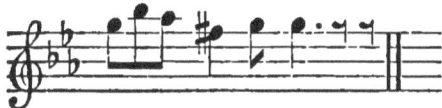

She. OH Love if a God thou wilt be,
Do Justice in Favour of me
For yonder approaching I see
   A Man with a Beard,
   Who as I have heard,
   Has often undone
   Poor Maids that have none,
   With sighing, and toying,
   And crying, and lying,
And such kind of Foolery.

He. Fair Maid by your Leave,
My Heart does receive
Strange Pleasure to meet you here,
   Pray tremble not so,
   Nor offer to go,
I'll do ye no Harm, I swear,
I'll do ye no Harm, I swear.

She. My Mother is spinning at Home,
My Father works hard at his Loom,
And we here a milking are come,
   Their Dinner they want,
   Pray Gentlemen don't
   Make more ado on't,
   Nor give us Affront,
   We're none of the Town
   Will lie down for a Crown,
Then away, Sir, and give us Room.

By

He. By *Phœbus*, by *Jove*,
By Honour, by Love,
I'll do ye dear sweet no harm,
    Y're as fresh as a Rose,
    I want one of those,
Ah, how such a Wife would charm,
Ah, how such a Wife would charm.

She. And can you then like the old Rule,
Be Conjugal, honest, and dull,
And marry, and look like a Fool,
    For I must be plain,
    All Tricks are in vain,
    There's nothing can gain
    The Thing you'd obtain,
    But moving, and proving,
    By Wedding, true Loving,
My lesson I learnt at School.

He. I'll do't by this Hand,
I've Houses, I've Land,
Estate too in good Free-hold,
    My Dear, let us joyn,
    It all shall be thine,
Besides a good Purse of Gold.

She. You make me to blush, now I vow,
Oh Lord, shall I too baulk my Cow,
But since the late Oath you have swore,
    Your Soul shall not be,
    In danger for me,
    I'll rather agree,
    Of two to make three,
    We'll Wed, and we'll Bed,
    There's no more to be said,
And I'll ne'er go a Milking more.

The British Muses *an* ODE, *occasion'd by the Hearing of Five fine* Ladys *at a Man of Qualitys House in the Country, playing a* Sonata *in Consort.*

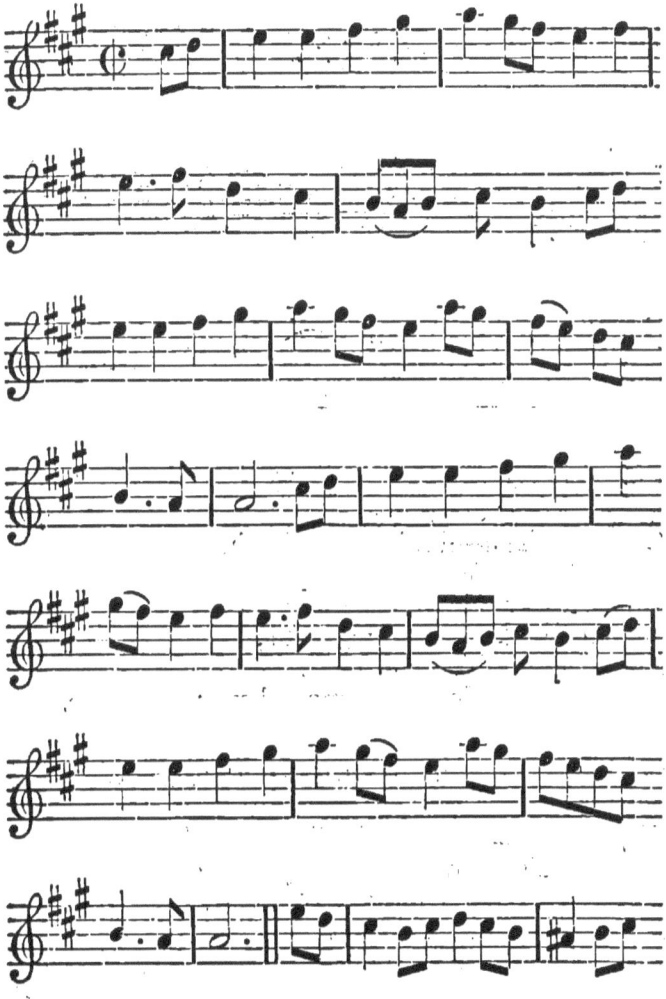

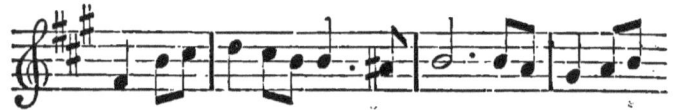
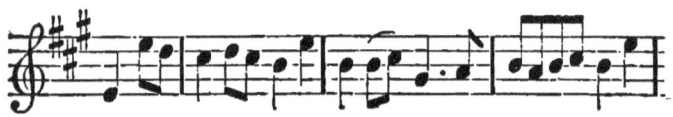
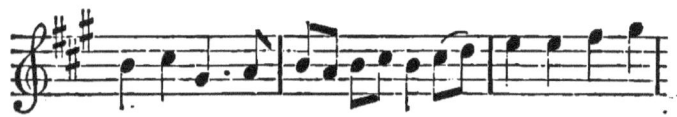
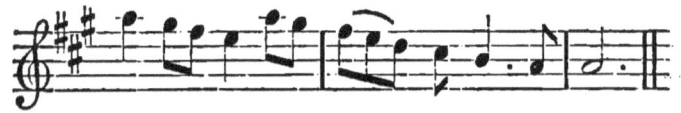

AS the *Delian* God, to fam'd *Halcyon*,
    From Heavens high Court descended down,
There the Tuneful *Muse's* playing he found,
    A *Sonata* Divinely rare:
When *Thalia* touch'd the charming Flute,
Errato Struck the warbling Lute;
And *Clio's* Treble joining to't,
    Made the Harmony beyond compare.

Then *Euterpe's* full Bass, the sweet Consort did raise,
And with pleasure each Sence alarm'd,
E'ry Note was enjoy'd, e'ry Hand was imploy'd,
With sounds of Joy the Flowery Valley rung:
Apollo gaz'd, and silent was his Tongue,
But when his dear *Calliope* Sung,
    Ah, then the *God* was charm'd.

Pleasant and Divertive.

A Song *in the* Modern Prophets.

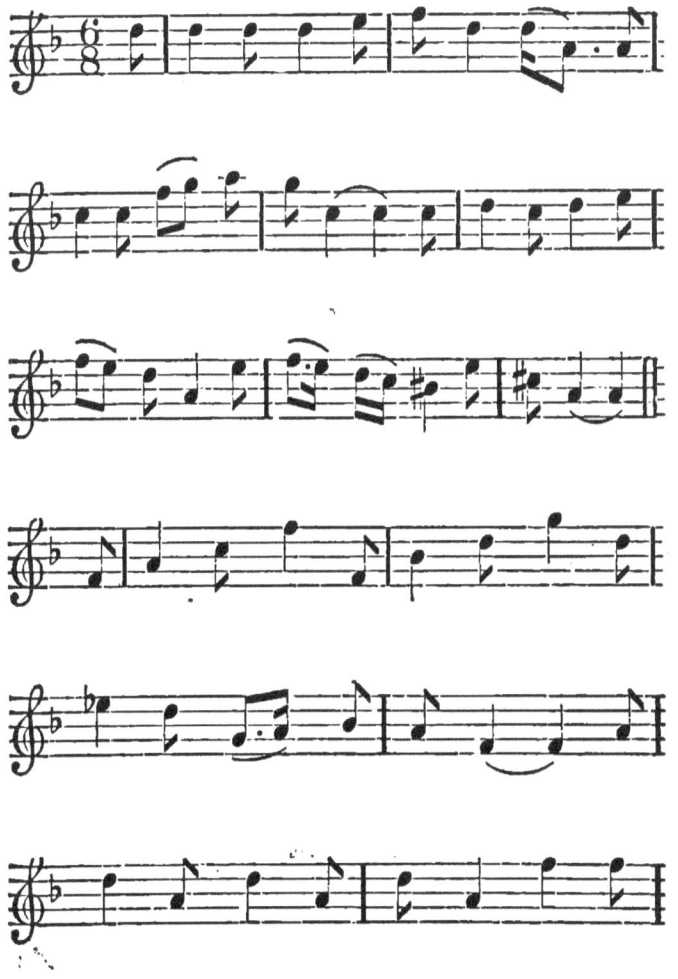

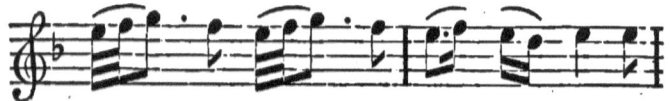

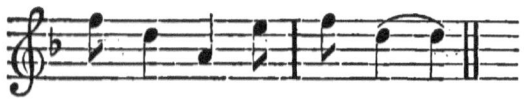

WE *Prophets* of the *Modern Race*,
  To hide rebellious Evil,
Pretend we all excel in Grace,
  And fight against the Devil:
We range, we roam, we quake, we foam,
  We breed by Inspiration,
We own the Call the Spirit moves,
And then the chosen Sister proves
  By frequent Agitation.

Strange Miracles we ne'er unfold,
  We scorn to understand 'em,
Those shewn the Mob in Days of Old,
  Provok'd, but did not mend 'em;
    We Cant in Tone,
    We sigh, we groan,
Nor do our Whimseys tire us;
And tho' our Preaching be hum drum,
And writing senseless as *Tom Thumb*,
  We still have Fools admire us.

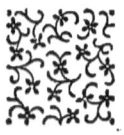

An Epithalamium *on the Marriage of the Honourable* Charles Leigh.

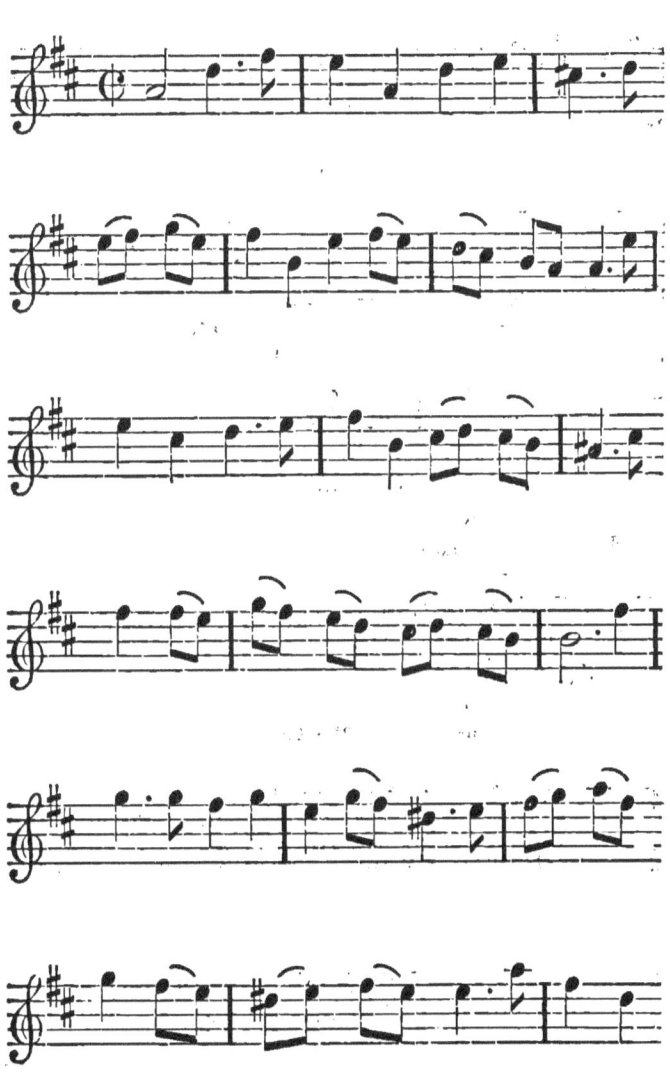

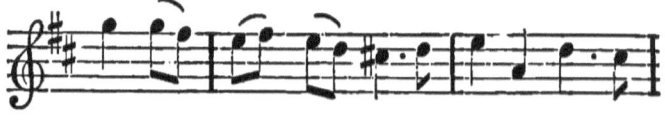

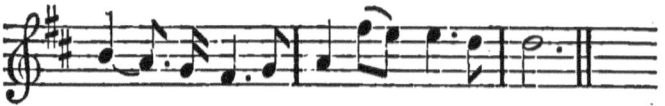

Draw, draw the Curtain, fye, make hast,
  The panting Lovers long to be alone,
The precious Time no more in talking wast,
  There's better Business going on:
Our Absence will their Wishes crown,
The next swift Moment's not too soon,
Our artful Song sounds like a Drone,
For now all Musick, but their own,
  Is harsh, and out of Tune.

Now Love inflames the Bridegroom's Heart,
  How weak, how poor a Charmer is the Flute;
And when the Bride's fair Eyes her Wishes dart,
  How dully sounds the warbling Lute.
If this Divine, harmonious Bliss
  Attends each happy Marriage Day,
Who such a blessed State would miss,
And such a charming Tune as this,
  Who would not learn to play?

Oh, Joy too fierce to be exprest,
  Thou sweet Atoner of Life's greatest Pain,
By thee are Men with Love's dear Treasure blest,
  And Women still by losing gain.
Smile then divine, propitious Pow'rs,
  Upon this Pair let Blessings flow,
Let Care mix with their Sweets, not Sowers,
But may succeeding Days and Hours
  Be charming all as now.

A New Dialogue: *Set by Mr.* Henry Purcell, *Sung by a* Boy *and* Girl *at the* Playhouse.

He.   Celemene, pray tell me,
      Pray, pray tell me *Celemene*,
   When those pretty, pretty, pretty Eyes I see,
   Why my Heart beats, beats, beats, beats in my Breast,
   Why, why it will not, it will not, why, why, it will not let me rest:
   Why this trembling, why this trembling too all o'er?
   Pains I never, pains I never, never, never felt before:
   And when thus I touch, when thus I touch your hand,
   Why I wish, I wish, I wish, I was a Man?
She. How shou'd I know more than you?
   Yet wou'd be a Woman too.
   When you wash your self and play,
   I methinks could look all day;
   Nay, just now, nay, just now am pleas'd, am pleas'd so well,
   Shou'd you, shou'd you kiss me, I won't tell,
   Shou'd you, shou'd you kiss me, I won't tell.
   No, no I won't tell, no, no I won't tell, no, no I won't tell,
   Shou'd you kiss me I won't tell.
He. Tho' I cou'd do that all day,
   And desire no better play:
   Sure, sure in Love there's something more,
   Which makes *Mamma* so bigg, so bigg before.
She. Once by chance I hear'd it nam'd,
   Don't ask what, don't ask what, for I'm asham'd:
   Stay but till you're past Fifteen,
   Then you'll know, then, then you'll know what 'tis I mean,

Then you'll know what, then you'll know, what
    'tis I mean.
He. However, lose not present bliss,
    But now we're alone, let's kiss :
    But now we're alone let's kiss, let's kiss.
She. My Breasts do so heave, so heave, so heave,
He. My Heart does so pant, pant, pant ;
She. There's Something, something, something more
        we want,
    There's Something, something, something more
        we want.

*The Happy Country Gentleman;
a New* SONG.

The Words made to a pretty Italian *Air:
Sung by* Nicolini, *in the opera of* Rinaldo,
Il tricerbero humiliato, &c.

ALL the World's in Strife and hurry,
    And the Lord knows when 'twill cease ;
Some for Interest, some for Glory,
    Tho' their Tongues run all of Peace :
Since the High-Church then and Low,
Make our daily Mischiefs grow,
And the Great, who sit at the Helm in doubt,
Are not sure, how quickly they may turn out :
    How blest is the happy he,
Who from Town, and the Faction that is there, is
        free ;
    For Love and no ill ends,
    Treats his Neighbours and his Friends,
    He shall ever in the Book of Fame,
    Fix with Honour a glorious Name.

He that was the High Purse-bearer,
    At his Levy no Crowds you see ;

He

Pleasant and Divertive.

He that was the Grand Cause hearer,
  Now no longer makes Decree :
Nay, to prove her wavering evil,
And that Fortune is the Devil,
The Hero leading our Arms abroad,
Whom they late did Celebrate like a God,
Scarce has any to Drink his Health,
If a Friend does not kindly put it round by stealth ;
    A *Whigg* is out of grace,
    And a *Tory* in his place :
Riddles all, and something is amiss,
What a Whimsical world is this.

A Pindarick ODE, *on* New Years-Day : *Perform'd by Vocal and Instrumental Musick, before their Sacred Majesties King* WILLIAM *and Queen* MARY. *Set by Dr.* John Blow.

BEHOLD, how all the stars give way ;
  Behold, how the Revolving Sphere,
Swells to bring forth the Sacred Day,
  That ushers in the mighty Year ;
Whilst *Janus* with his double Face
Viewing the present Time and past,
In strong Prophetick Fury sings,
Our Nation's Glory and our King's.

See *England's* Genius, like the dazling Sun,
Proud of his Race, to our Horizon run
To welcome that Cœlestial Power,
That of this Glorious Year begins the Happy Hour :
    A Year from whence shall Wonders come ;
    A Year to baffle *France* and *Rome*,
And bound the dubious Fate of Warring *Christendom.*

Move

Move on with Fame, all ye Triumphant Days,
To *Britain*'s Honour, and to *Cæsar*'s Praise;
Let no short Hour of this Year's bounded Time,
Pass by without some Act sublime :
Great William, Champion of the Mighty States,
And all the Princes the Confederates :
Ploughs the Green *Neptune*, whilst to waft Him o'er,
The Fates stand smiling on the *Belgick* Shore;
   And now the *Gallick* Genius Trembles,
   How e'er she Pannick Fear dissembles;
To know the Mighty League, and view the Mighty
   Pow'r :
So when the *Persian* Pride of old,
   Disdain'd their God the Sun,
With Armies, and more powerful Gold,
   Did half the World o'er run,
Brave *Alexander* chang'd their Scorn to Awe,
And came and fought, and Conquer'd like *Nassau*.

Then welcome Wondrous Year,
   More Happy and Serene,
Than any ever did appear,
   To bless *Great Cæsar* and his Queen :
May every Hour encrease their Fames;
Whilst Ecchoing Skies resound their Names :
And when Unbounded Joy, and the Excess }
Of all that can be found in Human Bliss, }
Fall on 'em, may each Year be still like this, }
Health, Fortune, Granduer, Fame, and Victory,
And Crowning all, a Life, long as Eternity.

          CHORUS.
Come ye Sons of Great Apollo,
Let your Charming Consorts follow;
Sing of Triumph, sing of Beauty,
Sing soft Ayres of Loyal Duty;
   Give to Cæsar's *Royal Fair,*
   Songs of Joy to Calm her Care;
Bid the less Auspicious Year Adieu,
And give her joyful Welcomes to the New.

The first SONG *in the first Part of* Massaniello, *Sung by Mr.* Pate, *Representing* Fate.

From Azure Plains, blest with Eternal day,
    Celestial flow'ry Groves, that ne'er decay;
From Lucid Rocks that *Sol*'s bright Rays let in,
      Where, with unclouded Brow,
        I sate and view'd the deeps below,
And saw my Female drudges Spin;
I Fate am come, thy Courage to improve,
'Tis the Eternal's Doom, Engrav'd in Adamant above;
      And oh! thou drowzy Deity,
        That dost in slumbers bind,
        The Body of Mortality,
        And calm the Stormy Mind;
No more, no more his Brain possess,
With the soft charm of gentle Peace,
He must awake to bloody Wars,
Unbounded Fury, civil Jars,
And is by Heav'ns decree for wonderous deeds design'd.

St. Genaro, *Protector of* Naples, *descends and Sings.*

St. *Gen.* Tho' mighty Fate all must obey,
    And conq'ring Hero's greatest King,
    Amongst the rest of human things,
Yield to his dreadful sway;
Yet view thy Book of Dooms once more,
Thou there wilt find one happy hour,
When *Naples* shall be free from Rebel power,
    'Tis sure as the revolving year,
    And I her darling Saint appear
To stop thy fury, least it should exceed,
And tell thee tho' permission of this ill
Is sacred mystery, and th' Eternal's Will;
      Yet he that does the deed,
      For doing it, must bleed. *Ascends.*

Fate. Hear each Neighbouring Destiny.
   Who the Souls of Mortals free,
   Hear my Voice and straight obey,
Heaven Commands, the Work must stay.
Such a number, and no more, ⎫
Must Encrease your fatal store, ⎬
And he must die the task being o'er; ⎭
   Remember all 'tis so decreed,
   That he that does this mighty deed,
   For doing it must bleed.

An ODE *on the Assembly of the Nobility and Gentry of the City and County of* York, *at the Anniversary Feast,* March *the* 27th. 1690. *Set to Musick by Mr.* Henry Purcell. *One of the finest Compositions he ever made, and cost* 100l. *the performing.*

OF Old, when Heroes thought it base
 To be confin'd to Native Air,
And Glory brought a Martial Race,
 To breath their towring Eagles here,
The Sons of Fam'd *Brigantium stood ⎫
Disputing Freedom with their blood; ⎬
Undaunted at the Purple flood, ⎭
Brigantium honour'd with a Race Divine;
Gave Birth to the Victorious *Constantine.*
Whose Colony whilst Planted there,
With blooming Glories still renew'd the Year,
The bashful *Thames* for Beauty so renown'd,
In hast ran by her Puny Town;
And poor †*Augusta* was asham'd to own.
Augusta then did drooping lye,
Though now she rears her towring front so high,

 * York. *Anciently so call'd.*   † *London.*
             The

The Pale and Purple * Rose, *The Houses*
That after cost so many Blows *of* York, *and*
When *English* Barons fought; Lancaster.
A Prize too dearly bought:
By the fam'd Worthies of that Shire,
Still best by Sword and Shield defended were.
And in each Tract of Glory since,
For their Lov'd Country and their Prince;
Princes that hate *Rome's* Slavery,
And join the Nations Right with their own Royalty,
None were more ready in distress to save,
None were more Loyal, none more Brave.

And now when the Renown'd *Nassau*
Came to restore our Liberty and Law,
The work so well perform'd and done,
They were the first begun;
They did no storms or threatenings fear,
Of Thunder in the grumbling Air,
Or any Revolutions near:
The Noble work large hopes of freedom told,
Freedom Inspir'd their minds and made 'em bold,
And gave them *English* Hearts like those of Old,
To welcome their Redeemer when he came,
   Whose Vertue and whose Fame,
Made our long smother'd Joys burst into brighter flame.
So when the Glittering Queen of Night,
With black Eclipse is shadow'd o're,
   The Globe that swells with sullen Pride,
   Her dazling Charms to hide,
   Does but a little time abide,
And then each Ray is brighter than before,

        CHORUS *of all.*
   Let Musick joyn in a Chorus Divine,
   In praise of all, of all, of all,
   That Celebrate, that Celebrate,
   This Glorious Festival.
   Sound Trumpets sound, beat every Drum,
   Till it be known through Christendom;

This is the Knell of falling Rome,
To him that our Mighty Defender has been,
   Sound all,
And to all the Heroes invited him in,
   Sound all,
And as the chief Agents of this Royal Work,
Long flourish the City and County of York.

Vive le Roy.
The Poet's humble Address to the King. The Words made to a pleasant Tune.

NOW over *England* Joy to express,
   Sing, sing *vive le Roy;*
The Town and the Countrys have made an Address,
   And sing *vive le Roy.*
For Loyalty many, and many for Place;
   True Hearts duty employ,
   Whiggs, now Publish your Joy;
High-Church and *Low-Church,*
The True *Church*, and No *Church*,
   All Sing, sing *vive le Roy,*
   All Sing *vive le Roy.*

A Glorious Feast *Great Britain* may boast,
   Sing, sing *vive le Roy;*
Where since Royal *George*, Treat us all at his cost,
   Who sing *vive le Roy:*
The Muses 'tis hop't, may have share of the roast,
   Sound, sound far as the Sky;
   Fame, fame never to dye,
For the Cause Royal, Obedient and Loyal:
   They Sing, sing *vive le Roy,*
   All Sing *&c.*

Poets

Poets affirm to fix their renown,
  Sing, sing *vive le Roy ;*
In all Revolutions, some up and some down,
  Sing, sing *vive le Roy :*
Not one out of Forty, was false to the Crown,
  Rare, rare carols of joy ;
  Bear, bear fancys on high,
Common-wealth haters, Abhorring all Traitors:
  They sing, sing *vive le Roy,*
  All sing *&c.*

Humours go round the Town at each meal,
  Sing, sing *vive le Roy ;*
And if we in Wit, as in Metals may deal,
  Sing, sing *vive le Roy :*
Tho' some are of Lead, yet the best are in Steel,
  Round, round *Europe* they fly ;
  Wide, wide Nations supply,
Loyal Spectators, with Morals and Satyrs :
  Still sing, sing *vive le Roy,*
  Sing, sing *&c.*

If the wise Members ripe for a Fray,
  Would Sing *vive le Roy ;*
And take my Advice in a moderate way,
  Or sing *vive le Roy :*
Chuse quiet two Bottles, and three Meals a day,
  No more Strife would destroy,
  No more Malice supply ;
Virulent stories, the *Whiggs,* and the *Tories,*
  Would end all, *vive le Roy,*
  All, all *&c.*

But if vile humours lasting and long,
  Wont sing *vive le Roy ;*
Both sides to support it, with Libel that's strong,
  To sing *vive le Roy :*
         Must

Must hire *Tom D'urfey* to make a smart Song,
   Where, where, as in a glass,
   They'll see plainly each face ;
Lyrick, and *Crambo*, to *vy el de Gambo*,
   Would soon sing, &c.

Thus mighty Sir, thus finishing all,
     Sing, sing *vive le Roy ;*
I wish you long Life, and your Fame to extol,
     And sing *vive le Roy :*
You'd throw down *Mardyke*, and you'd build up
   Whitehall,
   Hark, hark Muses on high,
   Chant loud Carols of Joy :
Britain's Reliever, Reign o're us for ever,
   And long, long *vive le Roy,*
   Long, long *vive le Roy.*

A New SONG *on the late* Peace, *and the present turn of Times. The Words made to a pretty Playhouse Tune.*

Now some Years are gone,
   Since you saw *Apollo* smiling,
Britain's cares exiling ;
When the Dove was flown :
To crop the Branch, the sign of Peace,
   Then flew o're the Nation,
   A Royal Proclamation ;
     Human gore,
     Should flow no more,
     Nor Crimson o're,
     The *Flemish* shore :
All hated feuds abroad, should ever cease,
                     [*Second*

[*Second Movement.*]
Above twenty Years did France oppose,
 With hopes of Empire blinded;
Castile, to frighted Peace with blows,
 Tho' now they think fit to mind it:
The *Hogan* that plunder'd our Fishing before,
 Tho' grumbling agreed to secure his gain:
And the greedy *Spread-Eagle* that gap'd to have
 Spain
At last too was forc'd to come o'er.

But if this sham Peace do at last bring
 France upon us;
High-Church has undone us,
That caused War to cease:
Had ruin'd else the *Mounsieur* quite:
  Then if Forces slender,
  Can bring in the *P——r:*
   Waft him here,
   Thro' plains of Air,
   And turn the State,
   In spight of Fate:
You may affirm, the *Tories* plotted right.

[*Third Movement.*]
But let Royal *George* live long in Health,
 He'll prop the sinking Nation;
If Peace don't bring us Fame and Wealth,
 Mardyke shall have small Cessation:
Our Council are wise, and their Policy sure,
 That against all our fears, will our Rights maintain;
 By *Marlborough*'s Arms, and the *Chancellour*'s Brain,
Our Country shall still be Secure.

The

The Coronation HEALTH; *the Words made to a pretty new Tune.*

GReat *Cæsar* is Crown'd,
   To the Skies let it sound;
Tho' the *Tories*, the *Tories*, the *Tories*, the *Tories*
   With Malice, do grumble and lower:
      Whilst *Whiggs* raise their Joys,
      With a general Voice;
And with Boo, huzza boo, huzza boo, huzza,
   The great Cannon go off at the *Tower*.

   Prince *Wallia* along,
   Gave such Grace through the throng;
That you'd fancy, you'd fancy, you'd fancy, you'd fancy,
   Some God had descended:
      His Goddess look'd on,
      And with joy heard each Gun;
Give a boo, huzza a boo, huzza a boo, huzza,
   By her brace of young Angels attended.

   Then fill Glasses high,
   For methinks I am dry,
'Till I'm toping, I'm toping, I'm toping, I'm toping,
   Success to the King and the Nation:
      'Twill wit too Inspire,
      And we'll second the Fire;
Of the boo, huzza boo, huzza boo, huzza,
   Never was a more Glorious occasion.

MUSIDORA

MUSIDORA:

A New Song. The Words made to a pretty Scotch Ayre.

Opening Budds began to shew
    The Beauty of their vernal Treasure,
Spring had routed Frost and Snow,
    Obeying *Flora's* Pleasure:
Damon by a River's side,
Whose silver Streams did gently glide,
Compar'd his Blessings to the Tide,
    That flow'd beyond all Measure.

Musidora Fair and Young
    With panting Rapture still alarms me,
Motion, Shape, or Charming Tongue,
    All raise a Flame that warms me:
Eyes excelling *Titan's* Ray;
But when she's most divinely gay,
And kindly designs to sing and play,
    Oh *Venus!* how she charms me.

Sylvia, dearest of all Dears,
    Charm'd by Nature to content ye,
In her Face the Figures wears
    Of Pleasure, Joy, and Plenty:
Kindling Hopes, and Doubts, and Fears,
The Young inchants, the Old she chears,
So well she makes dull seventy Years,
    Grow brisk as Five and Twenty.

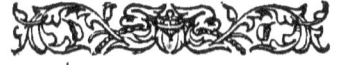

On the Warwickshire Peers. A New Sonnet.
The Words made to a pretty Tune.

Ride all *England* o'er,
 East and West, South or Nore,
And try every *British* Peer;
 The *Warwickshire* Lords
 Will excel what affords,
Any other remaining Shire.
 Peer *Den——gh* is kind,
 And a hearty true Friend, [1]
Lord *Cr——n* the same we know,
 He'll still hold ye to't,
 From the Dram to the Flute,
And ne'er give ye a Hint to go.

 North——ton of Fame
 Should have first here a Name,
Whose Deserts great Applause have gain'd,
 His brave Loyal Race,
 To their Country a Grace,
In Old Times the Crown's Right maintain'd:
 Lord *Brook* by his Choice
 Would make *Warwick* rejoyce,
Would his Spleen let him Harbour there,
 But since that plagues his Head,
 For his Cure let him read
* *Le Malade Imaginaire.*

 Lord *Willoughby's* Old,
 But couragious and bold,
For the Rights of the Church and Crown,
 Who though ninety Odd,
 Was freezing his Blood,
For the Cause would rise post to Town:
 But, oh, to its Shame,
 There is one without Name,

  * *A Play of* Molieres.

Tho'

Tho' the *French* have it plain, *un fou*,
    I say nought of his Face,
    But his stigmatiz'd Dress,
You'll find is a *Coventry* Blue.

    And now this is past,
    To dear *Stonely* I hast,
That its Patron my Praise may share,
    Spite do what it can,
    He that looks like a Man,
May still find a Welcome there:
    The Queen still goes round,
    And the Warriours renown'd,
The Church too, and all its Sons,
    Who cry, let's go there,
    Some good News we shall hear,
Lord *Thomas* has fir'd his Guns.

    Lord *Digby* of late
    Is so wondrous sedate,
That 'tis counted a kind of Crime,
    Condemn'd to his house,
    Without sometimes a Loose,
He'd be sainted before his time;
    A regular Life,
    Free from Faction and Strife,
Gains Applause still amongst the Wise;
    But who shuns all Converse,
    Lives as 'twere in a Hearse,
And is dead now, before he dies.

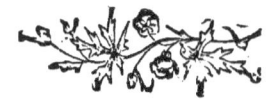

The Brisk COMPANION.

Reflecting on the Party Humours and Discourse of WHIGG *and* TORY. *A New* Song; *Written in the Great Snow. The Words made to a pretty New* Minuet.

Flow the flowry Rain,
    That blanches round the Plain,
Filling the Hills and the Dales so fast,
    Snow will soon be gone;
        Then, then the vernal Sun
        Brightly will right ye
        From Troubles past,
    When his Glory does restore me,
        Wine his Creature,
        Charms my Nature,
Drink, drink then to the Wise and Brave;
    Torys raise your little King,
    Whiggs, let all the *Tories* swing,
I, a Club more brisk will have.

    Rot 'em, crys the *Whigg*,
    Steeple Rogues grow so big,
To their New *Perkin* they roar a Song;
    Oh, says *High-Church* Brood,
    We can't be understood,
They take a King that can't speak our Tongue;
        This a Canter,
        This a Ranter;
        One for true Kings,
        One for New Kings;
Stark Mad, they often fall to Blows,
    Whilst our jolly Beaus esprits
    Drink, o're Wit and Harmony,
Hang the Sect can be our Foes.

LOVE *and* GRATITUDE : *Or, The* PARALELL; *A Lyrical* ODE, *taken from a Chapter in the famous* Italian *Boccace.*

IN Old *Italian* Tales we read
   A Youth, by Riot, and fond Love undone,
Had yet a Faulcon left of famous Breed,
His sole Companion in his fatal Need,
   And chief Diversion when he left the Town.

The Saint that did his Soul possess,
Touch'd with a generous Sense of his Distress,
   Made him a Visit at his poor Retreat,
Whom his Heart nobly feasted, but alas,
   His empty Purse could get;
Nothing was good enough for her to eat:

'Till rack'd with shame, and a long fruitless Search;
   He, more to make his perfect Love appear,
His darling Hawk snatch'd from the Pearch,
   And dress'd it for his Dear;
Which generous Act did so entirely gain her,
   She gave him all her Love and Wealth,
And nobly paid her Entertainer.

PARALELL.

So when my Love, with Fate at Strife,
   In hope was lost to gain the Fair,
And Nature's darling Hawk, my Life,
   Was doom'd a Feast for sad Despair.
     Divine *Olympia* chang'd the sad Decree,
     And with infallible Divinity,
     Gave a new Being to my Soul and me.

The Yeoman of Kent, A Ballad.

Relating how the Parson of S———b *finding long* George *in his Shirt under his favourite Maid's Bed, beat him, and turn'd him home without his Cloaths.*

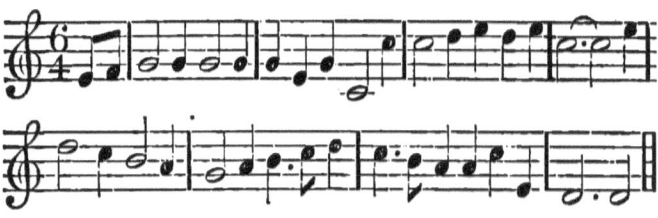

IN *Kent* I hear, there lately did dwell
   Long *George*, a *Yeoman* by trade,
Plump, lively and young, brisk, jolly and strong,
   Who fugell'd the Parson's fine Maid,
And her Ruffdom, Ruffdom, frizledom Madg,
   Her Hey Rump, frizlerump de,
Rowze about, towze about, seek all the House about,
   Under the Bed was he.

It once fell out, a Moon-shiny Night,
   It seems his Passion did move,
He thought fit to wooe her, and do something to her,
   So great was the Power of his Love,
      To her Ruffdom, &c.

At Window then he softly did call,
   Sweet Amber *Mary* pray rise,
Since *May-day* our dancing, Love has been advancing,
   And thou art my beautiful Prize;
      With thy Ruffdom, &c.

Fye *George*, she crys, these Words are but Toys,
   My Master sleeps in his Bed,
The Door it is lock'd, and I'm in my Smock,
   Be gone, there's no more to be said
      To my Ruffdom, &c.

The God of Love, says he, wounded me,
   And bade me fly to thy Arms,
I must, and I will, this night have my Fill,
   And tast of the luscious Charms
      Of thy Ruffdom, &c.

Did Love command, dear *Georgy*, thy Hand?
   For then it can be no Sin;
He scrawling, she tugging, with hawling and lugging,
   Through Window at last he got in
      To her Ruffdom, &c.

They were so fierce, they made the Bed squeak,
   The Parson heard them, as 'tis said,
Who Marriage obeying, and with his Wife praying,
   Found one did the same to his Maid
      In her Ruffdom, &c.

Then both soon rose, but *Georgy* was gone,
   Who heard the Noise that they made,
That they might not find him, and afterwards bind him,
   He screw'd himself under the Bed
      From her Ruffdom, &c.

But 'twould not do, the Wife found him out,
   Brown Bum blaz'd under the Bed;
Oh *Mary*, she swore, Odswoons y'are a Whore,
   And soon you in Jayl shall be laid,
      With your Ruffdom, &c.

The Parson crys, ye wicked young Dog,
   How durst you do such a Folly?
For tho' to save Strife, I may preach with my Wife,
   I sometimes sing Anthems with *Molly,*
      And her Ruffdom, &c.

Then out he pull'd Tall *George* in his Shirt,
   And gave with Bedstaff some Blows,
Then sent him away to his Farm before Day,
   But without ever a Rag of his Clothes,
From the Ruffdom, Ruffdom, frizledom Madg,
   The Hey Rump, frizlerump Dee,
Rowze about, towze about, seek all the House about,
   Under the Bed was he.

The Courtier and Country Maid. A Ballad.
[CHORUS first.]

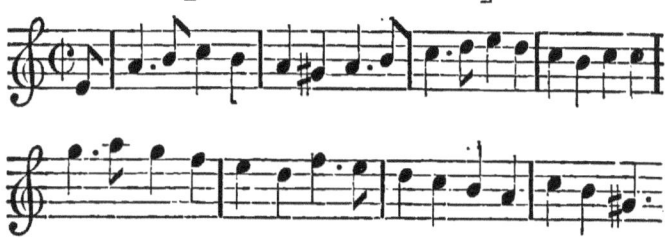

[*Second Movement, like a* Chorus.]

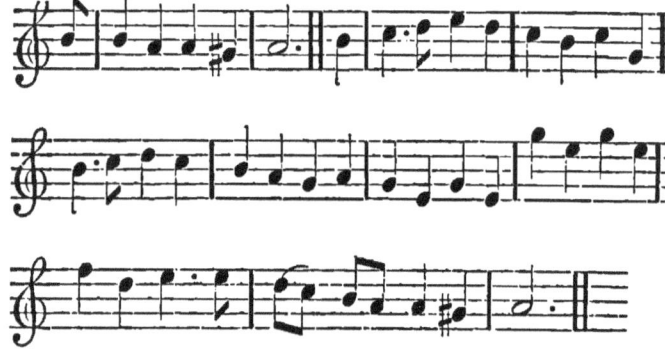

'Twas in the flowry Spring,
The Linnet, Nightingale and Thrush,
Sate on the fresh green hawthorn Bush,
And Jug, jug, jug, and twee, twee, twee,
Most sweetly they did sing.

[*Bombuy* and *Doppa.*]

Bom.   ALL you that either hear or read,
        This Ditty is for your Delight:
Dop.   'Tis of a pretty Country Maid,
        And how she served a courtly Knight.
    'Twas in the flowry Spring, &c.

Bom

Pleasant and Divertive.

Bom. This courtly Knight, when Fields were green,
Dop.   And *Sol* did genial Warmth inspire,
Com. A Farmer's Daughter late had seen,
  Whose Face had set his Heart on Fire,
    'Twas in the flowry Spring, &c.

Dop. Oft to her Father's House he came,
Bom.   And kindly was receiv'd there still,
Dop. The more be added to his Shame,
  Since only 'twas to gain his Will.
    'Twas in the flowry Spring, &c.

One Evening then amongst the rest
  He came to visit the good Man,
But needs must know where *Clara* was,
  And heard she was a milking gone.
    'Twas in the flowry Spring, &c.

Then call'd he for his pamper'd Steed,
  With Pistols at his Sadle Bow,
And to the Meadow rode with Speed,
  Where she was milking of her Cow.
    'Twas in the flowry Spring, &c.

Her pretty Hands that stroak'd the Teats,
  From whence the Milk down streaming came,
Inform'd his Thoughts of other Sweets,
  That more encreas'd his raging Flame.
    'Twas in the flowry Spring, &c.

Then off he lights, and tyes his Horse,
  And swore she must his Pain remove,
If not by fair Means, yet by Force,
  Since he was dying for her Love,
    'Twas in the flowry Spring, &c.

The pearly Tears now trickling fall,
  That from her bashful Eyes do flow,
But that he heeded not at all,
  But does her strait his Pistols shew.
    'Twas in the flowry Spring, &c.

But first pull'd out a fine gay Purse,
  Well lin'd within, as she might see,
And cry'd, before it happens worse,
  Be wise, and take a Golden Fee.
    'Twas in the flowry Spring, &c.

Oh keep your Gold, reply'd the Maid,
  I will not take your golden Fee,
For well you hope to be repay'd,
  And greater Treasure take from me,
    'Twas in the flowry Spring, &c.

A thundering Oath then out he sent,
  That she should presently be dead;
For were his Heart not eas'd, he meant
  Point blank to shoot her thro' the Head.
    'Twas in the flowry Spring, &c.

Then making hast to seize her, went
  And laid the Fire-Arms at her Feet,
Whilst *Clara* seeing his Intent,
  Has no recourse to Aid, but Wit.
    'Twas in the flowry Spring, &c.

She feigns a Smile, and clinging close,
  Cry'd out, I've now your Courage try'd,
Y'have met no simple Country Mouse,
  My Dear, you shall be satisfied.
    'Twas in the flowry Spring, &c.

My Father takes me for a Saint,
  Tho' weary of my Maiden Geer,
That I may give you full Content,
  Pray look, Sir Knight, the Coast be clear.
    'Twas in the flowry Spring, &c.

Look out, and see who comes and goes,
  And you shall quickly have your Will;
For if my Father nothing knows,
  Then I shall be a Maiden still.
    'Twas in the flowry Spring, &c.

Pleasant and Divertive.

The witless Knight peeps o'er the Hedge,
   As one well pleas'd with what he heard,
Whilst she does both the Pistols snatch,
   And boldly stood upon her Guard.
      'Twas in the flowry Spring, &c.

Keep off, keep off, Sir Fool, she cry'd,
   And from this Spot of Ground retire,
For if one Yard to me you stride,
   By my sav'd Maiden-head I fire.
      'Twas in the flowry Spring, &c.

My Father once a Soldier was,
   And Maids from Ravishers would free,
His Daughter too, in such a Case,
   Can shoot a Gun as well as he.
      'Twas in the flowry Spring, &c.

For Soveraign too, when Foe invades,
   Can on Occasion bravely kill,
Not shoot, like you, at harmless Maids,
   That wont obey your Savage Will.
      'Twas in the flowry Spring, &c.

Who when the good old Man, whose Cheer
   Shew'd welcome, tho' of little cost,
A Rape thought on his Daughter dear,
   Most grateful way to pay your Host.
      'Twas in the flowry Spring, &c.

Go home, ye Fop, where Game's not dear,
   And for half Crown a Doxey get,
But seek no more a Partridge here,
   You could not keep, tho' in your Net.
      'Twas in the flowry Spring, &c.

At this the Knight look'd like a Mome,
   He sues and vows, but vain was all,
She soon convey'd the Trophies home,
   And hung up in her Father's Hall.
      'Twas in the flowry Spring, &c.

A Song *in the last* Act *of the* Modern Prophets. *Sung by Mr.* Pack.

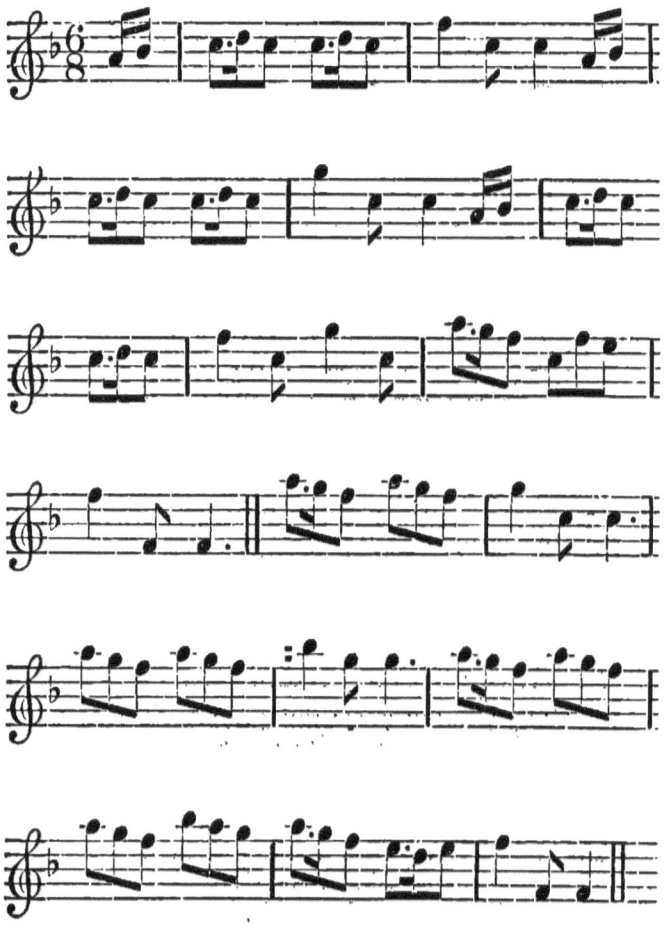

WOuld ye have a young Virgin of fifteen Years,
You must tickle her Fancy with sweets and dears,
Ever toying, and playing, and sweetly, sweetly,
Sing a Love Sonnet, and charm her Ears :
Wittily, prettily talk her down,
Chase her, and praise her, if fair or brown,
    Sooth her, and smooth her,
    And teaze her, and please her,
And touch but her Smicket, and all's your own.

Do ye fancy a Widow well known in a Man ?
With a front of Assurance come boldly on,
Let her rest not an Hour, but briskly, briskly,
Put her in mind how her Time steals on ;
Rattle and prattle although she frown,
Rowse her, and towse her from Morn to Noon,
Shew her some Hour y'are able to grapple,
Then get but her Writings, and all's your own.

Do ye fancy a Punk of a Humour free,
That's kept by a Fumbler of Quality,
You must rail at her Keeper, and tell her, tell her
    Pleasure's best Charm is Variety,
Swear her much fairer than all the Town,
Try her, and ply her when Cully's gone,
    Dog her, and jog her,
    And meet her, and treat her,
And kiss with two Guinea's, and all's your own.

134 SONGS *Compleat,*

A SONG. *On Young* Olinda.

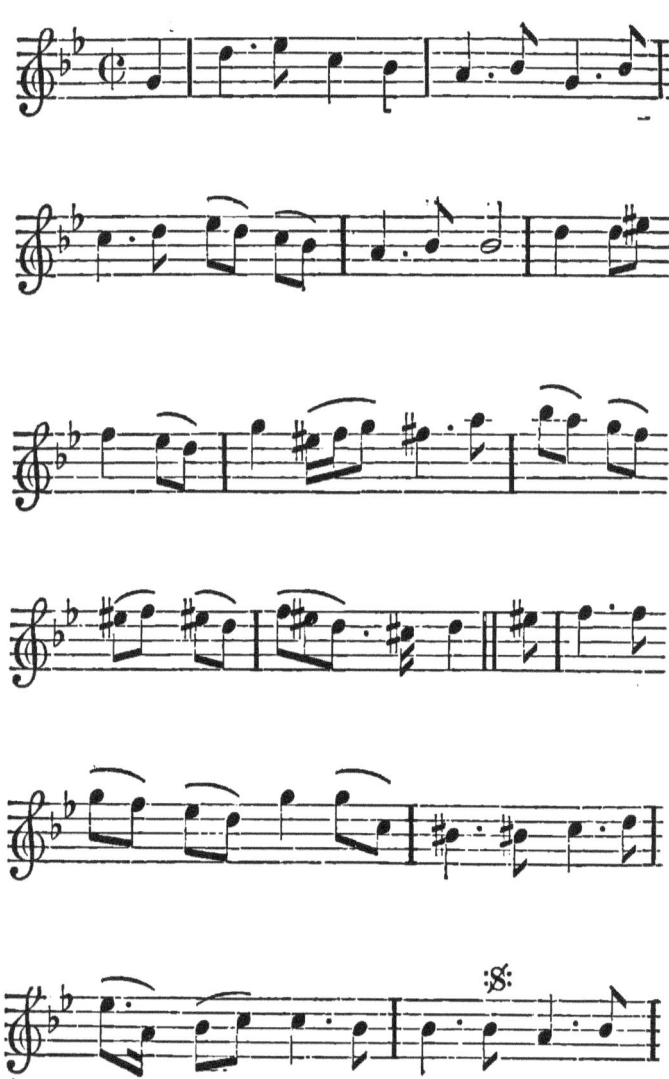

Pleasant and Divertive.   135

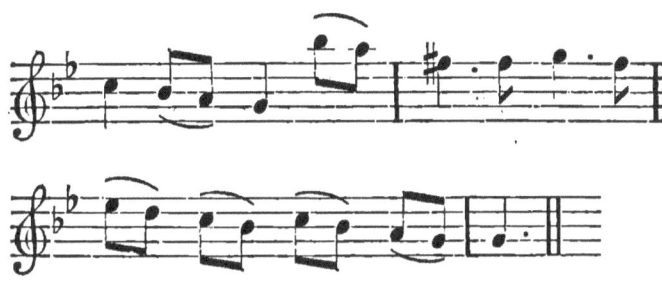

WHen Innocence, and Beauty meet,
  To add to Lovely Female Grace,
Ah, how beyond Expression sweet
  Is every Feature of the Face:

By Vertue, ripened from the Bud,
  The flower Angelick Odours breeds,
The fragrant Charms of being good,
  Makes gawdy Vice to smell like Weeds.

Oh Sacred Vertue, tune my Voice,
  With thy inspiring Harmony;
Then I shall sing of rapting Joys,
  Will fill my Soul with Love of thee.

To lasting Brightness be refin'd,
  When this vain Shadow flyes away,
Th' eternal Beauties of the Mind
  Will last, when all Things else decay.

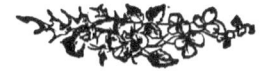

An

An ODE *on* Musidora, *walking in the Spring - Garden.* *The Tune by Mr. Croft.*

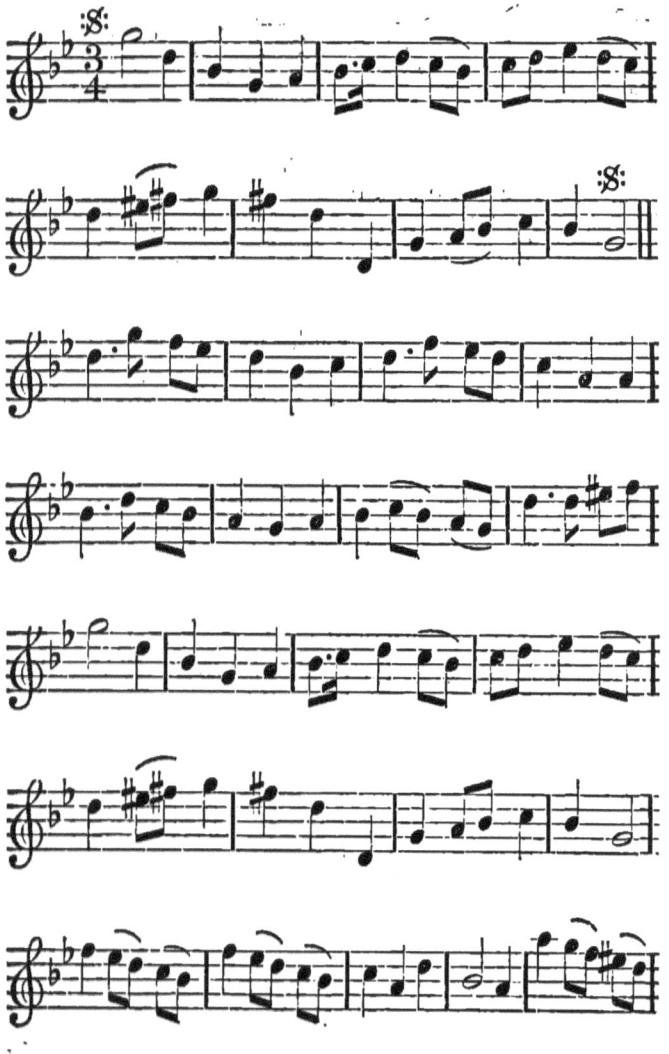

Pleasant and Divertive. 137

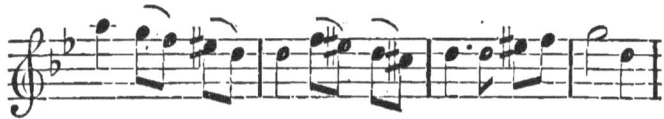

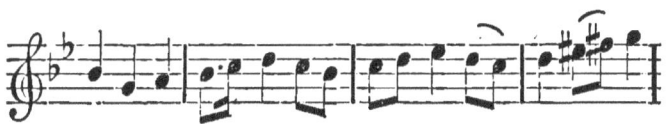

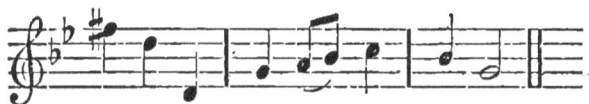

AH, how sweet are the cooling Breez,
 And the blooming Trees,
  When into his Bower Love guides *Musidora*,
When we meet there, the Nightingales sing pretty Tales,
 Mistaking my Dear for the Goddess *Aurora*,
  Jessamines and Roses,
  A thousand pretty Poses,
  The Summer's Queen discloses,
  And strews as she walks.

Oh *Venus*, oh, how sweet are the cooling Breez,
And the blooming Trees,
 When into his Bower Love guides *Musidora*,
Passion, Devotion, she gains with each Motion,
Lutes too, and Flutes too, are heard when she talks.
Oh *Venus*, oh, how sweet are the cooling Breez,
And the blooming Trees,
 When into his Bower Love guides *Musidora*.

A

A Farewel to the Town.
A New Song.

FArewel the Towns ungrateful Noise,
    Hurry, Strife, that damps all Joys,
Where Reason proud Ambition blinds,
Frenzy of unquiet Minds,
        Ease and Pleasure,
        Blest with Leasure,
In sweet Groves my Choice shall be,
        Cælia smiling,
        Time beguiling,
Dear Content's a World to me.

Late manag'd Peace does nought avail,
Lawyers bawl, and Parsons rail,
A Friend against a Friend must be,
And darling Brothers disagree;
        Yet their Stories,
        Whiggs and *Tories*,
Both would change did gain appear,
        Charming Graces
        In a Place is
Of a thousand Pound a Year.

Great *Pan* has left his foreign Powers,
Where Peace sat smiling crown'd with Flowers,
To govern *Albion*'s stubborn Flocks,
Whose Hearts are harder than their Rocks;
        He that's Royal
        Loves all Loyal
Hearts like mine, from Treason free,
        Peace when lasting,
        Love ne'er wasting,
Is a World to him and me.

Oh, State and Glory unconfin'd,
Thou burning Feaver of the Mind,

Pleasant and Divertive. 139

I, midst the Grandeur thou dost bear,
In Content more blest appear;
  Flowers when springing,
  Birds when singing,
In my Rural Shade I see,
  Plots ne'er making,
  Heart ne'er aking,
Dear Content's a World to me.

A Dialogue *in the Kingdom of the Birds, to the famous* Cebell *of Signior* Baptist Lully.

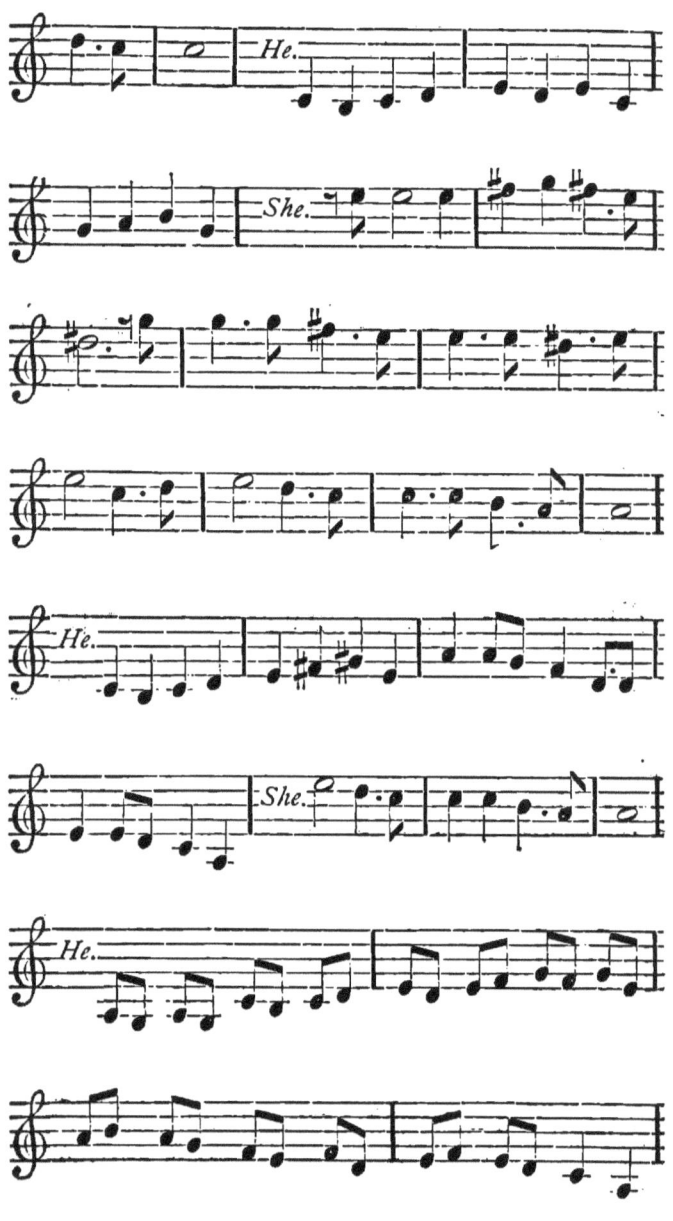

Pleasant and Divertive. 141

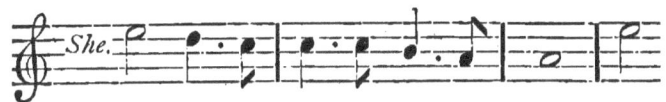

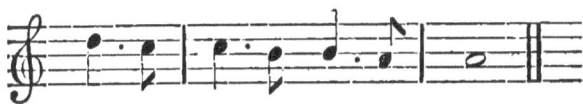

She. P Ray now *John*, let *Jug* prevail,
Doff thy Sword and take a Flail,
Wounds and Blows, with scorching Heat,
Will abroad be all you'll get.
He. Zooks y'are mad, ye simple Jade,
Begone and don't prate;
She. How think ye I shall do with *Hob* and *Sue*,
And all our Brats, when wanting you :
He. When I am rich with plunder,
Thou my Gain shalt share, *Jug*.
She. My Share will be but small, I fear,
When bold Dragoons have been pickering there,
And the Flea flints, the *Germans* strip 'em bare.

He.   Mind your Spinning,
        Mend your Linnen ;
        Look to your Cheese too,
        Your Piggs and your Geese too :
She. No, no, I'll ramble out with you ;
He.   Blood and Fire,
        If you tire,
        Thus my Patience,
        With Vexations, and Narrations,
    Thumping, thumping, thumping
        Is the fatal Word, *Joan;*
She. Do, do, I'm good at thumping too.
He. Morbleau, that Huff shall never do.

                                              She

She. Come, come *John*, let's buss and be Friends,
    Thus still, thus Love's Quarrel ends;
    I my Tongue sometimes let run,
    But alas, I soon have done.
He.   'Tis well y'are quash'd,
            You'd else been thrash'd,
            Sure as my Name's *John*:
She. Yet fain I'd know for what
    Y'are all so hot,
    To go to fight where nothing's got.
He. Fortune will be kind,
    And we shall then grow great too;
She. Grow Great,
    Yet want both Drink and Meat,
    And Coin, unless the pamper'd *French* you beat;
    Ah, take care *John*, take care,
    And learn more Wit.
He.   Dare you prate still,
            At this rate still,
            And like a Vermin,
            Grudge my Preferment;
She. You'll beg, or get a wooden Leg.
He. Nay if Bawling, Caterwawling,
    Tittle tattle, prittle prattle,
    Still must Rattle,
    I'll be gone, and straight aboard,
She. Do, do, and so shall *Hob* and *Sue*,
    Jugg too, and all the ragged Crew.

The Play-house Saint; Or, Phillis *unmasked*.
A New Ballad.

Near famous *Covent-Garden*
    A Dome there stands on high;
       With a fa, la, la, la, &c.
Where Kings are represented,
    And Queens in Metre dye;
       With a fa, la, la, la, &c.
The Beaus and Men of Business
    Diversions hither bring,
To hear the wanton Doxies prate,
    And see 'em dance and sing;
       With a fa, la, la, la, &c.

Here *Phillis* is a Darling,
    As she her self gives out,
       For a fa, la, la, la,
As tight a Lass as ever
Did use a Double Clout,
       On her fa, la, la, la, &c.
She's brisk and gay, and cunning,
    And wants a Wedlock Yoke,
Her Mother was before her
    As good as ever strook
       For a fa, la, la, la, &c.

Young Suitors she had many,
    From 'Squire, up to the Lord,
       For her fa, la, la, la, &c.
And daily she refus'd 'em,
    For Vertue was the Word;
       With her fa, la, la, la, &c.
A Saint she would be thought,
    And dissembled all she could,
But jolly Rakes all knew she was
    Of Play-house Flesh and Blood,
       And her fa, la, la, la, &c.

Her Mother when incourag'd
  With warm *Geneva* Dose,
    And a fa, la, la, la, &c.
Still cry'd, take care dear *Philly*,
  To keep thy Hanches close,
    And this fa, la, la, la, &c.
This made her stand out stoutly,
  Opposing all that come,
Though twenty Demi-Cannon
  Still were mounted at her Bum,
    And her fa, la, la, la, &c.

The Knight and Country Squire
  Were shot with her disdain,
    And her fa, la, la, la, &c.
The Lawyer was outwitted,
  The hardy Soldier slain,
    By her fa, la, la, la, &c.
The bluff Tarpolian Sailor
  In vain cry'd hard a Port,
She buffled Shirks at Sea,
  As the Country, Town, and Court;
    With her fa, la, la, la, &c.

The God of Love grown angry,
  That *Phillis* seemed so shy,
    Of her fa, la, la, la, &c.
Resolv'd her Pride to humble,
  And rout her pish and fie;
He sent a splayfoot Taylor,
  Who knew well how to stitch,
And in a little time had found
  A Button for her Britch,
    And her fa, la, la, la, &c.

Yet was it not so close,
  But 'tis known without all Doubt,
    With a fa, la, la, la, &c.
A little humane Figure
  Has secretly dropp'd out,
    From her fa, la, la, la, &c.

And

Pleasant and Divertive.

And tho' some petty Scandal
Pursue this Venial Fact,
Her Mother she swears Zoons and C——t
Her Honour is intact,
  And her fa, la, la, la, &c.
Oh *Phillis,* then be wise,
And give Ease to Lover's rack'd,
  For your fa, la, la, la, &c.
Let Coyness be abated,
You know the Pitcher's crack'd,
  By a fa, la, la, la, &c.
For shame, let lowsie Taylors
No more your Love trapan,
Since nine of 'em, you know 'tis said,
Can hardly make a man;
  With a fa, la, la, la, &c.

❖❖❖❖❖❖❖❖❖❖❖❖❖❖❖❖❖❖❖❖❖❖❖

A SONG, *in my Comedy of the* Marriage Hater *match'd: Set by Mr.* Henry Purcell. *The Tune to be found prick'd in his* Orph. Brit.

AS soon as the *Chaos* was turn'd into Form,
  And the first Race of Men knew a Good from a Harm,
    They quickly did joyn
    In a Knowledge divine,
That the World's chiefest Blessings were Women and Wine:
Since when by Example, improving Delights,
Wine governs our Days, Love and Beauty our Nights;
    Love on then, and drink,
    'Tis a Folly to think
    On a Mystery out of our Reaches;
    Be moral in Thought,
    To be Merry's no Fault,

Tho'

Tho' an Elder the contrary preaches;
   For never my Friends,
      Never, never my Friend,
Never, never my Friends, was an Age of more Vice,
Then when Knaves would seem pious, and Fools
   would seem wise.

The Queen's Health: Or, New Gillian of Croydon. The Remarks of three Jolly Lasses over a Bottle, on the present Affairs, and News.

FAme loudly thro' *Europe* passes,
   And sounds of many a Wound and Bruise,
Once more then *Croydon* Lasses
   Were met to settle the foreign News,
      The same that the Healths began,
      In Master *Willy's* late Reign,
Brown *Nelly*, black *Joan*, and *Gillian* of *Croydon*,
Gillian, young *Gillian*, plump *Gillian*, bold *Gillian* of
Croydon, fill a new Glass cry'd *Gillian* of *Croydon*,
   Here's to our new Mistress *Nan*.

What ails this mad *Bavary*,
   Crys *Nell*, Old *Nick's* in that beaten Duke,
For playing a strange Vagary,
   For which he lately had found Rebuke;
      And they'll ferret him in the Ban,
      Let the Bishop relieve if he can,
A Brace of false Loons, cry'd *Gillian* of *Croydon*,
Gillian of *Croydon*, *Gillian*, blunt *Gillian*, jolly *Gillian* of
Croydon, let 'em be damn'd, cry'd *Gillian* of *Croydon*,
   Fill round to our Mistress *Nan*.

Nell dress'd as sprunt as a Daizy,
   Cry'd, what a Plague ails our King of *Spain*,
That getting Ground he's so lazy,
And what's become of brave Prince *Eugene?*

Who

Pleasant and Divertive.

Who the Marshall you know did trapan,
  And snapt like a Frog by a Swan;
'Twill ne'er be forgot, cry'd *Gillian* of *Croydon*,
Gillian of *Croydon*, *Gillian*, pert *Gillian*, merry *Gillian* of *Croydon*, take off your glass, cry'd *Gillian* of *Croydon*,
  A Bumper to Mistress *Nan*.

Dutch Hums our Health may wish too,
  We sav'd their Herrings with Pain and Toyl,
For had we not cook'd their fish so,
  Their Butter all had been turn'd to Oyl;
    I'll pawn all the Things in my Room,
    To welcome the General home,
And I my best Smocks, cry'd *Gillian* of *Croydon*,
Gillian of *Croydon*, *Gillian*, blunt *Gillian*, frolick *Gillian*
Of *Croydon*, but the mean time, cry'd *Gillian* of *Croydon*,
  Put round to our Mistress *Nan*.

Proud *Lewis*, for all his Incomes,
  Says Nell, now finds that his Hands are full,
The Old Queen too has got the Crincums,
  And her Advices now prove but Dull:
    Then hey for the Squabble in *Spain*,
    When both the Boys meet on the Plain,
Fight Dog and fight Bear, cry'd *Gillian* of *Croydon*,
Gillian of *Croydon*, *Gillian*, stout *Gillian*, shrew'd *Gillian*
Of *Croydon*, brim it then round, cry'd *Gillian* of *Croydon*,
  Long Life to our Mistress *Nan*.

Thus setling of foreign Matters,
  They top'd till Civil Wars broke at home,
Joan lisping her Liquor scatters,
  And *Nelly* hiccuping calls her Mome,
    Then told her of *Robin* and *John*,
    Till strait the Quoif tearing began;
Y'are two drunken Jades, cry'd *Gillian* of *Croydon*,
Gillian of *Croydon*, *Gillian*, sly *Gillian*, bowzy *Gillian* of *Croydon*, but to make Friends, cry'd *Gillian* of *Croydon*,
  Once more to our Mistress *Nan*.

A New Scotch Song. *The Tune by Mr.* Corbet. *Within the Compass of the* Flute.

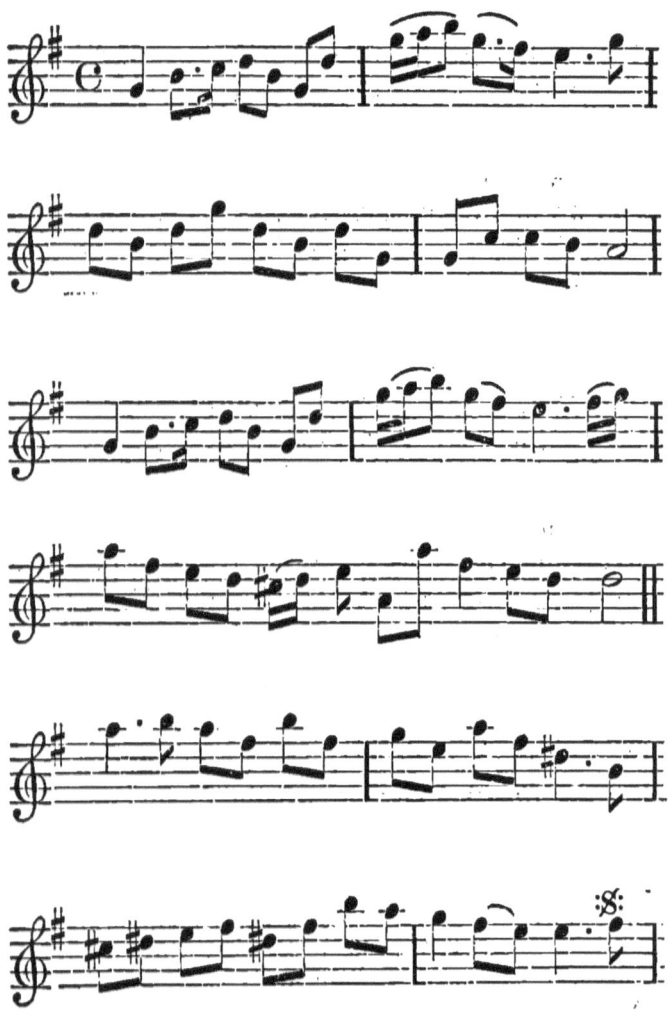

Pleasant and Divertive.

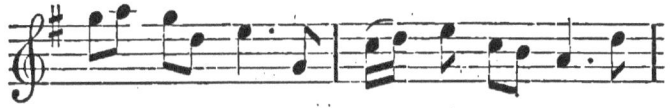

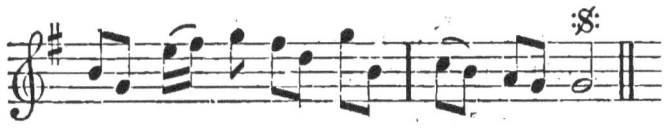

MAD Loons of *Albany*, what is't you do?
You'll find your wrangling, and your jangling,
    Playing aw the Foo;
Bread, why dee heed the *Mounsieur's* wily Tales?
Or plague your Noddles to bring in the Prince of *Wales*.
Wiser Pates than yours have laid Succession right,
And aw the bonny Highlanders for that should fight;
    Unite then as one Man,
    And leave what you began,
To gang to *Kirk*, and beg long Life for geud Queen *Ann*.

Well aided *Portugals*, our Allie true,
    Our High and Mighty,
    Friends to right ye,
    Will send *Quota's* too,
Aw joyn'd in muckle Power the *French* pursue;
Geud Feth 'tis fit the doughty Scot should do so too.
In Cabals no more than let your Bosoms swell,
But sing with Joy, for glorious things have late befel,
    Nor raise the jarring Vein,
    Who shall hereafter Reign,
But gang to *Kirk*, and beg long Life for geud Queen *Ann*.

A

A New Song.

Made in honour of the Worthy Society of Archers, meeting the 11*th of* January, *Anno* 1711. *By* T. D'Urfey. *The Words made to a pretty Tune;* She turns up her Silver hair.

OF all noble Sports
    Us'd in Country or Court,
For our Health or our true Delight,
    The Wise have confest
    That an Archer's is best,
As 'tis also the noblest Sight;
    He firmly does stand,
    And looks like a Man,
When the Shaft strongly drawn does go:
    Drink away then my Boys,
    And to heighten our Joys,
Sing in praise of the brave long Bow.

    Britain's Father's did chuse,
    E'er damn'd Guns were in use,
With this Weapon to end their Frays;
    Fam'd *Agin* Court,
    Shews at this Royal Sport,
How we conquer'd in *Henry's* Days;
    The *Mounsieur* was mawl'd,
    And the *English* extoll'd,
From the *Thames* to the Gallick *Sein:*
    And were Guns laid aside,
    And our Archers were try'd,
We are sure we could do't again.

Health that we gain to our Body and Brain,
To the World has been clearly shewn;
    Who e'er can say,
    He that shoots e'ry Day,
Has the Strangury, Gout, or Stone?
    He firmly does stand, &c.

A DIRGE.

Sung in the First Part of Don Quixote *by a Shepherd and Shepherdess. Set by* Mr. Eales.

Sleep, sleep poor Youth, sleep, sleep in Peace,
    Reliev'd from Love, and mortal Care,
Whilst we that pine in Life's Disease,
    Uncertain, blest less happy are.

Couch'd in the dark and silent Grave,
    No Ills of Fate thou now canst fear,
In vain would Tyrant Power enslave,
    Or scornful Beauty be severe.

Wars that do fatal Storms disperse,
    Far from thy happy Mansion keep,
Earthquakes that shake the Universe,
    Can't rock thee into sounder Sleep.

With all the Charms of Peace possest,
    Secure from Life's Tormentor, Pain,
Sleep and indulge thy self with Rest,
    Nor dream thou e'er shalt rise again.

CHORUS.

Past is the Fear of future Doubt,
    The Sun is from the Dial gone,
The Sands are sunk, the Glass is out,
    The Folly of the Farce is done,
The Folly of, &c.

A Satyr, *or* Ditty *upon the jarring of the Two East-India* C——*ys.*

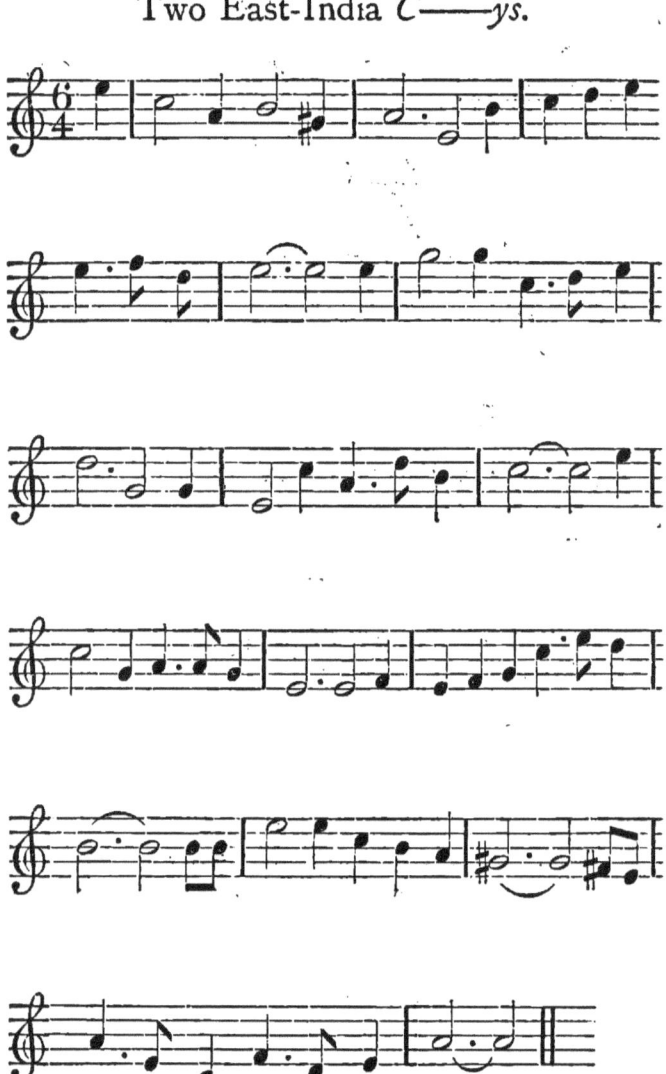

ONE Morn as lately musing,
  I went to the City to Poll,
Where Members then were a chusing,
  I chanc'd to take up a Scrowl;
A stinging Jest by my Soul,
  It afterwards happen'd to be,
For the first Words as I unroul'd
  Were, *Agree, you rich Cuckolds, agree.*

Tho' the Author's Brains did ramble,
  The Sence was poynant and strong,
I soon found by the Preamble,
  'Twas made of the Trading Throng,
That to *East India* belong,
  As by the matter you'll see,
For the Burthen still of the Song
  Was, *Agree, ye rich Cuckolds, agree.*

Their golden Bags increasing,
  The Old Company purse proud grew,
Till at last two Million raising,
  Some others set up a New:
And they were for Trafficking too,
  And cheating by Land and by Sea,
And swore they'd t'other undo,
  Come agree, ye rich Cuckolds, agree.

Resolv'd to be thought thrifty,
  They got Subscriptions like mad,
Some wrote Ten Hundred and Fifty,
  A Thousand more than they had:
I thought 'em bewitch'd be gad,
  Or that I some Vision did see,
But the Old to truckle they made;
  Come agree, ye rich Cuckolds, agree.

A thousand Rogues and Cheaters,
  In *Cornhill*, you'd hear them call,
The *Tories*, and the *Tub-Meeters*,
  That roosted near *Leadenhall.*

Oh

Oh how *Cheapside* too did bawl
  At those in the *Poulterey*,
For shame, leave acting your Droll,
  And agree, ye rich Cuckolds, agree.

To the Senate then with Vigour,
  The Old soon after address'd,
Tho' half were chous'd by the Tyger,
  That wondrous politick Beast.
The whilst the unfortunate Rest,
  In course outvoted must be,
Was ever known such a Jest,
  Come, agree, ye rich Cuckolds, agree.

Tho' baulk'd by this Digression,
  Yet moving another Spring,
They made amends the next Session,
  And clearly carried the Thing:
To Court their Case then they bring,
  And Reverence made on the Knee,
But the Answer got from the K——
  Was, *Agree, ye rich Cuckolds, agree.*

Tho' kept a while at Distance,
  Yet least they should totally drop,
They got a legal Existence,
  And then were strait cock-a-hoop:
But when the New ones did stoop,
  The t'other as huffing would be,
For now again they got up,
  Come agree, stubborn Cuckolds, agree.

The New with false, sham Storys,
  Of which each Noddle was full,
Equip'd Sir *W. N*——
  An Envoy to the Mogul:
And he did the Colony fool,
  With Tydings that never will be,
Were e'er Stockjobbers so dull,
  Come agree, ye rich Cuckolds, agree.

Pleasant and Divertive.

The Old that knew this Passage,
   And what Commission he bore,
A jolly Lad, with a Message,
   To contradict it sent o'er:
Another Packet he wore,
   Five Hundred Pounds was his Fee,
It should have been as much more,
   Come agree to that, Mizers, agree.

Ye jarring Powers that rule us,
   What foolish doings are here?
Whilst these two Factions fool us,
   No honest Man can appear,
No Major be chose for the year,
   But that some Trick in't will be,
Nor Knight can stand for the Shire,
   Come agree, ye rich Cuckolds, agree.

What hopes to have free Senates,
   Whilst you are playing this Game,
And bribe the Boors and Tenants
   Thro' Spite, each other to tame:
The Church too, Faith, has a Maime,
   Whilst *Whiggs*, and High *Tories* there be;
Reform, reform then for shame,
   And agree, ye rich Cuckolds, agree.

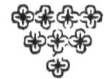

A SONG *in my Comedy, call'd the* Bath, *or the* Western *Lass. Set by Mr.* Jeremy Clark. *Sung by Mrs.* Lucas.

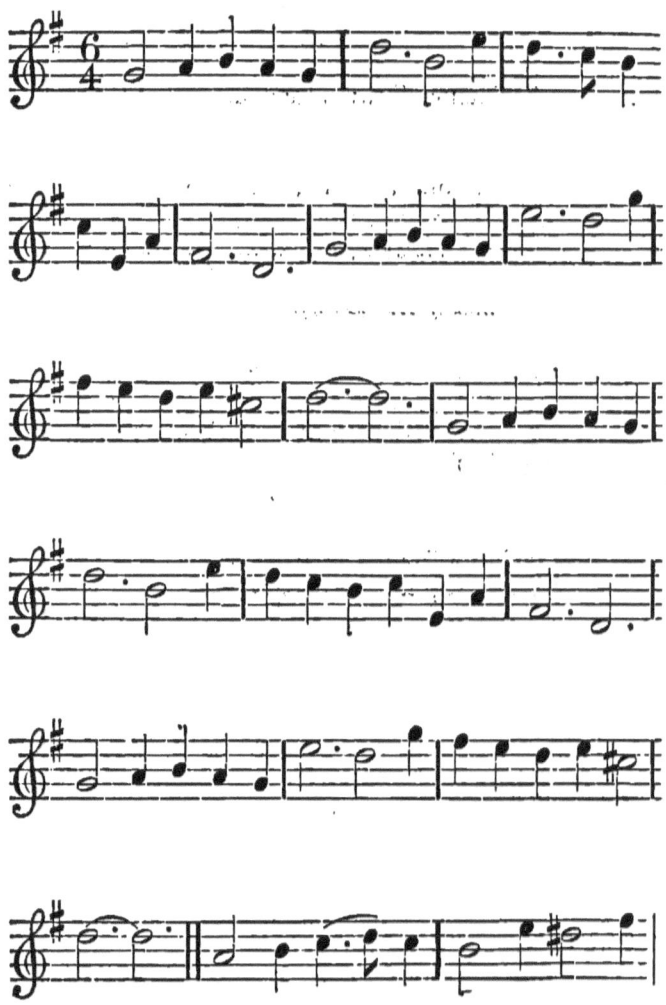

Pleasant and Divertive.

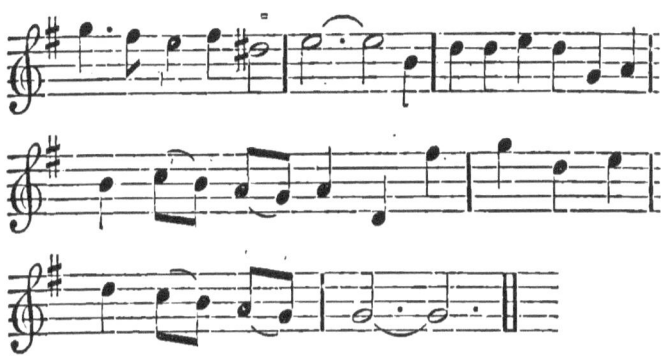

Lord! what's come to my Mother,
     That every Day more than other,
My true Age she would smother,
     And says I'm not in my Teens;
Tho' my Sampler I've sown too,
My Bib and my Apron out-grown too,
Baby quite away thrown too,
     I wonder what 'tis she means;
When our *John* does squeeze my Hand,
     And calls me sugar sweet,
          My Breath almost fails me,
          I know not what ails me,
My Heart does so heave and so beat.

I have heard of Desires,
From Girls that have just been of my Years,
Love compar'd to sweet Bryers,
     That hurts, and yet does please:
Is Love finer than Money,
Or can it be sweeter than Honey,
I'm poor Girl such a Toney,
     Evads that I cannot guess,
But I'm sure I'll watch more near,
There's something that Truth will shew,
     For if Love be a Blessing,
     To please beyond Kissing,
Our *Jane* and our Butler does know.

A

A SONG *in praise of Soldiery, sung in Don
Quixote, and set to Musick by Mr.* Henry
Purcell, *which is compos'd in his* Orpheus
Britannicus.

SIng, sing all ye Muses, your Lutes strike around,
When a Souldier's the Story, what Tongue can
want Sound?
      Who Danger disdains,
      Wounds, Bruises, and Pains,
And the Honour of Fighting is all that he gains;
Rich Profit comes easy in Cities of Store,
But the Gold is earn'd hard where the Cannons do rore;
      Yet see how they run
      At the storming a Town,
Thro' Blood, and thro' Fire, to take the Half-moon;
      They scale the high Wall,
      Whence they see others fall,
Their Heart's precious darling, bright Glory pursuing,
'Tho' Death's under foot, and the Mine is just blowing;
      It springs, up they fly,
      Yet more will supply,
As Bridegrooms to marry, they hasten to die,
      'Till Fate claps her Wings,
      And the glad Tydings brings,
Of the Breach being enter'd, and then they're all Kings;
      Then happy's she, whose Face
      Can win the Soldier's Grace,
      They range about in State
      Like Gods, disposing Fate.
      No Luxury in Peace,
      Nor Pleasure in Excess,
Can parallel the Joys the Martial Heroes crown,
When flush'd with Rage, and forc'd by Want, they
storm a wealthy Town.

The PEROQUETTE.

An ODE; *occasion'd by the seeing a very beautiful one, belonging to the Right Honourable the Earl of* Leicester; *with a small Remark upon his Lordship's fine Seat at* Penshurst.

WELL mayst thou prate with mirthful Cheer,
    And pick thy plumy green,
Who in delightful *Penshurst* here,
    Art seated like a Queen.

Thou call'st upon a Widow oft,
    Tho' few of them are known;
With Look so sweet, and Touch so soft,
    Dear Creature, as thy own.

Thus too in Groves, and Gardens fair,
    Of Old, the *Sylvan* Gods,
Perfum'd with Breeze of fragrant Air,
    Contriv'd Divine Abodes.

Others, *sic siti*,* may express,
    Possess'd with Fancy vain,
Thou, only in thy Bower of Bliss,
    That Phrase canst well maintain.

---

* *Sic siti lætantur Lares.*

160   SONGS *Compleat*,

A SONG, *occasion'd by the speedy Addition of two Million, made to the* Bank *of* Great Britain. *Sung in the* Modern Prophets.

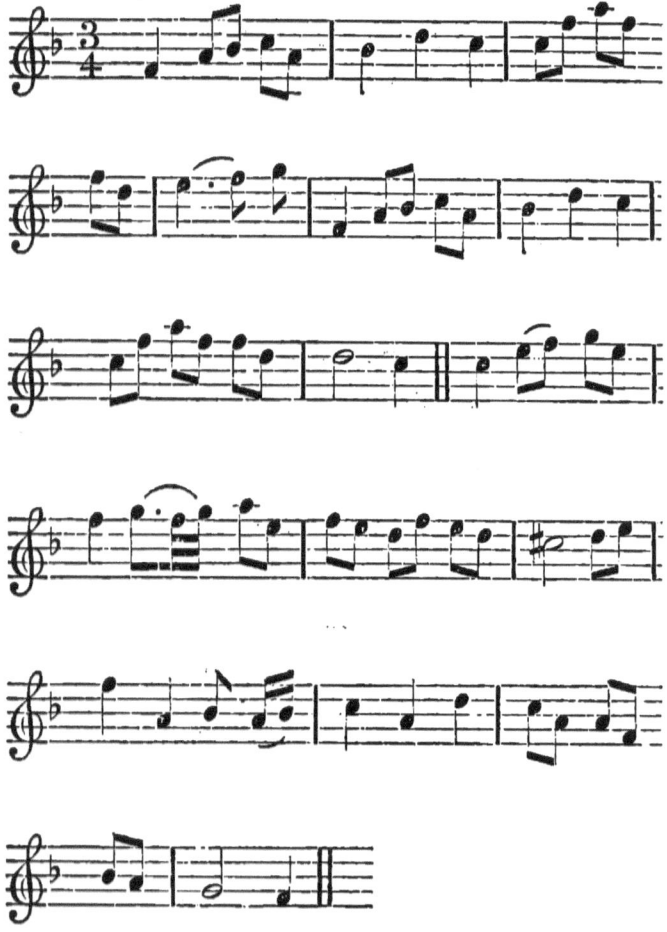

MOunsieur looks pale, and *Anjou* quakes,
  Weakly stands the Thrones they sit on,
Dull is *Versailles*, th' Escurial shakes,
  Hearing of the *Bank* of *Britain*.
Lewis storms to think the Foe,
  Instead of sinking down grows stronger,
Morbleu, says he, their Millions grow,
  'Tis in vain to fight 'em longer.

When K. of *Spain*, I crown'd young *Phill*,
  And to fix him made such Offers,
Jernie, thought I, the *Bullion* will
  All be cram'd now in my Coffers:
But these Bougers drink and whore,
  And riot on each small Occasion,
And yet *begar* will ne'er be poor,
  Le Grand Diable's in *de* Nation.

The *Spanish* Indies I possess,
  Yet they bear a Purse above me,
And that I no Bank can raise,
  Shews how well my People love me:
Former grand Success is gone,
  Bruges, *Ghent*, and *Lisle* is taken,
Then whilst my Capital's my own,
  I'll make Peace, and save my Bacon.

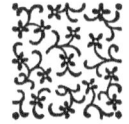

The fond Keeper's RELAPSE:
A New Song.

Inscrib'd to all whom it may concern: The Words made to a pretty Play-house Tune, call'd, Pretty Poll.

C*Eladon* the gay,
    In the merry, merry Month of *May*,
When the gawdy Flowers enamell'd lay,
    Was with *Cælia* walking,
        She to move
        Talk'd of Love,
        What could prove
Fitter for the Season, or the Theam of talking;
    Celadon was angry, you may guess,
    He return'd no amorous Look nor Kiss,
    But thus teas'd pretty Miss,
        But thus, &c.

Go Seducer, go——
Let the World no more my folly know,
Nor let odious Names of Miss and Beau
    Shame succeeding Ages;
        Hast away,
        Nothing say,
        I'll go pray,
Reason now at Folly past my Soul enrages:
    I have been your Cully, Slave and Beast,
    Thrown away ten Thousand Pound at least,
        On pretty, pretty Miss,
        On pretty, &c.

                      Rich

Pleasant and Divertive.

Rich Brocadoes so fine,
Phœbus never did so gayly shine,
And luxurious Flasks of *Cyprus* Wine
    Swallow'd at our feasting;
        Curse on Pride,
        Lets divide,
        I a Bride
Now resolve on chusing, thus a Joy more lasting:
    You have drain'd my Purse, and rais'd my Sins,
    I have given Five Hundred Pound for Pins,
        For pretty, pretty Miss,
        For pretty, &c.

Farewel *Venus* Joys,
That my Heart so long did vainly prise,
Welcome Wedlock now to close my Eyes,
    Never loud nor craving;
        Skin like Snow,
        Eyes like Sloe,
        And will go
In Callicoe, or lowly Chinse, to be more saving:
    Can there any Life compare with this?
    Yet methinks I long for one more Kiss
        From pretty, pretty Miss,
        From pretty Miss, &c.

She t' improve the Mood,
Seeing like a Fool he gazing stood,
Peeping first, then turning up her Hood,
    Runs in t' embrace him;
        Young and sly,
        Had by th' By,
        I'en scay quoy,
An Artifice that never, never fails caressing:
    Soon was now forgot the Wedlock Bliss,
    He that was subdu'd with one false Kiss
        Went home with pretty Miss,
        With pretty, pretty Miss.

The first Song to a Minuet of Don Quixote, in the first Act.

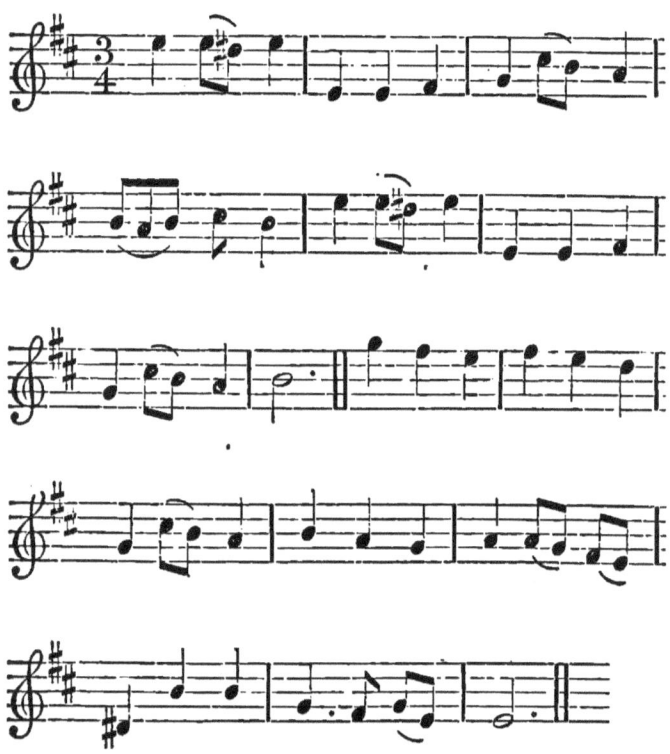

IF you will love me, be free in expressing it,
 And henceforth give me no cause to complain;
Or if you hate me, be plain in confessing it,
 And in few Words put me out of my Pain.
This long delaying, with sighing and praying,
Breeds only decaying in Life and Amour,
    Cooing and wooing,
    And daily pursuing,
Is damn'd silly doing, therefore I'll give o'er.

If you'll propose a kind Method of ruling me,
 I may return to my Duty again;
But if you stick to your old way of fooling me,
 I must be plain, I'm none of your Men;
Passion for Passion on each kind Occasion,
With free Inclination does kindle Love's Fire,
  But tedious prating,
  Coy folly debating,
And new Doubts creating still make it expire.

The Lady's Answer. The second Song to a Minuet, at the Duke's Entertainment of Don Quixote *in the first Act.*
[*To the same* Tune.]

YOU love, and yet when I ask you to marry me,
 Still have recourse to the Tricks of your Art,
Then like a Fencer you cunningly parry me,
 Yet the same time make a Pass at my Heart.
  Fye, fye deceiver,
  No longer endeavour,
Or think this way ever the Fort will be won;
  No fond caressing
  Must be, nor unlacing,
Or tender embracing, 'till th' Parson has done.

Some say that Marriage a Dog with a Bottle is,
 Pleasing their Humours to rail at their Wives;
Others declare it an Ape with a Rattle is,
 Comfort's Destroyer, and Plague of their Lives:
  Some are affirming,
  A Trap 'tis for Vermin,
And yet with the Bait tho' not Prison agree,
  Ventring that chouse you
  Must let me espouse you,
If e'er my dear Mouse you will nibble at me.
                                    LOVE

LOVE and SATYR.

A New Song.

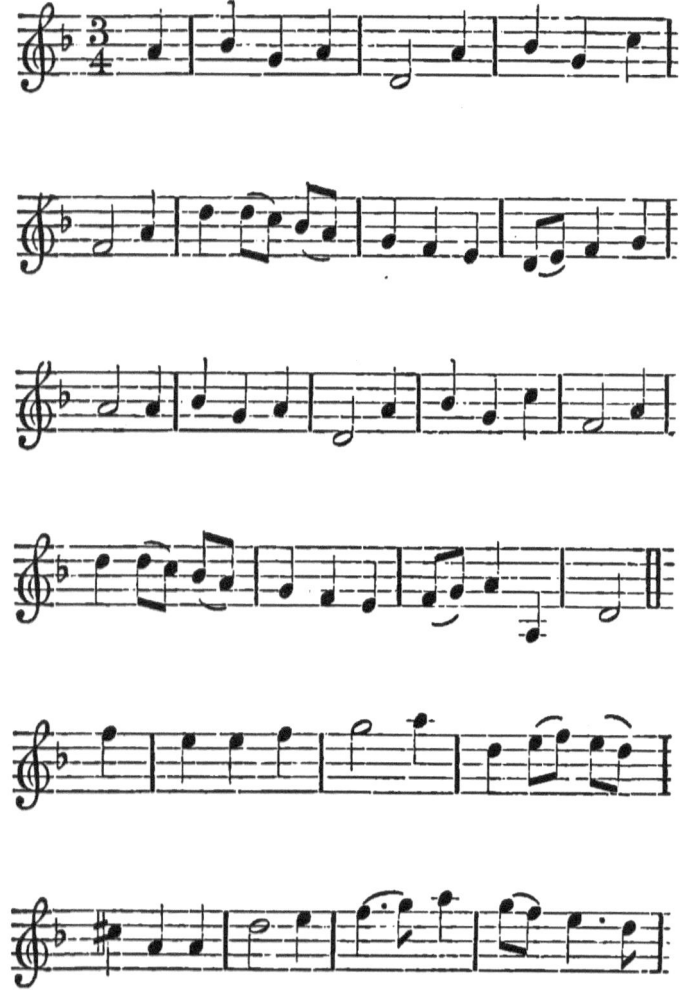

Pleasant and Divertive. 167

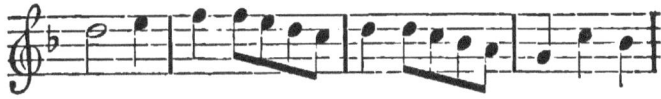

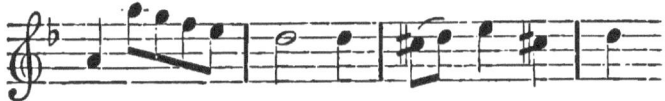

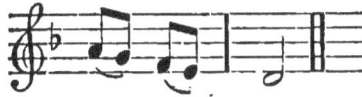

WHen *Phœbus* does rise, the Flow'rs raise their Heads,
And charm'd by his Influence, smile o'er the Meads,
When *Cælia's* bright Eyes with kindness meet mine,
New Hopes and new Raptures, my Joys make divine.
We laugh and we sing, the Hours fly with Pleasure,
Affairs abroad we care not to know,
   In Youth at our Leisure,
   Loves happy Treasure,
   Makes Blessings flow,
Mortally averse to Brawlings of *High-Church* and *Low*.

   Ye Wits of the Town,
   Ye Chiefs of the Gown,
Ye Law-making Sages that flatter the Crown,
   How dare you address?
   How can you profess?
To honour your Soveraign, yet still make her less,
Whilst Factions reign of *Whigg* and of *Tory*,
Your Zeal's a Banter to all Men of Sence;
   'Tis Gain moves your Fury,
   And not her Glory,
   Nor our Defence,
And the solemn Word, *Religion*, is meerly Pretence.
            The

The Second Movement.

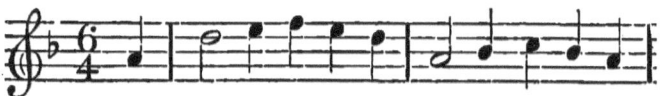

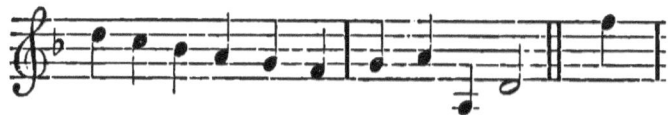

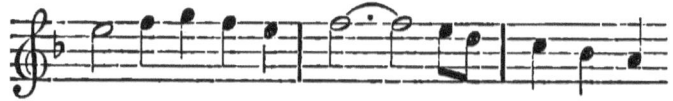

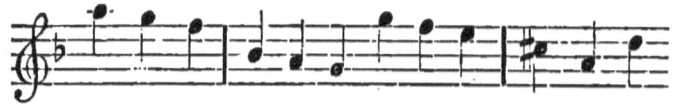

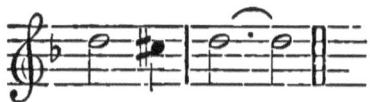

No Feuds desiring,
From Town retiring,
Let's hast then, and share in the flourishing Bloom,
Where Noise and Cares never come,
Nor the jarring
Of National warring,
That yearly is plaguing all Christendom.

The Willoughby WHIM.
A Scotch SONG.
In a DIALOGUE *between two Sisters.*

Molly. OH *Jenny, Jenny,* where hast thou been?
    Father and Mother are seeking for thee,
  You have been ranting, playing the Wanton,
    Keeping of *Jockey* Company.

Jenny. Oh *Molly,* I've been to hear Mill clack,
    And grind Grist for the Family,
  Full as it went I've brought home my Sack,
    For the Miller has tooken his Toll of me.

Molly. You hang your Smickets abroad to bleach,
    When that was done, where could you be?
Jenny. I slipt down in the quickset Hedge,
    And *Jockey* the Loon fell after me.

Molly. My Father you told you'd go to Kirk,
    When Prayers were done, where could you be?
Jenny. Taking a Kiss of the Parson and Clerk,
    And of other young Laddys some two or three.

Molly. Oh *Jenny, Jenny,* what wilt thou do,
    If Belly should swell, where wilt thou be?
Jenny. Look to your self for *Jockey* is true,
    And whilst Clapper goes will take care of me.
                                The

The SONG *of* Orpheus *charming the Birds, Beasts, Trees,* &c. *to follow him*: *Sung in the* Kingdom of the Birds. *Set to the Tune call'd the* Czar.

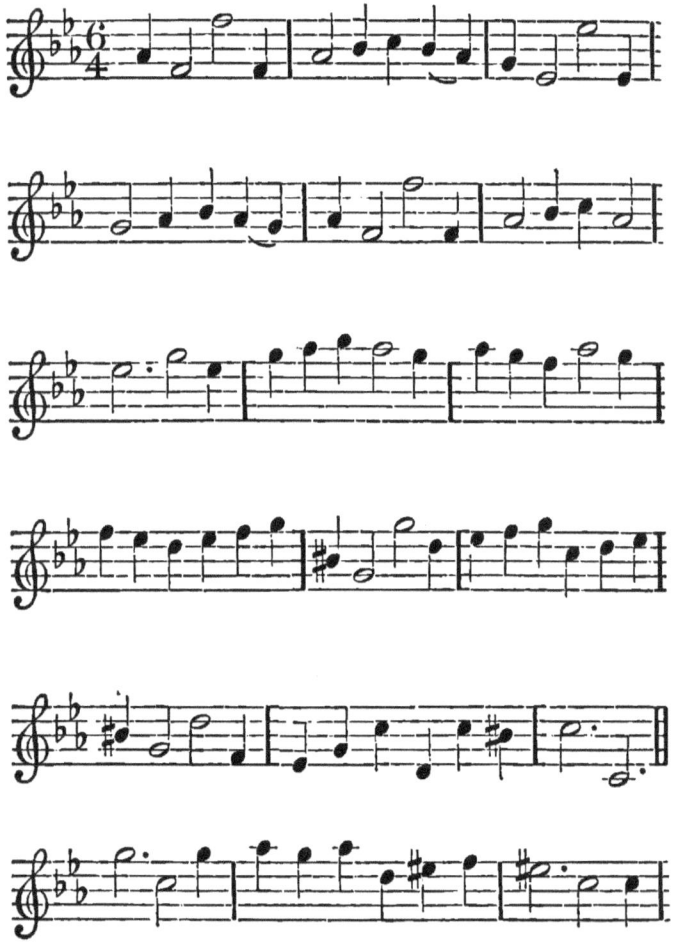

Pleasant and Divertive.

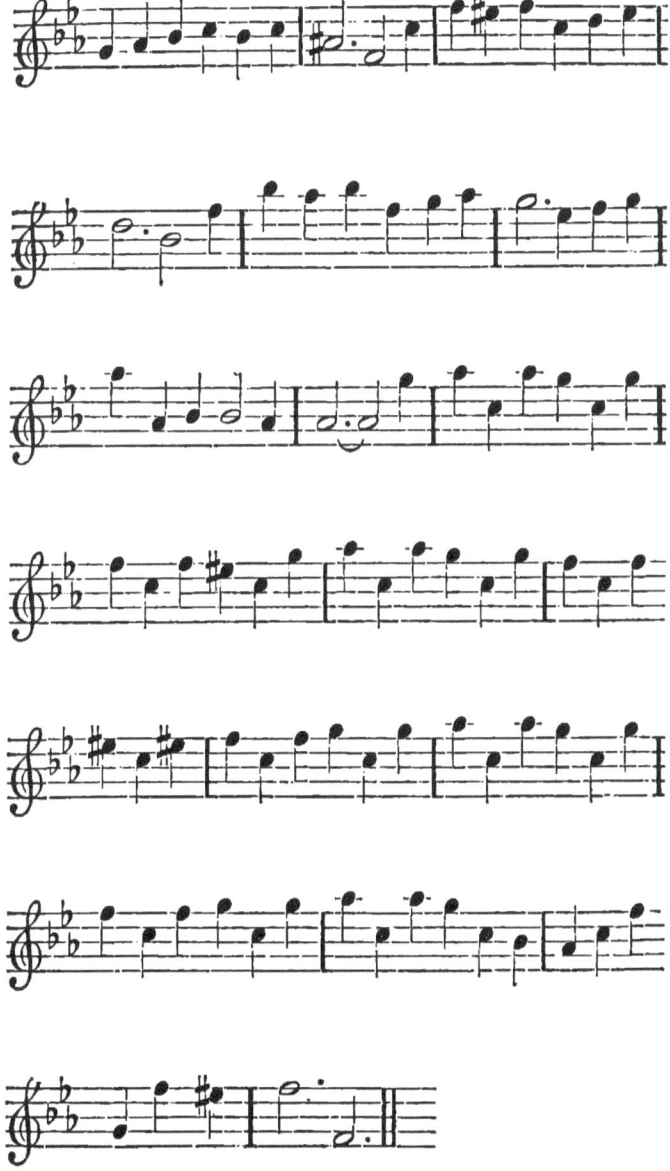

Groves and Woods, high Rocks and Mountains,
Springs and Floods, clear Brooks and Fountains,
Birds and Beasts that range with Pleasure,
   Hear, hear the Charm of my Voice,
Make hast and appear to dance a gay Measure,
And *Phœbus* please with Nature, and Arts valu'd treasure,
   Hast and see that no Sluggard refuses:
Flora, delightful as blushing *Aurora*,
To banish the Pest of *Pandora*,
I summon thy Jessamine and Roses,
Ye pretty young Nymphs with your Poesies,
Come away when I sing and play,
    No Creature in Nature
    Be late here, but wait here,
    From *Vulcan*'s hot Bellows,
    Air *Neptune* and *Tellus*,
    The Thrushes from Bushes,
    And Prickets from Thickets,
    Come whisk it and frisk it,
    And skip it and trip it,
In honour of Love and the Muses.

The first Song *in the* Modern Prophets.
Sung by Mr. Pack.

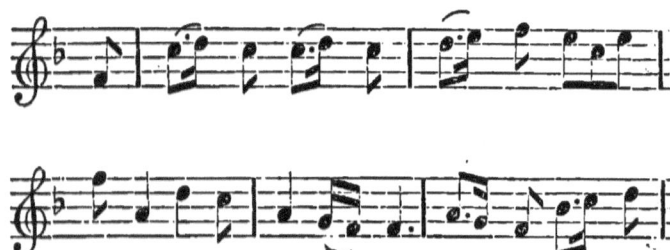

Pleasant and Divertive. 173

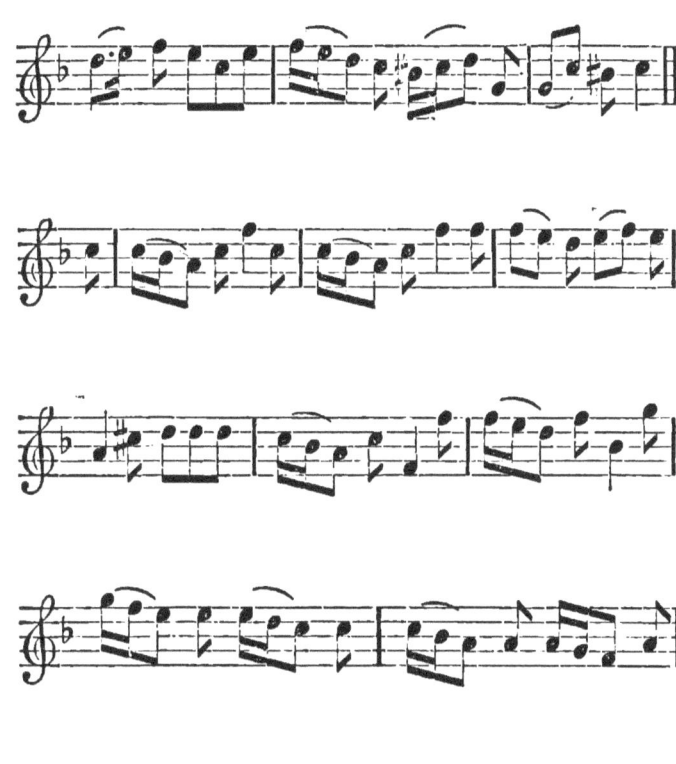

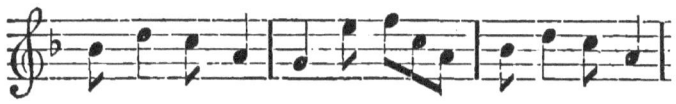

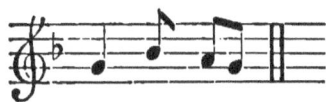

WE *London* Valets all are Creatures,
   No Modern Beau can live without,
Who tho' the Devil be in our Natures,
   Divinely bring Intrigues about:

We

We wait, we run, cajole each Dun,
　Who threatens with the Laws Disasters,
In Taverns snore, on Bench 'till four,
Then bring the Miss for Morning Bliss,
　　And often snack her with our Masters.
　　And often snack her with our Masters.

At Seasons when the Senate's sitting,
　We mimick each Law-maker there,
Without Doors those within outwitting,
　And act the Speaker in the Chair;
　　　With Votes and Pleas,
　　　And Means and Ways,
We ape the Legislative Jurys,
　　　At th' end o' th' Day
　　　We see a play,
　　　There full of Ale
　　　The Gallery scale,
And roar, and clatter like the Furys.

Oft-times by Order 'tis our Duty,
　To go to the Play-house and take Rooms,
There cheek by jole we sit with Beauty,
　And out-do clearly all Perfumes,
　　　Or if no Play
　　　Will please that Day,
We're hurried strait to *Hide-Park* Corner,
　　　There Crambo sing
　　　Of all the Ring,
　　　What wanton Wives
　　　Lead Modish Lives,
And who's the Cuckold, who's the Horner.

The

The Bell ASSEMBLY,

An ODE, *occasion'd by K*. William's *entertaining the Ladies at Court every* Wednesday. *The Words made to a pretty New Ayre.*

FOR too many past Years with *Belonia's* Alarms,
   Has poor *England* been made a meer stranger to Bliss,
But the Goddess of concord now spreads her soft Charms,
  And new Gallantry shews us the Fruits of a Peace;
     Mighty *William* fast binds
     The Hearts of both Kinds,
Either Sex so oblig'd makes his Foes turn his Friends;
     When our Land he releas'd,
     Then all Mankind he eas'd,
But now far greater reigns, since the Ladies are pleas'd.

As the Offspring of Light new adorning the Night,
With their glittering Blaze make the Firmament bright,
All the Nymphs shon so gay on great *Nassau's* Birthday,
Had *Apollo* been there, had out-dazled each Ray,
     Which the Sovereign so fir'd,
     He nobly desir'd,
To shew how Love and Beauty Valour inspir'd,
     And tho' Glory in view,
     He like *Cæsar* pursue,
That he could, when he pleas'd, be *Mark-Anthony* too.

So the fam'd *Macedon*, that the World overran
  With the Terour of Arms, and his Wonders in Fight,
When the Ladies came down his new triumphs to crown,
  By their Beauty subdu'd gave a Loose to Delight;
     All the Toyls of past Days
The great *Mars* of the Battle unarms him and plays,
     Court Gallantry own'd,
     Jolly Revels went round,
And the Captives late sorrow new pleasure soon drown'd.

A SONG *on a dressing Fop, in the* 3d Act *of the* Modern Prophets. *The Tune by Dr.* Crofts.

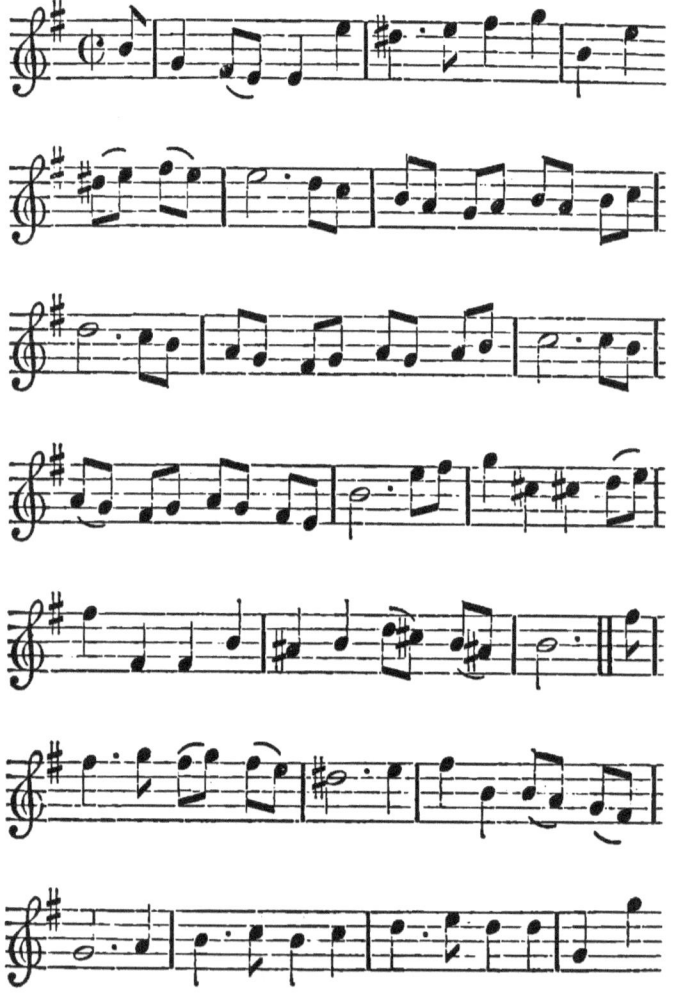

Pleasant and Divertive.

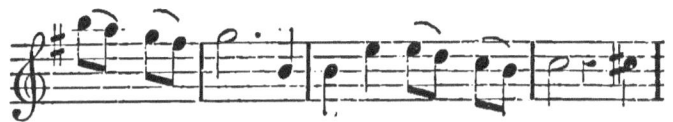

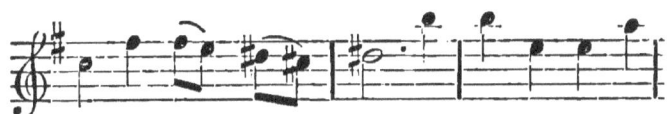

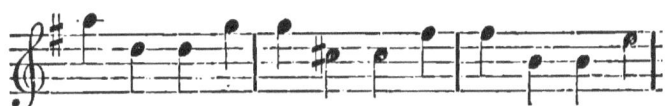

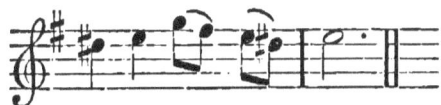

I Hate a Fop that at his Glass
   Stands prinking half the Day,
With a sallow frowzy olive colour'd Face,
And a powder'd Peruke hanging to his Wast,
Who with ogling imagines to possess,
And to shew his Shape does cringe and scrape,
      But nothing has to say;
    Or if the Courtship's fine,
    He'll only cant and whine,
    And in confounded Poetry,
    He'll Goblins make divine;
    I love the bold and brave,
    I hate the fawning Slave,
     That quakes and crys,
     And sighs and lyes,
      Yet wants the Skill,
      With Sence to tell,
What 'tis he longs to have.

A SONG, *Sung by Mr.* Leveridge *in the Comedy call'd,* The Country Miss with her Furbelow.

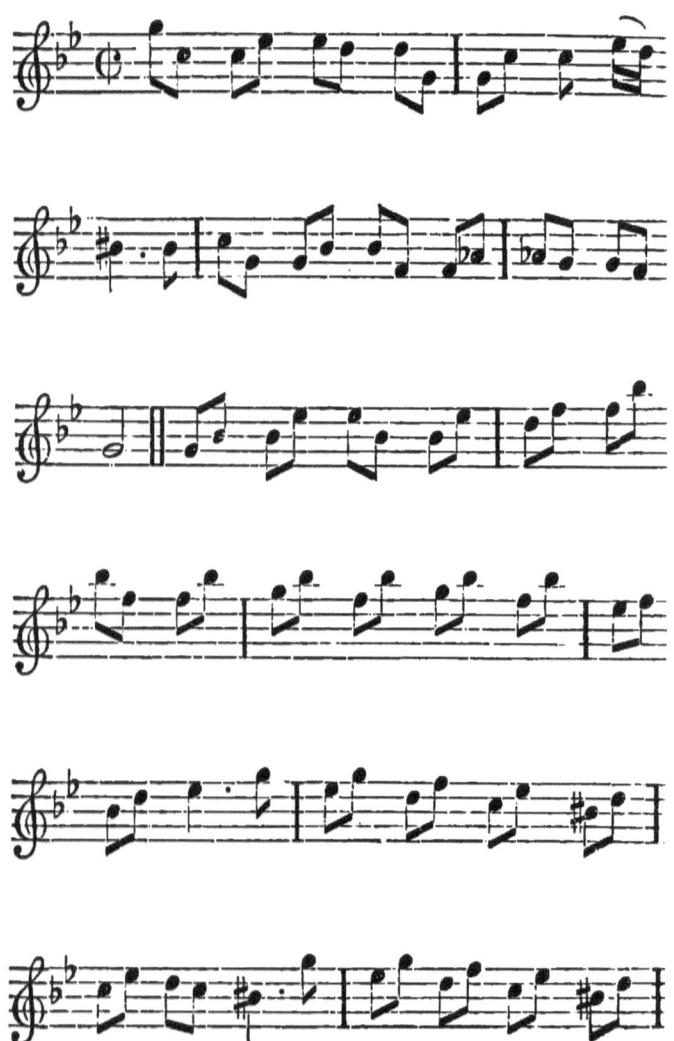

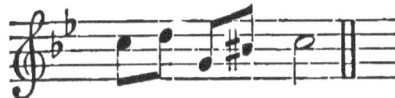

Celladon, when Spring came on,
    Woo'd *Sylvia* in a Grove,
Both gay and young, and still he sung
    The sweet Delights of Love:
Wedded Joys in Girls and Boys,
    And pretty Chat of this and that,
The honey kiss, and charming Bliss
    That crowns the Marriage Bed;
He snatch'd her Hand, she blush'd and fann'd,
    And seem'd as if afraid,
Forbear, she crys, your fawning Lyes,
    I've vow'd to die a Maid.

Celladon at that began
    To talk of Apes in Hell,
And what was worse the odious Curse,
    Of growing old and stale,
Loss of Bloom, when Wrinkles come,
    And offers kind, when none will mind,
The rosie Joy, and sparkling Eye,
    Grown faded and decay'd,
At which when known, she chang'd her Tone,
    And to the Shepherd said,
Dear Swain give o'er, I'll think once more,
    Before I'll die a Maid.

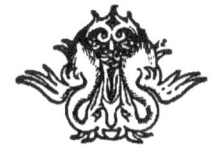

A drinking Song, *in praise of our Three fam'd Generals.*

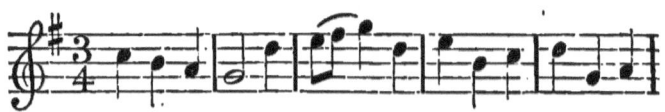
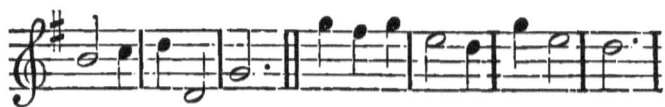
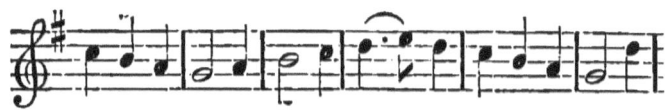
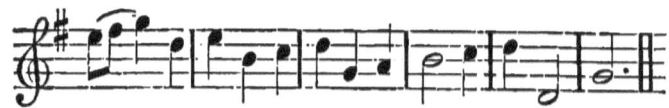

QUE chacun remplisse son verre,
  Pour boire a nos trois Generaux,
Par tout ou marchent ces Heros,
  Ils menent a pres eux la victoire,
Que chacun remplisse son verre,
  Pour boire a nous trois Generaux.

Que jamais Brille dans l'histoire
  La Glorie du brave *Marlborough*;
    Que jamais, &c.
  Auxson des verres et des Pots,
Celebrons ici sa victoire;
    Que jamais, &c.

Beu-

Pleasant and Divertive.

Beuvons a se Grand Capitaine
   Eugene, l'amour des ces Soldats ;
      Beuvons, &c.
Si tost qu'il paroit an Combat,
Tourjours le victoire est certain ;
      Beuvons a se, &c.

A *D'Auverquerque* en pleinetasse,
   Qu'on fasse raison pour ces exploits ;
      A *D*'Auverquerque, &c.
Sil n'est pas la premier des trois,
En Zele aucun nelny surpasse ;
      A *D*'Auverquerque, &c.

Que chacun devous a la ronde,
   Reponde et fasse comme moi ;
      Que chacun, &c.
C'est a la Reine que je bois,
Quelle reigner sur tout le monde ;
      Que chacun, &c.

Le pretendu Prince de *Galle*,
   De Batte soy disant notre Roi ;
      Le pretendu, &c.
Comme en *Eccosse* en diserroy,
A fuis d'une Ardeur sans *Esgale* ;
      Le pretendu, &c.

Si nous Amions autant la Glorie,
   Qua boire nous serrions des Heroes ;
      Si nous, &c.
Car parmis les verres le Pots,
Nous sommes seurs de la victoire ;
      Si nous, &c.

Translated from the *French*.

Fill every Glass, and recommend 'em,
   We'll drink our three Generals Healths at large,
For whereso'er these Heroes march,
Conquest renown'd is sure t'attend 'em ;
Fill every Glass, and recommend 'em,
We'll drink our Three Generals Healths at large.

What ever shone so bright in Story
   As Fame, that adorns brave Marlborough;
      What ever shone, &c.
Shocking our Glasses that o'erflow,
Celebrate then his lasting Glory ;
      What ever shone, &c.

Drink next then to that Grand Commander
   Eugene, *the Delight of all the Brave;*
      Drink next, &c.
Who laurel Wreaths is sure to have,
Where e'er he comes, like Alexander,
      Drink next, &c.

To Auverquerque *exalt your Glasses,*
   And just to his Valour let us be,
      To Auverquerque, *&c.*
Who tho' not youngest of the Three,
For brave Exploits there's few surpasses ;
      To Auverquerque, *&c.*

But now around Boys, Joy maintaining,
   Fill, fill 'em like mine up to the Brink ;
      But now around, &c.
Health to the Glorious Queen I drink,
Let her o'er all the Globe be reigning,
      But now, &c.

The sham Pretender Prince of W——
    The Prig, they sent o'er to be our K——
        The sham, &c.
    When the bold Scots own'd no such thing,
    Fled like a Devil home to Gallia ;
        The sham, &c.

Did we love Honours kind Caresses,
    Like toping we all Heroes should be ;
        Did we love, &c.
    For 'mongst our Cups perpetually,
    We should be sure of grand Successes ;
        Did we love, &c.

The Solemn LOVER. *A New* SONG, *made to entertain the Persons of Quality, and other my Friends at my Play. The Words made to a pretty Minuet, Compos'd by Mr.* Hendell.

WHEN the *Spring* in Glory,
    Fragrant and flowery,
Just had thrust Winter out, storming and showery,
    Celladon gallanting
    Celia, was chanting
A pleasant Tale of his Fortunes past ;
    Ah ! my dearest Pleasure,
    Joy beyond Measure,
Richer than all the Jems of *India*'s Treasure :
    When alluring Beauty
    Prostrates my Duty,
                                Ah,

Ah, then I own my self wholly blest
    State Affair Simplicity
    Has my Felicity,
Robb'd to a high Degree of sweet Delight,
High, *Low*, jangling all in a hurry,
    Nothing witty, nothing gay,
    Politicks rule e'ry Day,
Nor can the dear Bottle relieve the Night.

    He to Court that wanders
    Walks in Meanders,
Treading the Maez of Detraction and Slanders;
    In the Hall the News is
    Hot from both Houses,
Some Statesman snapt to his Tryal comes,
    Coffee Citts do prattle,
    Smoak, Tope, and Tattle,
Telling a foreign Lye of some great battle;
    Of the Czar's prevailing,
    Who we taught Sailing,
And gave a Rod to lash all our Bums,
    Poland's Ability,
    Prussia's Hostility,
Make no Account of bold *Sweden*'s Frowns,
    War, War, regale the Glory Lover,
    Let but my *Cælia* be mine,
    Happiness I'll ne'er resign,
Or change for the State of the Northern Crowns.

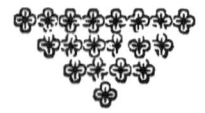

The Jolly Miller.

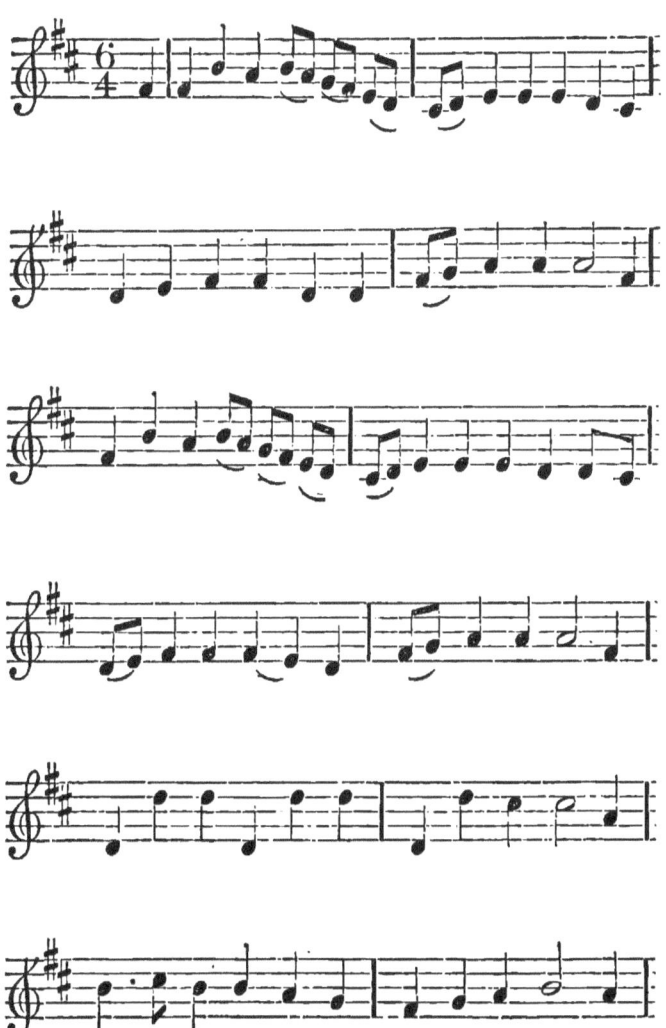

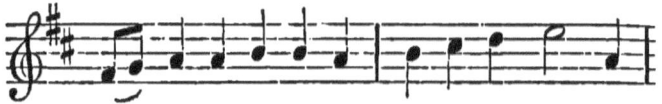

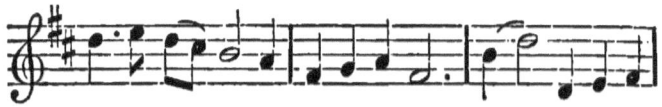

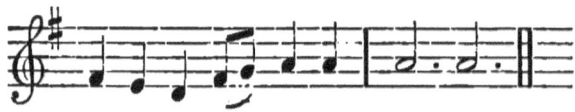

THE old Wife she sent to the Miller her Daughter,
   To grind her Grist quickly, and so return back,
The Miller so work'd it, that in eight Months after
   Her Belly was fill'd as full as her Sack;
Young *Robin* so pleas'd her, that when she came home,
She gap'd like a stuck Pigg, and star'd like a Mome,
She hoyden'd, she scamper'd, she hollow'd and hoop'd,
      And all the Day long,
        This, this was her Song,
Was ever Maiden so lericompoop'd.

Oh *Nelly*, cry'd *Celie*, thy Cloths are all mealy,
   Both Backside and Belly are rumpled all o'er,
You moap now and slabber, why what a pox ail you?
   I'll go to the Miller, and know all ye Whore:
She went, and the Miller did grinding so ply,
She came cutting Capers a Foot and half high,
She waddled, she stradled, she hollow'd and whoop'd,
      And all the Day long,
        This, this was her Song,
Hoy, were ever two Sisters so lericompoop'd.
                              Then

Pleasant and Divertive.

Then *Mary* o'th' Dairy, a third of the Number,
   Wou'd fain know the Cause they so jigg'd it about,
The Miller her Wishes long would not incumber,
   But in the old manner the Secret found out.
Thus *Celie* and *Nelly*, and *Mary* the mild,
Were just about Harvest Time all big with Child,
They danc'd in the Hay, they hallow'd and whoop'd,
     And all the Day long,
     This, this was her Song,
Hoy, were ever three Sisters so lericompoop'd.

And when they were big they did stare at each other,
   And crying, Oh Sisters, what shall we now do,
For all our young Bantlings we have but one Father,
   And they in one Month will all come to Town too:
O why did we run in such hast to the Mill,
To *Robin*, who always the Toll Dish would fill,
He bumpt up our Bellies, then hallow'd and whoop'd,
     And all the Day long,
     This, this was their Song,
Hoy, were ever three Sisters so lericompoop'd.

A New SONG,

Made in Honour of the Renown'd Prince Eugene *of* Savoy, *and to welcome him to* England.

The Words made to a pretty Tune.

NOW is the Sun
   From the Horizon gone,
That the Empire so long did cheer,
   Weak stands the Court
   Without wonted Support,
              We

We have got the main Pillar here :
To Sea from the Shoar
Let loud Cannons roar,
Let the Trumpet too sound between,
  Whilst from each *Brittish* Voice
  We are venting our Joys,
In honour of great *Eugene*.

  Hail mighty Prince,
  Whose bright Glory from hence
Soon will spread o'er the wandring Isle,
  You we possess,
  Should we ne'er see your Face,
Who remember *Turin* and *Lisle* ;
  Your Twin, Brother Star,
  The Soul of the War,
Bright as *Phœbus* was always seen,
  For search all *Europe* o'er,
  Never Heroes before
Shone like *Marlborough* and great *Eugene*.

  Each Day and Night,
  To promote your Delight,
Let the Muses their Art employ ;
  Janglings are guest
  From the Dome in the West,
That I wish may not curb your Joy ;
  Jarrs have long while
  Been the Plague of our Isle,
The Effects of our Wealth and Spleen ;
  May they fly like the Wind,
  And let all be enclin'd
To sing Welcome to Great *Eugene*.

CHANSON en Francois.

LE printems, r'apelle aux armes, Couller mes larmes;
  Le printems, r'apelle aux armes, ah quel tourment,
Grand Dieu parmis, tant d'allarmes, epargnezmon,
  Cher amant bis.

Ne revenez point encore Charmante Flora,
  Ne revenez point encore tendre Zephire,
Chaque fleur qu'on voit eclore,
  Me causer mille soupirs.

Arbre dont l' epaix femlage former ruiage,
  Arbre dont l' epaix femlage cacher le jour,
Emittee par ton ombrage le devil,
  De mon tendre amour.

Translated from the French.

Spring invites, the Troops are going, let Tears be flowing,
  Spring invites, the Troops are going, ah, cruel smart,
    Midst alarming, dreadful harming,
  Spare him Fate, who charms my Heart.

Flora, bring no more with Pleasure, thy gaudy Treasure,
  Zephire, bring no more with Pleasure, refreshing Joys,
    Each Flower growing, sweetly blowing,
  Make me vent a thousand Sighs.

Ye tall Trees, whose gloomy shading, the light invading,
  Ye tall Trees, whose gloomy shading, the day conceal,
    Shew by Sorrow, Night and Morrow,
  Cloudy Woes, like those I feel.

The Italian SONG,

Call'd Pastorella; *made into an* English Dialogue.

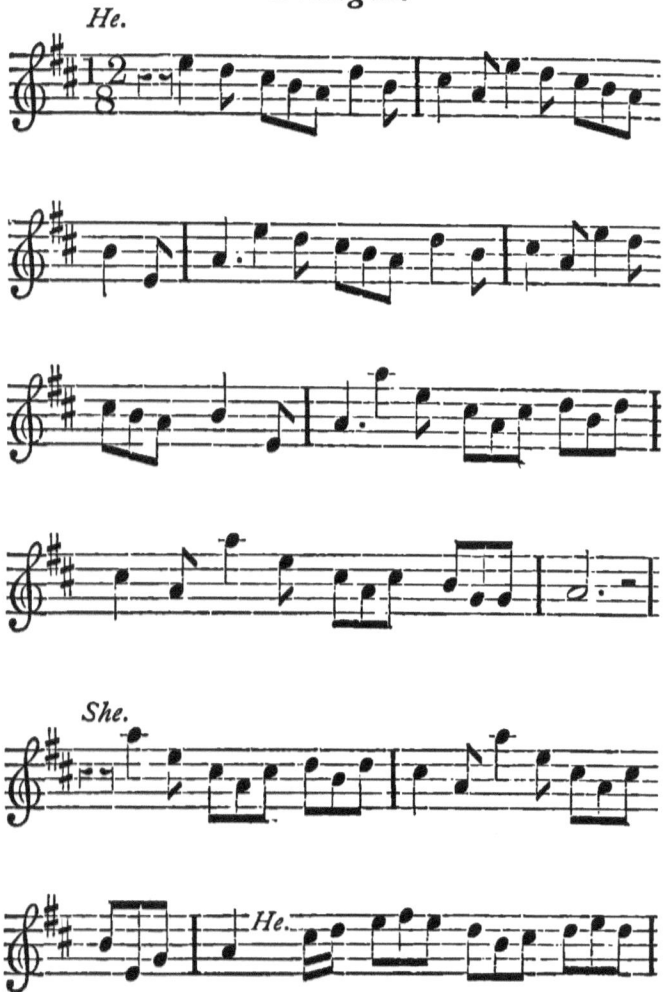

Pleasant and Divertive.

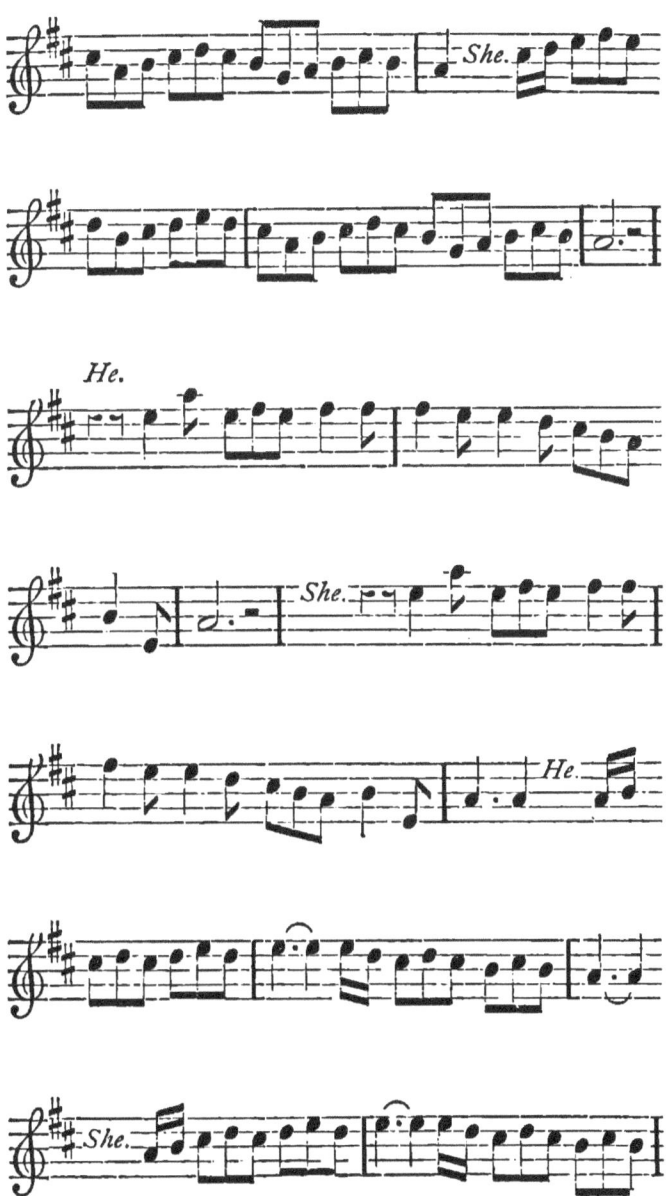

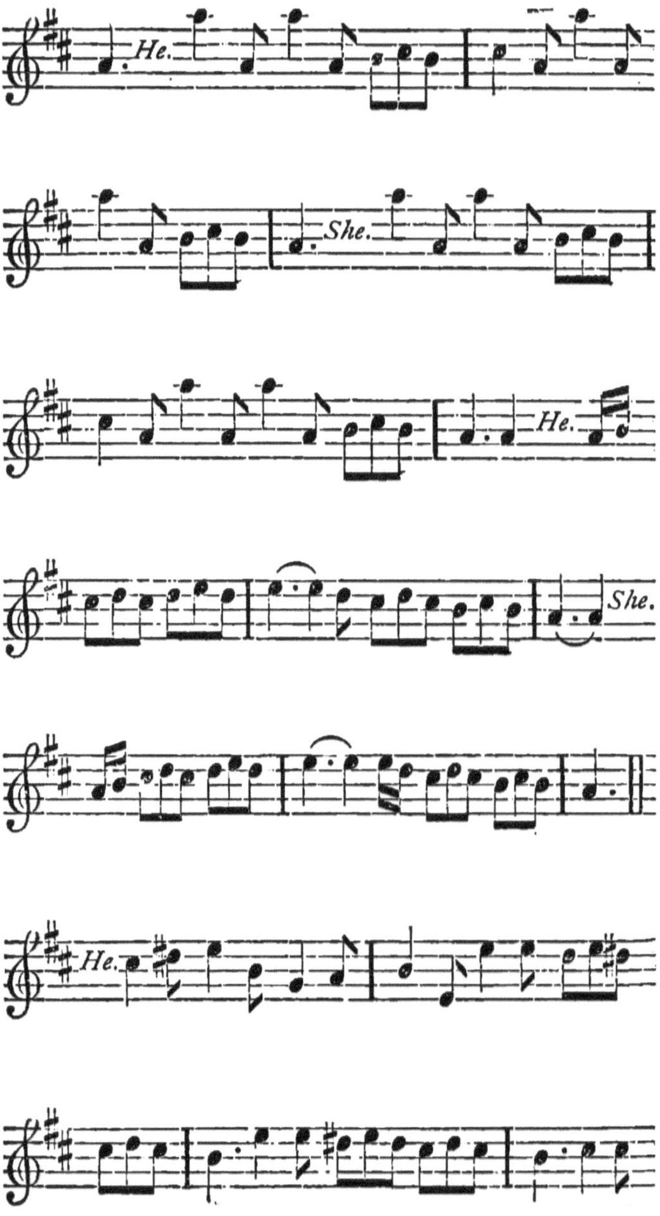

192   SONGS *Compleat*,

Pleasant and Divertive.

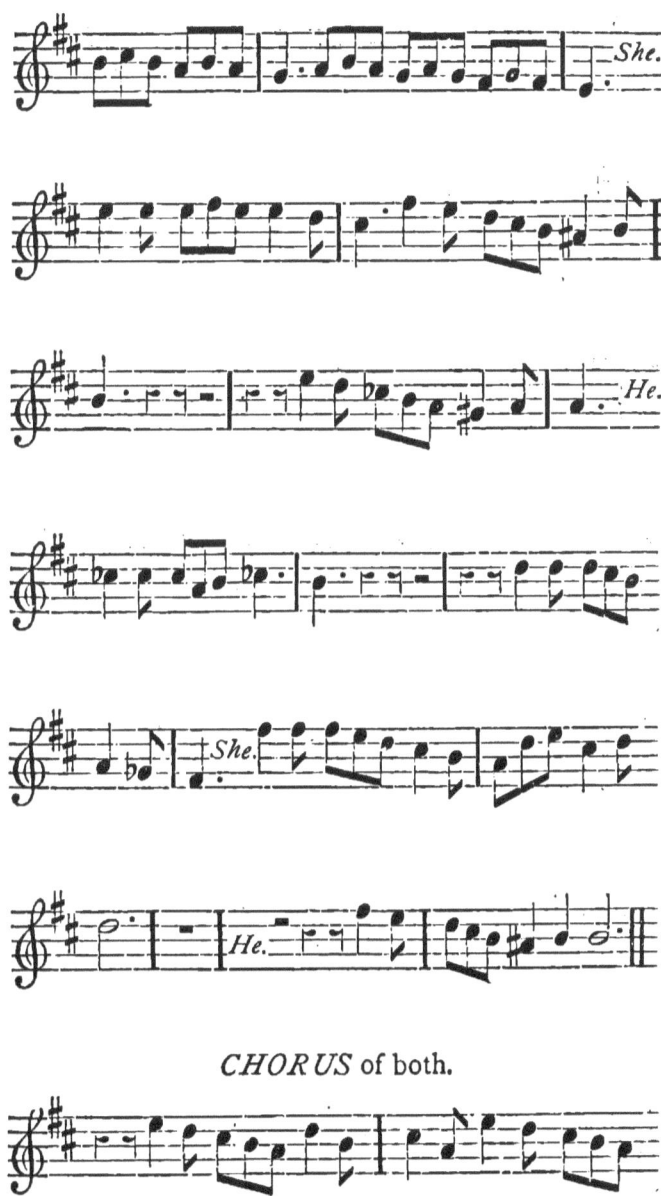

CHORUS of both.

194 SONGS *Compleat,*

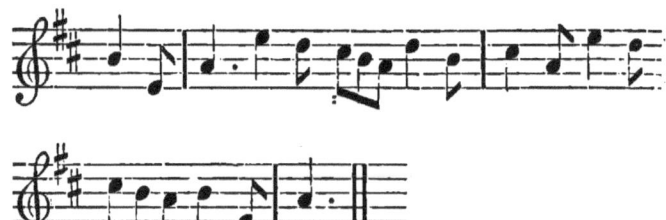

B*Lowzabella* my bouncing Doxie,
  Come let's trudge it to *Kirkham* Fair,
There's stout Liquor enough to Fox me,
  And young Cullies to buy thy Ware.
She. Mind your Matters ye Sot without medling
  How I manage the sale of my Toys,
Get by Piping as I do by Pedling,
  You need never want me for supplies.
He. God-a-mercy my Sweeting, I find thou think'st fitting,
  To hint by this twitting, I owe thee a Crown;
She. Tho' for that I've been staying, a greater Debt's paying,
  Your rate of delaying will never Compound.
He. I'll come home when my Pouch is full,
  And soundly pay thee all old Arrears;
She. You'll forget it your Pate's so dull,
  As by drowzy Neglect appears.
He. May the Drone of my Bag never hum,
  If I fail to remember my *Blowze*;
She. May my Buttocks be ev'ry ones Drum,
  If I think thou wilt pay me a Souse.
He. Squeakham, Squeakham, Bag-pipe will make 'em,
  Whisking, Frisking, Money brings in;
She. Smoaking, Toping, Landlady groping,
  Whores and Scores will spend it again.
He. By the best as I guess in the Town,
  I swear thou shalt have e'ery Groat;
She. By the worst that a Woman e'er found,
  If I have it will signify nought;

He

Pleasant and Divertive.

He. If good Nature works no better,
 Blowzabella I'd have you to know,
 Though you fancy my Stock is so low,
 I've more Rhino than always I show,
 For some good Reasons of State that I know.
She. Since your Cheating I always knew,
 For my Ware I got something too,
 I've more Sence than to tell to you.
He. Singly then let's imploy Wit,
 I'll use Pipe as my gain does hit,
She. And If I a new Chapman get,
 You'll be easy too,
He. Easy as any worn out Shoo.

[CHORUS of both.]
Free and Frolick we'll Couple Gratis,
Thus we'll show all the Human Race;
That the best of the Marriage State is,
Blowzabella's *and* Collin's *Case.*

A Serenading ODE;

The Words made to the foregoing Italian Pastorella, *and humbly Dedicated to the Right Honourable the Earl of* FINGALL.

P*Astorella*, Inspire the Morning,
 Your bright Eyes will create a Day;
Envious *Phœbus* is just returning,
 Shame him back with a brighter Ray,
A brighter Ray, Ray, each adorer with flaming heart,
 Before thy beauty Divine does kneel;
With Devotion in every part,
 Much stronger than any *Persian* Zeal.

          Arise,

Arise, then sweet Angel arise,
A Lover dispairing relieve;
Who values a Smile from your Eyes,
    More than all the worlds Treasure can give.
    Thus let Man do,
    What he can do, can do, can do;
    Mighty Love will for ever be,
    Mighty Love will for ever be
    Potent Lord of our Liberty,
    Potent Lord of our Liberty.
    Pastorella, let Day break,
    On thy Votary pity take;
    Venus rising from out the Sea,
    Will be foil to thee:
    Charm the World then, and Ravish me,
    Charm the World and Ravish me.

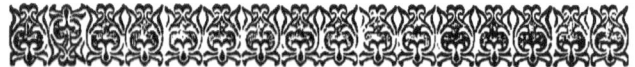

An ODE *on Queen* ANN.

The Words Made to an Excellent Tune of Mr. Henry Purcell*'s*.

SOund, Fame thy Golden Trumpet sound,
   Sound, sound thy Golden Trumpet sound;
Fly from the Arches of the Firmament,
    Inspire the Muses all around:
To Sing of Peace and then disperse,
In Artful numbers and well chosen Verse;
    Great *Albiona*'s Story,
    Great *Albiona*'s Glory.

                                    The

The Occasional BALLAD.

Being a Supplement *to the last, on the* Occasional Bill; *And upon the Bishops and Parsons preaching down the Playhouses: The Words fitted to a Comical Tune, call'd* Hobb's Wedding.

Since long o'er the Town
   My Fame has been blown
For Sonnets, that suit with each Palate;
   Tho' I dare not maintain
   Ye Wits, your bold Strain,
I can add an *Occasional Ballad.*

   For as you were right
   In a Satyr to bite,
When the Cause was so near Desolation,
   So mine is a Theam
   Of as great an Extream,
The confounding all Wit in the Nation.

   But I am, you must know,
   Not for *High-Church* nor *Low,*
A *Medium,* my Intelect chooses;
   And some think it wou'd
   Do the Nation much good,
If ye all trimm'd like me, in both Houses.

   For by moderate Sense,
   That can Reason dispense,
Sullen *Britains* are soonest confuted,
   As a mild gentle Breez
   Still refreshes the Trees,
That by wild roring Tempests are rooted.

   Calm Wit will prevail
   More in a smooth Tale
Then lashing Reproof, that sounds louder,
   Better ways we may use
   Oft, to quench a fir'd House,
Than by blowing up all with Gunpowder.

And therefore my Song
None o'th' Senate shall wrong,
Nor I'll ruffle no Collars of Esses,
But with Royal *Anne*,
A renown'd happy Reign,
And a hundred Year more than Queen *Besses*.

No Peers grown too great,
Nor no *Commons* Wit
Shall swell up my Lines to the Margent,
Since the first at their Nod
Have a swinging black Rod,
And the last, a rough thing call'd a Serjeant.

No Statesman that rise
By Publick Employs
With Offence, here shall trouble the Reader,
No takers of Bribes,
Nor potent State Scribes
Low as Shrubs, or as tall as a Cedar.

I'll not search into Ills
Of *Occasional Bills*,
Nor the Gain, or the Loss of the Nation,
Nor scan the moot Case
Of the Snake in the Grass,
Late imagin'd in point of Succession.

Great Ladies at Court
That make Profit their Sport,
When lucky at *Ombre* or *Bassett*,
Who in Benefits swim,
So well I can trim,
To wish much Good do her that has it.

Old Dames boasting youth
Without e'er a tooth,
And *Beaus*, that have Breaths that can Purge ye
In short, a meer Ape
That's a Layman shall 'scape,
But I wont part so fair with the *Clergy*.

A

A Rabby of which
Who was fated to Preach,
When the Fast-day Ingag'd all our Prayers;
As his Zeal did provoke,
Gave a terrible stroke,
To knock down the *Poets* and *Players*.

Another Church Wit
Who near Woolpack did sit,
Shew'd a Play too, to prove their vile sinning,
Tho' 'twere better some thought,
That his Lordship had brought,
A good *Homily* of his own Penning.

But a Pamphlet late spread
Had charm'd his Wise head,
Wrote by one who well knew the Stage evil;
Some *Collier*-like Saint,
Who to publish the Cant,
Had rak'd a hodg podg for the Devil.

A Jargon of Phrase
Cull'd out of lewd Plays,
And patcht into Form by the vermin;
Just in such a way
As with dull hum— and ha,
Some of them use to Patch up a Sermon.

The Tempest long made
And by accident play'd,
Might shame them, that made such a pother;
Since no one can think,
That's not Mad or in Drink,
'Twas e'er done in Contempt of the t'other.

And tho' that abuse
I'll in Canters excuse,
Who good Music, or Wit never heard on;
Yet the *B———ps* those Rocks,
Of our sence Orthodox,
Who could second such Stuff, I wont Pardon.

They

They should favour the Age
That does cherish the Stage,
Since kind to their Ghostly performance;
Remembring late days
When *Lawn Sleeves*, and Plays,
Were cry'd down, an equal enormance.

But see the result
Of their *quicunque vult*,
Her Majesty made Proclamation;
'Twixt the Scenes that none stay,
That all Bullies should pay,
And sponge no more for Recreation.

That no Plays be rude
Immoral or lewd,
In *Betterton*'s Province or *Riches*,
All Masque's lay'd away,
Which is done since that day,
For now they come mobb'd up like Witches.

All this being obey'd
Is still of our side,
Since the Profit is our chiefest matter;
But of all that have been,
The commands of the *Queen*,
She has not forbid us our Satyr.

Which is a new * Case   [* *Doyley's Case*
We may properly raise,   *late try'd.*]
Where a Gown-man did furnish the matter;
For proof of it all
Ask at *Westminster Hall*,
How the *Clergyman* Marry'd his Daughter.

Good sence that is shewn
Without Blunder or Tone,
Preach'd by heart too, to make it more Charming;
A Devout sober life,
Never stirring up strife,
All prejudice must be disarming.

But

Pleasant and Divertive.

>   But if o'er the Town
>   I observe a Black Gown,
> Who is proper to make a fine Farce on ;
>   As they late made Essays,
>   To Preach down all the Plays,
> I shall make bold to Act up the Parson.

>   Thus changing advice
>   With the Grave and the Wise,
> Let each one reform in his station ;
>   And so I shall cease,
>   In the laudible phrase,
> Of Bless the good *Queen* and the Nation.

The Mournful and Passionate Complaint or Petition of Madamoiselle Gallia, *or the Statue of* France, *plac'd amongst the other Nations, before the Cathedral of St.* Paul's *in* London, *to the Statue of our late Soveraign Lady Queen* ANN, *now Expos'd to view in Honour of her Majestys coming to Hear the* Te Deum *for the Glorious* Peace. *The Words made in Jargon of* English *and* French, *to a Pretty St.* Germains *Air.*

> Madam *je vous prie* you will right me,
>   Injurys maka me cry ;
> Do late you had reason to spite me,
>   Now Ime your ver good Ally :
> Aw, let not your Vassal den slight me,
>   Now, now in dis Grand season of Joy.

De

De Carver (*Jernie* me want Patiance)
  Shewing your Soveraign rule;
In spite to dese happy occasions,
  With his base Hammer and Toole
Among all de rest of de Nations,
  Make, make, maka me look like one fool.

De East and Nort *Britains* are merry,
  Dresse and dere humours are fitt;
De *Irish* Smile as if down derry,
  Newly had tagg'd her great Witt;
But me, as if past *Charons* ferry,
  Look, look just as if me were Besh—t.

Brave Peace our Grand Monarch does give you,
  Blessing your Subjects at home;
And derefore me tink it should greive you,
  Seeing me look like a Mome;
Strong *Dunkirk* does likewise receave you,
  Which, which is begar ver pretty Plum.

Rare Mirth your wise Land is enjoying,
  Finding *mon Grand Maitre* true;
De Army he keep all defying,
  Give cause ver me to Laugh soe;
Yet here in dis Posture of crying,
  Mine Phiz lowrs as 'twould make a Dog spew.

In fine den me humbla Petition,
  Vor Majesty would appear;
And order one better Incission,
  Min clowdy visage to clear;
For in dis confounded condition,
  Mort dieu me have Grand shame for sit here.

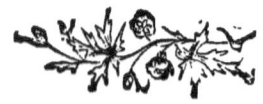

MAC

Pleasant and Divertive. 203

MAC BALLOR.

A comical Ditty, in Imitation of the Irish *Stile.*

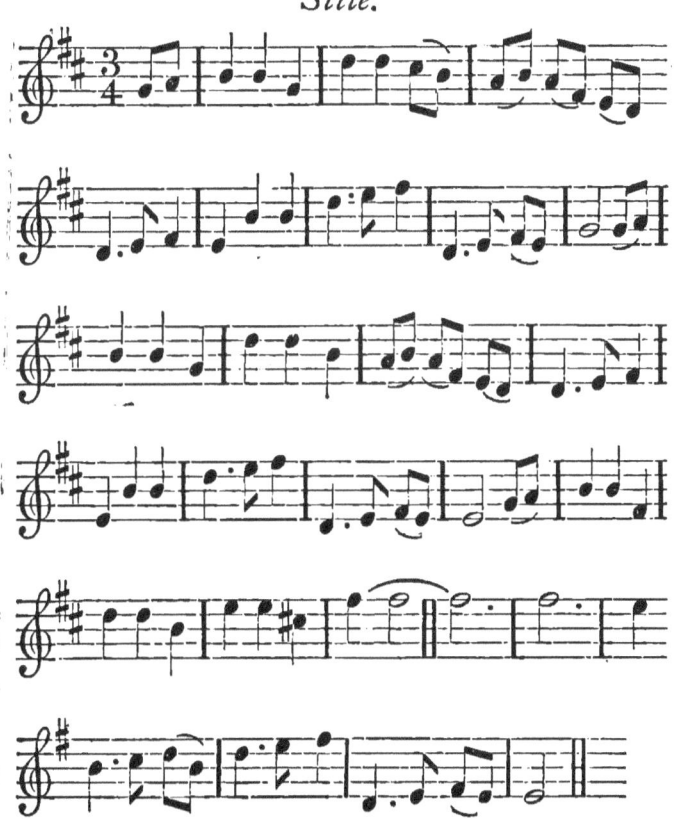

IF a woful sad Ditty to know thou art willing Man,
   Open thy Ears Joy, and then thou shalt see;
To *London*, *Mac Ballor* a stout *Iniskilling* Man,
   To seeking Brown *Kate*, by my Shoul am come eey;
My Heart is sore wounded, sore wounded, sore,
   A la Boo, boo, boo, boo, hone, Oh hone, hery Morah.
                                                          When

When the Valiant King *William* cross'd over the *Boyn* Joy,
    And with broken Pates, made *Jack Papishes* flee;
Of Dragoons a brave Troop made a Gallop to joyn Joy,
    And march with the foremost by Chreest did come eey;
They were beaten sore, Curst and Swore, and did roar,
    A la Boo, boo, boo, &c.

When I went on a Party, I Sung and was merry too,
    Tho' Hunger gives small occasion to Laugh;
I without any Grumbling, fought in *London-Derry* too,
    Without one Dram of Snush or Usquebaugh,
Where fed on Roots, stinking Fruits, old Jack-Boots.
    A la Boo, boo, &c.

In a Skirmish near *Limerick*, on the Bank of the *Shannon* there
    Many stout *Teagues* were slain in time of Yout;
And at *Agrim* I narrowly scap'd the damn'd Cannon there,
    Catching the Balls by my Shoul in my Mout,
But tho' the Guns spar'd my Bones, Love Gad Zoons,
    A la Boo, boo, &c.

The Bully-God *Mars*, tho' a Bug-bear they make him,
    All arm'd like a Gun-smith, with Bullets and Fire,
I defy, but the little Whelp *Cupid*, plague take him,
    Make me snort and grunt like a Hog in the Mire:
She had *Irish* Size, *English* Eyes, fat *Dutch* Thighs.
    A la Boo, boo, &c.

Heav'n make me a Cobler, or make me a Broom-man,
    Or cry Pudding, what a Plague call ye it i' th' Street;
So I may no more pogue the Hone of a Woman,
    Deel tauk me 't has har'd me quite out of my Wits:
For when I get drunk, toap a Funk, in comes Punk,
    A la Boo, boo, boo, boo, hone, Oh hone, herry morah.

Pleasant and Divertive. 205

A new Health *to* Prince Eugene : *A Triumphant* ODE *upon his return to* Vienna. *Sung by Mr.* Leveridge *in the Play call'd the Country Miss with her Furbelow.*

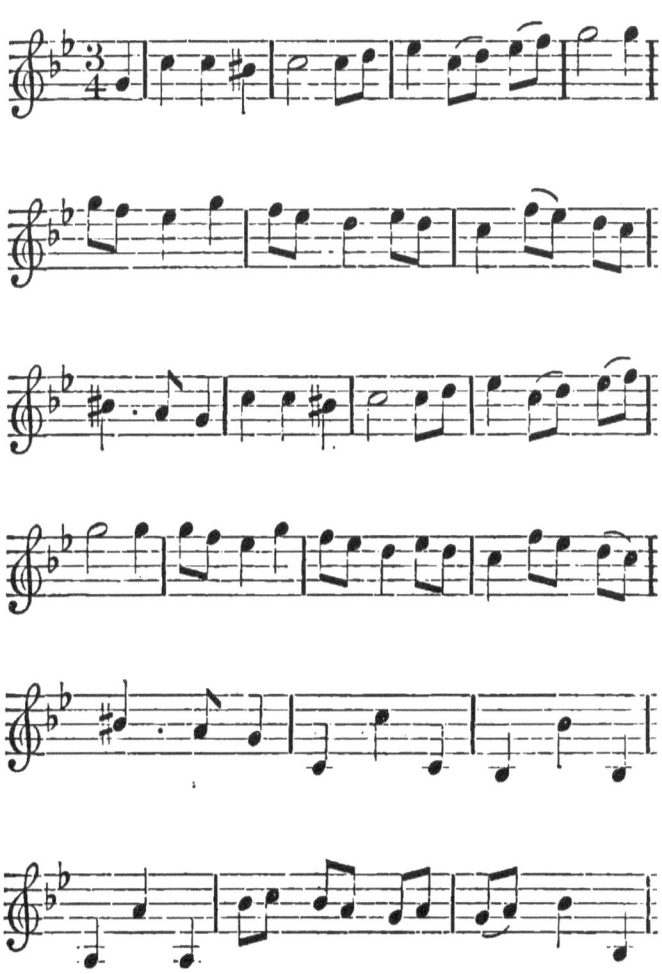

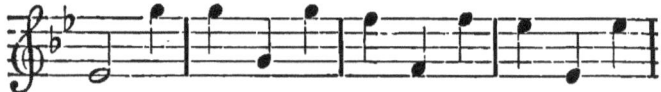
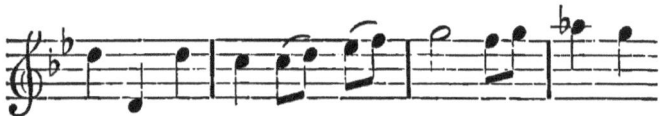
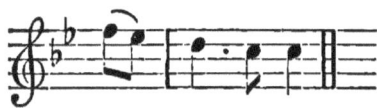

THE Valiant *Eugene* to *Vienna* is gone,
    And since deny'd,
    To be supply'd,
All his Troops are undone;
    For the haughty *Vendosme*,
    New Recruits being come,
    So proud is grown,
    Of two to one,
He Revenge swears to push home:
    And late Losses,
    Disgraces and Crosses,
Will soon retaliate now the General is gone;
    Oh *Leapold*, Oh *Baden*,
    What Fiend was perswading,
    Your Priest-ridden Clan,
    Simply to baulk so rare a Man.

Tho' *Carthage* grew proud, when story once shew'd,
    How well the Grand,
    Blind Affrican,
O'er the Alps hew'd out his Road;

All

Pleasant and Divertive.

All the Rocks in his way,
Were but Puff-past and Clay,
To those were seen,
When great *Eugene*,
Made his rugged Essay;
Where no Storm nor
Loud Thunder, this Wonder,
Could ever from his Purpose cause to hault or stay:
Tho' Watches, dispatches,
And lying their Frying,
His Youth did so decay,
Sable Locks turn'd into Grey.

Then *Latium* give o'er, name *Cæsar* no more;
Nor the *Macedon*,
Whose high renown,
Were so blaz'd on before;
But let Glorious *Eugene*,
That August Man of Men,
Be sounded high,
As far as Sky,
Or the Globe can contain;
For a braver,
Or bolder,
Good Soldier,
Did never on the bloody Field maintain his Ground:
Hell take those remove him,
And here's to those love him,
Drink, drink Boys around,
And his Foes *Pluto* confound.

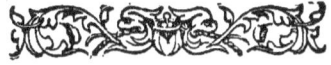

The

The new Blackbird; *A Satyr Musical.
Being Remarks on some of our Allies,
Occasioned by the* States *Deputys late refusing to assist the Duke of* Marlborough.

MOunsieur grown too mighty,
    Made half *Europe* grown;
Who for Causes weighty,
    Joyn'd to pull him down
The *Spread Eagle's* glory,
    Long Eclips'd had been,
Portugals John Dory
    Gladly too, came in;
Hogan mogan biters,
    Who our Fish devour,
Promis'd Troops of Fighters,
    To compleat the Power:
*Whilst in the Hawthorn Tree,
Terry, terry rerry rerry, sung the Blackbird,
Hey, terry rerry rerry, sung the Blackbird,
Oh what Allies have we.*

Now their Word and Honour,
    How these Chiefs regard;
Pray Sirs note the manner,
    'Twill good mirth afford;
First the *Imperial* Widgeon,
    Lately gone to rest,
Was for *Romes* Religion,
    Fool'd by each sham Priest;
Schemes of War were Riddles,
    Anxious to his Poll,
Whilst *Cremona* fiddles,
    Charm'd his thoughtless Soul;
Then in the Hawthorn Tree, &c.

He that rules at *Lisbon*,
    In next Scene survey;
Plagu'd ('tis said) in his Bone,
    The Venereal way;

Austerian

Pleasant and Divertive.

Austerian Charles inviting,
　To recover *Spain*;
He performance slighting,
　Forc'd him off again;
Arms we sent and Mony,
　English Boys to Horse,
But the Devil a Penny,
　Did they so disburse:
Whilst in the Hawthorn Tree, &c.

Prussia bravely true is,
　As in Action bold;
But the Godson *Lewis*,
　Gobbles up *French* Gold;
One great *Marlborough* aiding,
　Makes his Glory swell;
T'other Fight evading,
　Stinks on the *Mosselle*;
Shame pursue the great Ones,
　Who from Honour fall,
Fame renown the *Britains*
　Bear the brunt of all:
Whilst in the Hawthorn Tree, &c.

Lucky War maintaining,
　Pray observe the rest;
Bleinhim's Battle gaining,
　All the General blest;
Belgian Troops admiring,
　Courted his Command;
Conquest still acquiring,
　Through the *German* Land;
Hemskirk yet and *Shagen*,
　Baulk'd him late through fear,
Oh rare *Hogan Mogan*,
　Who shall lead next Year,
When in the Hawthorn Tree, &c.

Britains gain new Glory,
  Joyn like those of Old;
'Tis too plain a story,
  We are bought and sold;
Belgians still uniting,
  Mighty Sums have won;
Whilst pretending Fighting,
  Friendly Trade goes on:
Now to leave off writing,
  Skellums pine and grieve,
When we're next for Fighting,
  We'll not ask you leave,
When in the Hawthorn Tree,
Terry, terry rerry rerry, Sings the Blackbird,
Hey, terry rerry rerry, Sings the Blackbird,
  Then Jolly Boys we'll be.

A Satyr upon London, *and in Praise of the Country. The Words made to a pretty New Tune.*

WHO in Old *Sodom* would live a Day,
  Grow Deaf with Rattling of Coaches;
Where Folly and noise is call'd brisk and gay,
  And Wit lyes in studying Debauches.

With Stinks, which Smoke and rank Foggs display,
  Who'd be offending their Noses;
That in the sweet Shades of the Country may,
  Sit Cool under Bushes of Roses.

Town Fops in Riot consume every Day,
  The Citt will Cheat his own Brother;
And the Ladys haunt the Park and the Play,
  To Laugh, and Rail at each other.

Pleasant and Divertive.

Our Funds are wanting, our Credit decays,
  The *French* are publickly Arming ;
And for all the daily noise is of Peace,
  It never comes to confirming.

But we that Breath in a Fragrant Air,
  From News, Street noise, and such Howling ;
Our innocent Pleasures each Day prepare,
  With Fishing, and Shooting, and Bowling.

Some Mornings early we Hunt a Hare,
  Who Life to Pleasure us looses ;
Or else if the Weather proves not fair,
  At home we Regale on the Muses.

The charming Raptures of Beauty and Love,
  Sweet *Cloris* freely affords too ;
When we meet each Evening in a lone Grove,
  And sing and bill as the Birds do.

She feeds on Jessamin, and spring Nectar drinks,
  Whilst she we call a Town Madam ;
Is infected still with a foul Suburb stinks,
  And Damns her self in old *Sodom*.

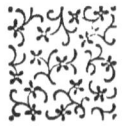

The Dame *of* Honour *or* Hospitality, *Sung by Mrs.* Willis *in the* OPERA *call'd the* Kingdom *of the* Birds.

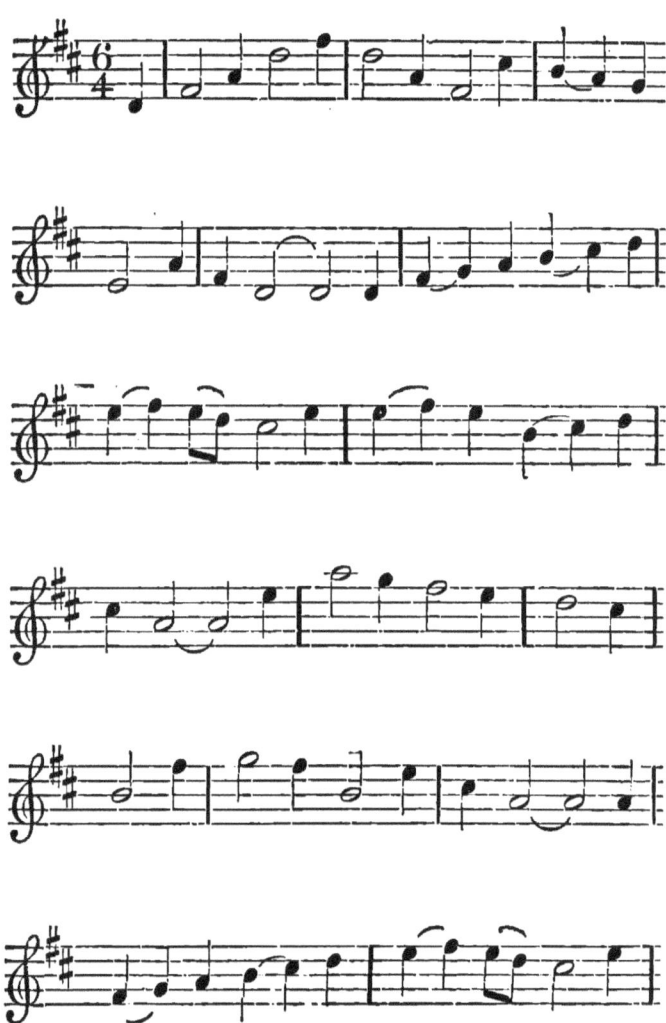

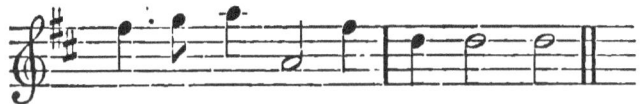

SInce now the world's turn'd upside down,
  And all things chang'd in Nature;
As if a doubt were newly grown,
  We had the same Creator:
Of ancient Modes and former ways,
  I'll teach you, Sirs, the manner;
In good Queen *Besses* Golden Days,
  When I was a Dame of Honour.

I had an ancient Noble Seat,
  Tho' now 'tis come to Ruin;
Where Mutton, Beef, and such good Meat.
  In th' Hall were daily Chewing:
Of Humming Beer my Cellar full,
  I was the Yearly Donor;
Where toping Knaves had many a Pull,
  When I was a Dame of Honour.

My Men of homespun honest Grey's,
  Had Coats and comely Badges;
They wore no dirty ragged Lace,
  Nor e'er complain'd for Wages;
For gawdy Fringe and Silks o'th' Town,
  I fear'd no threatning Dunner:
But wore a decent Grogram Gown,
  When I was a Dame of Honour.

I never thought *Cantharides*
  Ingredient good in Posset,
Nor ever stript me to my Stays,
  To play the Punk at *Basset*;
In *Rattafee* ne'er made debauch,
  Nor reel'd like toping Gunner;
Nor let my Mercer seize my Coach,
  When I was a Dame of Honour.

I

I still preserv'd my Maiden fame,
   In spight of Oaths and Lying;
Tho' many a long chinn'd Youngster came,
   And fain would be enjoying:
My Fan, to guard my Lips I kept,
   From *Cupid's* lewd o'errunner;
And many a *Roman* Nose I rapp'd,
   When I was a Dame of Honour.

My Curling Locks I never bought
   Of Beggar's dirty Daughters;
Nor prompted by a wanton thought,
   Above Knee ty'd my Garters;
I never glow'd with Painted Pride,
   Like Punk when the Devil has won her:
Nor prov'd a cheat to be a Bride,
   When I was a Dame of Honour.

My Neighbours still I treated round,
   And Strangers that come near me;
The Poor too always Welcome found,
   Whose Prayers did still endear me;
Let therefore who at Court would be,
   No Churl, nor yet no Fawner:
Match in old Hospitality,
   Queen *Besses* Dame of Honour.

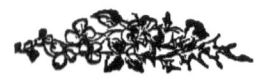

Pleasant and Divertive. 215

The 6th SONG *in the last Act of the* 2d *Part of* Don Quixote, *Sung by Mr.* Freeman *and Mrs.* Cibber. *Set by Mr.* Purcell.

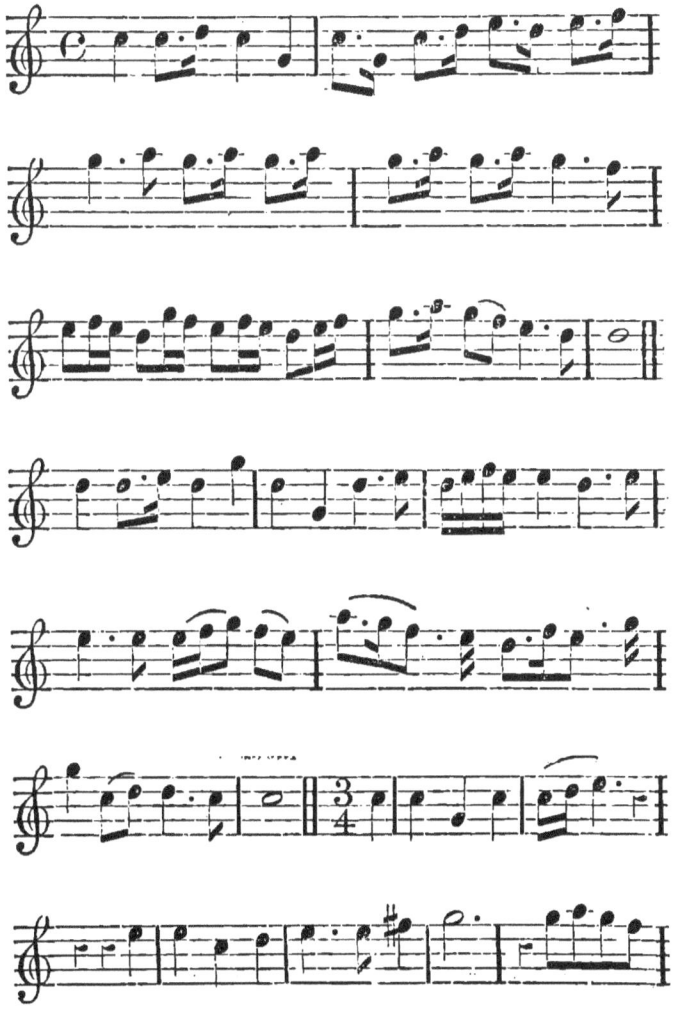

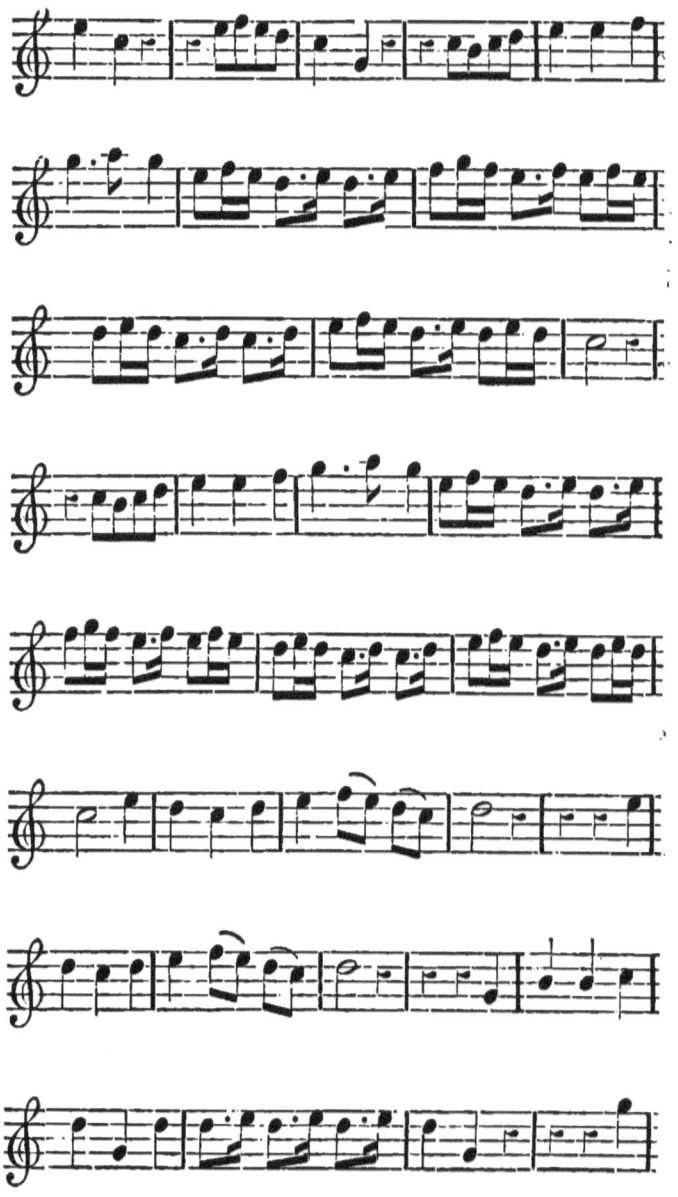

Pleasant and Divertive.

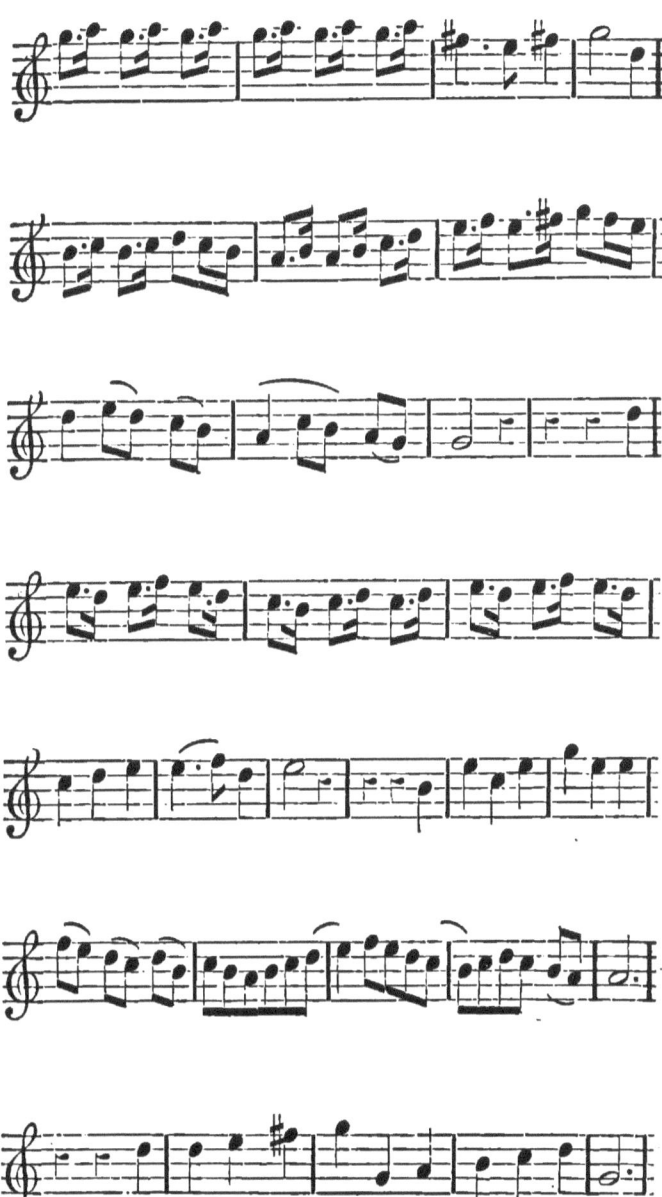

218   SONGS *Compleat,*

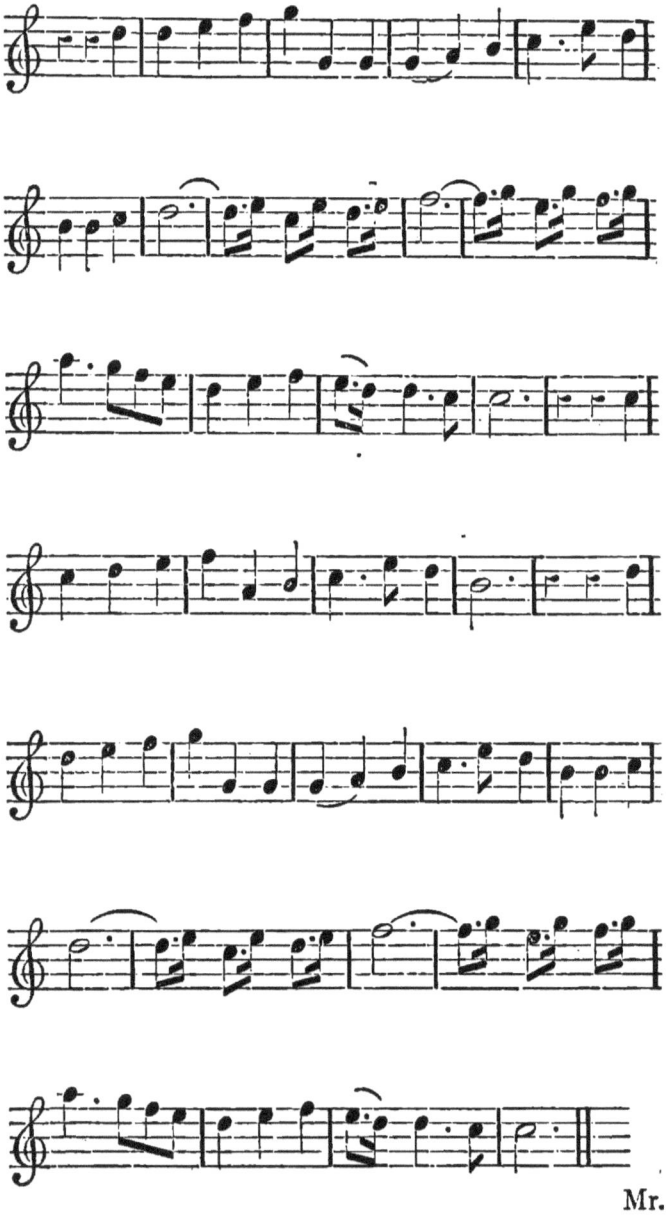

Mr.

Pleasant and Divertive.

Mr. *Freeman.*

Genius of *England,* from thy pleasant Bow'r of bliss,
Arise and spread thy sacred Wings;
Guard, guard from Foes the *Brittish* State,
Thou on whose smiles does wait,
Th' uncertain happy Fate of Monarchies and Kings.

Mrs. *Cibber.*

Then follow brave Boys, then follow brave Boys to the Wars,
Follow, follow, follow, follow, follow, follow
Follow, follow, follow bráve Boys to the Wars,
Follow, follow, follow brave Boys to the Wars;
   The Lawrel you know's the Prize,
   The Lawrel you know's the Prize:
Who brings home the Noblest, the noblest,
The noblest Scars looks finest in *Celia's* Eyes;
   Then shake off the Slothful ease,
Let Glory, let Glory, let Glory inspire your Hearts;
   Remember a Soldier in War and in Peace,
Remember a Soldier in War, in War and in Peace,
   Is the noblest of all other Arts:
   Remember a Soldier in War and in Peace,
Remember a Soldier in War, in War and in Peace,
   Is the noblest of all other Arts.

SON-

SONNET *Royal, made for one Voice to Instruments.*

THE Infant blooming Spring appears,
   Sol has his way through *Aries* made ;
And now this Wond'rous of all Years,
   The Prize of *Europe* must be play'd.

Crested *Belona* shakes her Lance,
   Her Sister *Britain* to defend ;
Whilst *Mars* of Old, in League with *France*,
   Dares proudly against both contend.

[*Second Movement.*]

But Rouze valiant *Britains*, and fear quite remove,
   You cannot of Victory fail ;
Our Goddess below, and our Goddess above,
      By force of their Charms,
      As that of their Arms,
   Have a right still to conquer the Male.

[*Third Movement.*]

March on then brave souls,
   You're sure of your Pay ;
And toping full Bowls,
   Warm valours allay,
This wish to the *Queen*, daily chant by the way :
   In wealth may she flow
   May she *Lewis* bring low,
   May her Fame spread and grow,
   Whilst Sun shines, or Wind blows,
   And Hang up Her foes.
In Wealth &c.

English

English *Words made to a Famous* Italian *Ayre, call'd* Scoca puero.

Life's short Hours, too fast are hasting
Sweet Amours, can never, never be lasting;
  Care and sorrow,
  May to morrow,
Hinder the dear design of Pleasure,
Nor grant the happy leasure,
To count our darling Treasure;
  Time, time *Celia* is flying,
  Whilst you are denying,
  Dissolution, and Confusion
  The passing Bell tolling,
  Relations condoling
  Horror will soon be surrounding,
  Nature confounding;
  Make then amends whilst you may,
  My dear for that sad Day,
  Our Loves kind advances,
  Our Songs and our Dances,
Age will conclude, and Amorous trances;
  Beauty with all 'tis charms,
Oh pitty, oh pitty will freez in my Arms.

Cursory Remarks on some Few, and partilarly the No Beauty of Tunbridge *Wells.*

To shew *Tunbridge* Wells,
  Other Waters excells,
In the various effects of the blessing;
  I can prove without pain,
  They can work on the Brain,
As well as the Bladder by P——sing.

For

For as they can Heal,
With the Iron and Steel,
And the Wretch, Paralitick recover;
   They can make lewd Dice Players,
   Go to Chappel to Prayers,
And a Brazen Physitian turn Lover.

They can make him disgrace,
A most Beautiful Face,
And adore a thing, Frowzy and Cloudy;
   Witness a brown Girl,
   Counted here for a Pearl,
Whom we all thought at *Clapham* a Dowdy.

A Face turn'd four-square,
Full of aukwardly Air,
Ne'er design'd for nice beauty's *Regalia*;
   With a Mouth, which each laugh,
   Spreads two Inches and half,
And a Skin like a Ham of *Westphalia*.

Then tho' Grazzet she wears,
Through her Sisterly fears,
Of what her whole Lineage may come too;
   Since her Daddy despairs,
   Yet she gives her self Airs,
And has got the Town Jett with her Bum too.

They can make the Precise,
The Demure and the Wise,
Applaud this fine Method of living;
   Tho' you never can keep
   Out the *Wolves* from the *Sheep*,
And it all ends, in Cheating and Thieving.

In short to conclude,
Without being rude,
They can give such a Tincture to Nature;
   They Fat Bawds can inure,
   To sell Fruit, and Procure,
In spight of the Jerks of a Satyr.

A

A SONG, *Made on the happy Occasion of our late Forcing the* French *Lines. The Words made to a pretty new Minuet.*

Grand *Louis* falls head-long down,
Since *Luxemburg's* Death, the Witchcraft is gone;
No Planet durst for him appear,
At *Helisheim* now, nor *Blenheim* last Year:
    Th' Arm's shouting,
    Bavaria's routing,
Shews just Fate too, that Rebel resigns,
    Once more flying,
    Hark how he's crying,
Jernie bleau, they have forc'd our strong Lines.

Sing *Muses*, the General's praise,
Baulk'd at the *Mosselle*, but not at the *Maes*;
Whilst Volumns with scandal are full,
On *Lewis* the Craz'd, and *Lewis* the Dull:
    One oppressing,
    Feigning redressing,
Seises Crowns without Title or Law;
    T'other marches,
    Very rarely charges,
Witness late, the long Siege at *Landau*.

Crown bowls then each *Brittish* brave Son,
Let *Bourbon* dispair, and *Baden* doze on,
Tell all who proud *France* dare defend;
What *Brabant* begins all *Flanders* shall end,
    Antwerp surrender,
    What can defend her,
Millian yield too, to Glorious *Eugene*;
    When that's gone too,
    Vendosme, Vendosme too,
Hey, for *Paris* next Summer's Campaign.

224   SONGS *Compleat*,

A New SONG *by way of* Congratulation *to her* Majesty, *on the Happy Frustrating the late* French *Invasion.*

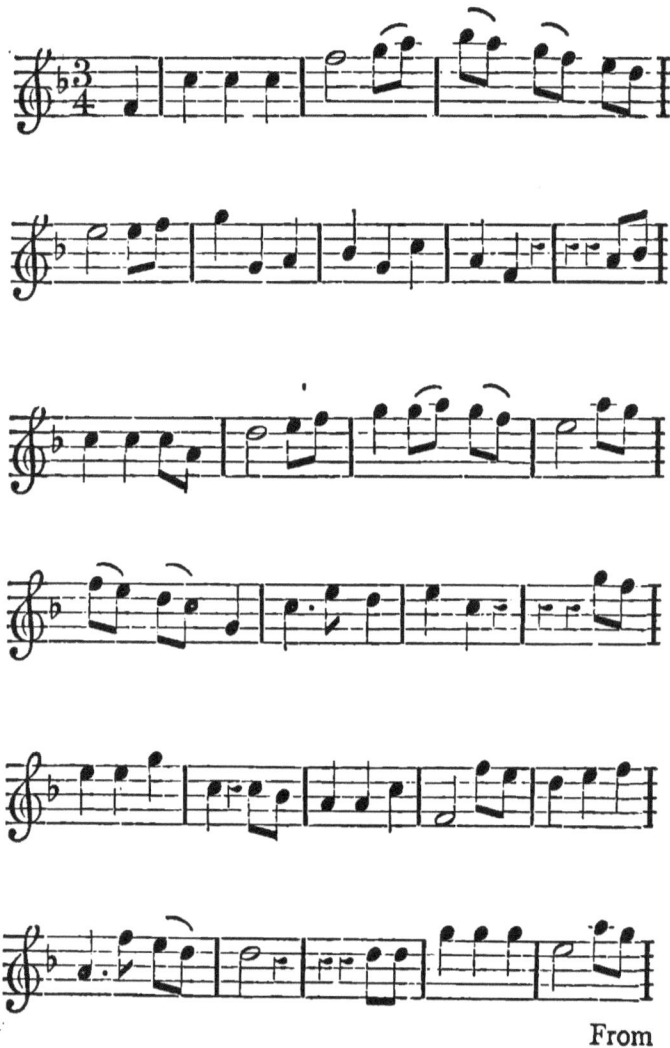

From

Pleasant and Divertive. 225

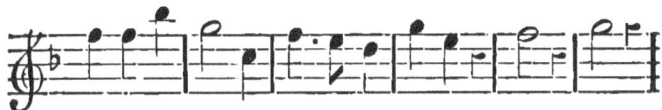

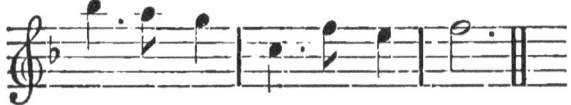

From *Dunkirk* one Night, they stole out in a fright,
    To Insult our Faith's Royal Defender;
But some *Dæmon* in th' dark, made 'em out-run the mark,
    And so baulk the invading *Pretender*:
Whilst the *Mounsieur* in heat, sent Express to each State,
    That in *Scotland* he straight should be Crown'd;
But instead of that Reign, he must take him again,
    Laugh Jolly bold *Britains*, laugh, laugh,
        Laugh at him *Europe* all round.

Would my Country-men know, how this comes to be so,
    And how He and his Slaves are so hearty;
Be ye Commons or Lords, in a few honest words,
    'Tis explain'd they are all of a Party:
And tho' poor as Rats, without Coyn or Estates,
    Only what the most *Christian* will spare;
They Unite against the Foe, ah, let us do but so,
    Ye Jolly bold *Britains* then, then,
        Then let 'em come if they dare.

Long live Gracious *Ann*, let her flourishing Reign,
    Give her safety and Glory for ever;
Let no more *Northern* Scribes, sell her Kingdom for bribes,
    Nor the *Brittish* to plague it endeavour:
Let the *Dutch* Troops obey, and give *Marlborough* his way,
    Let great *Hannover* mind his Affair;
Let brave Prince *Eugene*, lead his Troops once again,
    Ye haughty *French* boasters then, then,
        Then stand your Ground if you dare.

The

The Court LUNATICKS, *or Reflections on the late Changes. The Words made to the Tune of a pretty Country Dance, call'd* Hedg Lane.

SNUG of late, the Barons sate
    With Northern *Brittons* bonny,
Commons they, were every Day,
    On Ways and Means for Mony:
But there's now, the Devil to do,
    The high built *Tory* rory;
Plots maintain 'gainst Moderate Men,
    But have faln down a story:
Greg's harangu'd, but yet unhang'd,
    They want some more discovery;
H——ly's out, there's none can doubt,
    And *St——ns* past recovery:
M——hams Plot is piping hot,
    And all to change the Ministry;
They only mean, t' abuse the *Q——n*,
    With Loyal sham pretences,
Fie, *Tories* fie, you soar so high,
    Y' have all quite lost your Senses.

Who would put the General out,
    That is not strangely Frantick?
Who'd defame *Godolphins* name,
    That is not simply antick?
Who'd displace the Purse and Mace,
    That value Law or Reason?
Who'd discard the *Q——ns* best Guard,
    That is not fond of Treason?
Yet the Muse, can some produce,
    Who 'tis believ'd are much to blame;
Some who hope, to climb the top,
    And are too Great for me to name:
Who pretend, the Church to mend,
    Yet only do confound the same:

Pleasant and Divertive.

And meerly mean, to abuse the Q——n,
  With Loyal sham pretences;
Fie, Tories *fie,* &c.
H——*t's* Gown, is now laid down,
  The Court for't is in Mourning;
Yet the Cross, gives little loss,
  His Coat so well bears turning:
In all Reigns, his working Brains,
  Both sides have oft been trying;
Passive fear, he well could bear,
  But never self denying:
M——*sell* too, who all Men knew
  Of late, so wise and Politick;
Swears to joyn the Grand design,
  In spite of his Comptroling stick:
Several more were late brought o'er,
  But all were routed in the nick;
The Snake was seen the Flow'rs between,
  For all their Grave pretences;
Fie, Tories *fie,* &c.

Then in short 'tis well the Court,
  Can great Preferments vary;
Since they've chose, all now suppose,
  An honest Secretary:
One too Just a Knave to trust,
  Tho' Language he pronounces,
Or to make his Judgment weak,
  Employing Factious Dunces:
Let this Year our Ships of War,
  Be worth an able Penmans care;
Let the Plots of raving Sot,
  Ne'er draw our Party to a snare;
Nor the kind indulgent Q——n,
  Afflict with Heart disturbing care:
By doubts that rise, and Tales and Lies,
  And Loyal sham pretences;
Fie, Tories *fie, you Soar so high,*
  Y'have all quite lost your Senses.

A Song *for* Sancho *in the Fourth Act of* Don Quxiot. *Set by Mr.* John Eccles.

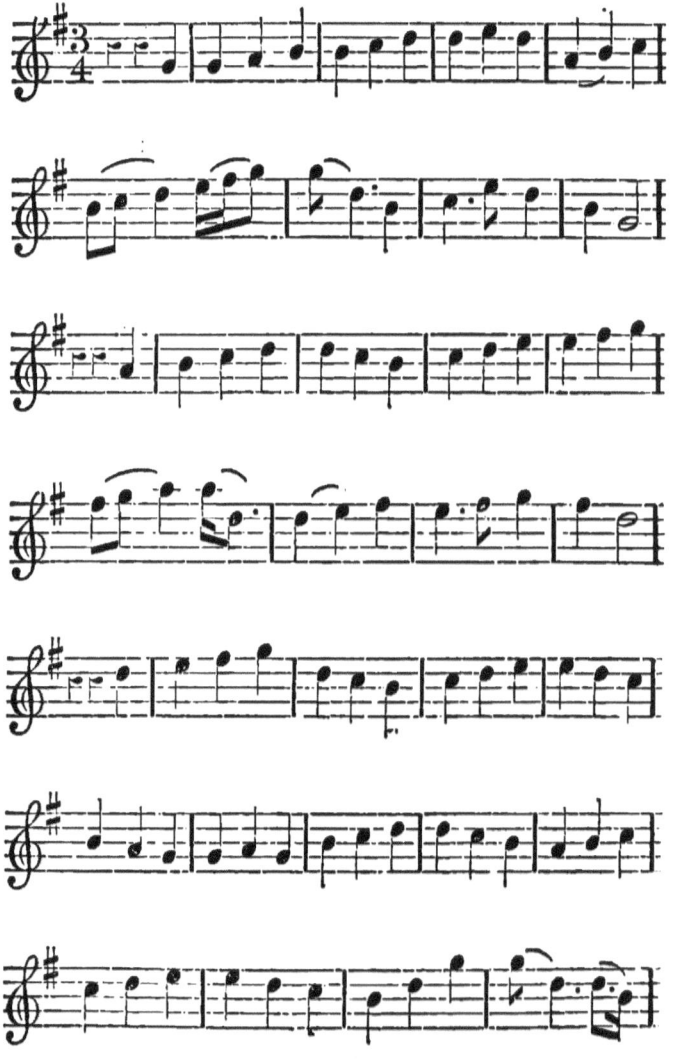

Pleasant and Divertive.

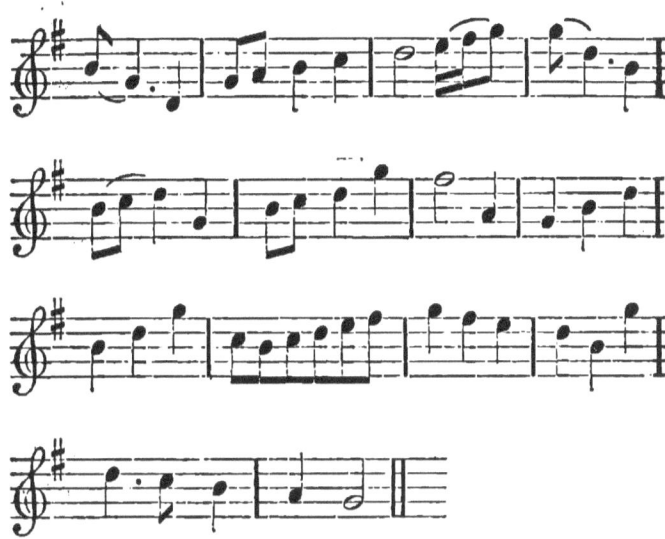

'TWas early one Morning, the Cock had just crow'd;
    Sing hey ding, hoe ding, langtridown derry;
My Holiday Cloaths on, and face newly Mow'd,
    with a hey ding, hoe ding, drink your brown Berry;
The Sky was all Painted, no Scarlet so Red,
For the Sun was just then getting out of his Bed,
When *Teresa* and I went to Church to be sped;
    With a hey ding, hoe ding, shall I come to Wooe thee,
    Hey ding, hoe ding, will ye buckle to me;
    Ding, ding, ding, ding, ding, ding derry, derry,
    Derry ding, ding, ding, ding, ding, hey lantridown derry.

Her Face was as fair, as if't had been in Print,
    Sing hey ding, &c.
And her small Ferret Eyes, did lovingly Squint;
    With a hey down, &c.
Yet her mouth had been damag'd with Comfits & plumbs,
And her Teeth that were useless, for biting her Thumbs,
Had late, like ill Tennants, forsaken her Gums;
    With a hey ding, hoe ding, &c.

But

But when Night came on, and we both were a Bed,
  Sing hey ding, &c.
Such strange things were done, there's no more to be said.
  With a hey down, &c.
Next Morning her head ran of mending her Gown,
And mine was plagu'd how to pay Piper a Crown,
And so we rose up the same Fools we lay down,
  With a hey ding, hoe ding, &c.

The Wedding, *or the Farmers Holliday; A New* Song. *The Words made to a Pleasant Tune.*

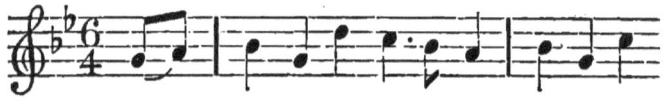

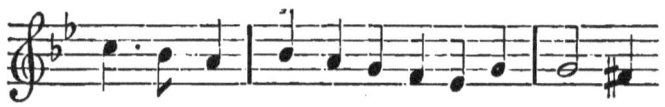

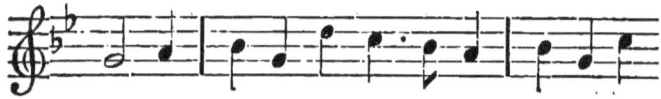

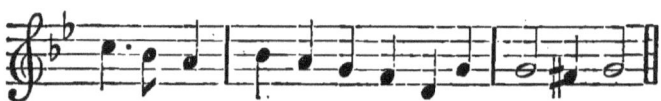

Pleasant and Divertive.

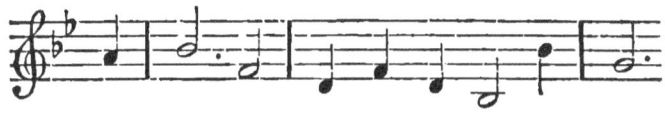
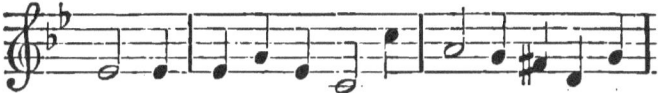
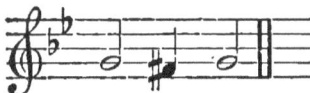

Ay's *Roger* to *Will*, both our Teams shall lye still,
   And no Hay shall be carry'd to make the Mow;
For what e'er betide, we must see the new Bride,
   And the Lads and the Lasses, and all the Show:
     Such fine folk never were seen,
     For all the Country comes in,
To Day, let's leave then our *hoy gee hoa*.

There's Flaxen, and Brown, and Slim, and full grown,
   There's Tall for your liking, and others low;
There's some that can Skip, and there's others can trip,
   There's grey Eyes, and Hazel, and black as Sloe:
     Their looks so pleasing and kind,
     They're sure all, all of one mind;
Zooks think no more then of *hoy gee hoa*.

There's Widdows and Maids, with their high cocking heads,
   Tho' some are unskilful, yet others know;
There's Batchelors brisk, who can Caper and Frisk,
   And the Art of fine footing can nimbly shew:
     When blood warms, Matches are made,
     Thus on goes love Jolly trade,
Then who'd be sweating at *hoy gee hoa*.
                               Windsor

Windsor Tarrass. *A New* Song.

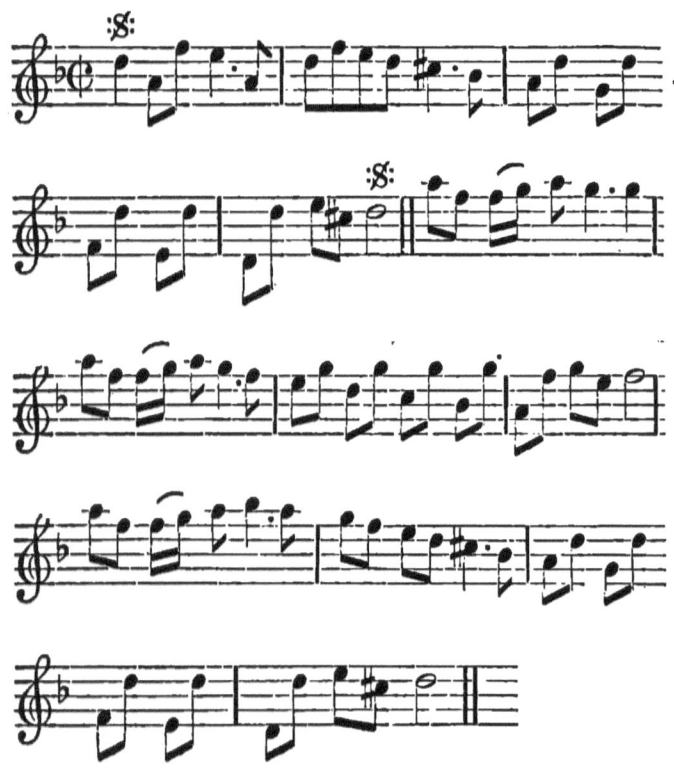

Using I late,
  On *Windsor* Tarras sate;
And hot, and weary,
  Heard a merry,
Am'rous couple chat;
  Words as they go,
The Nymph soon made me know,
  And t'other was,
  Tho' gay in dress,
A blund'ring Country Beau.

He

Pleasant and Divertive.

He had shown her all
The Lodgings, great and small;
 The Tower, the Bower,
 The Green, the Queen,
And fam'd St. *George's* Hall:
 Lastly brought her here,
 To court her for his Dear;
 To Wed and Bed,
 And swore he had,
A thousand Pound a Year.

Mony the crew
Of Sots, think all must do;
 And now this Fool,
 Unlearn'd at School,
It seems believes so too:
 But the rare Girl,
 More worth than Gold or Pearl,
 Was Nobly got,
 And brought, and Taught,
To slight the sordid World.

She then brisk and gay,
That lov'd a Tuneful Lay,
 In hast pull'd out,
 Her little Flute,
And bad him Sing or Play;
 He both Arts defy'd,
 And she as quickly cry'd;
 Who learnt no way,
 To Sing nor Say,
Shou'd ne'er make her a Bride.

An

An ODE, *or* Lyrical *Elegy, or Funeral* ODE, *Written in Sorrow ; on the Death of the late most Excellent and much Lamented Prince* GEORGE *of* Denmark.

S *Ilvander*, Royal by his birth,
    Divinely good, as well as great ;
'Mongst all the Kingdoms of the Earth,
    Chose happy *Albion*, for his seat :
The Queen of Hearts, and Queen of Isles,
    Possest him of their Fertile store ;
The first endear'd him with her smiles,
    The last gave Ease, and wealthy Ore :
Fame, he had purchas'd long before,
    Say *Cherubins* that sit on high,
    Ye radiant Inmates of the Sky,
Did Heavn e're give a Mortal more.

Hark, the Celestials answer no,
    None, more the powers above could bless ;
Nor 'mongst the human Race below,
    E'er stood desart in higher place :
'Twould pose the *Muses* to extend,
    On such extream of worth their praise ;
The noblest Master, truest Friend,
    The tend'rest Husband, Ancient days
Replete, with Conjugal Essays,
    Can scarce so just a pattern shew,
    Much less, Licentious rovers now,
To vertuous Love, such Altars raise.

The Gracious *Flora*, pain'd with fear,
    Who knew all days had Mortal date ;
That he might stay for ever here,
    Made league with every Power, but Fate,
                                        That

Pleasant and Divertive.

That barbrous Tyrant, Foe to th' Good,
  The Wise, the Vertuous, and the Brave;
Her pious Zeal, and Prayers withstood
  And still the more she press'd to crave
  A Grant, might lov'd *Silvander* save:
    The more was urg'd to a degree,
    His doom of frail Mortality,
  That sunk his Glory to the Grave.

The dark recess, to which all go,
  That breathe upon this Earthly ball;
And now the Royal *Flora's* woe,
  Admits no Patient interval:
Tears from her Eyes incessant fall,
  The State affairs too, weigh her down;
To none, she can for comfort call,
  The Partner of her Cares is gone,
  Who caus'd her oft to cease her moan,
    Whilst Grief, that precious Life decays,
    And Sighs, such storms in *Britain* raise,
As shakes the Nation from the Throne.

Rest then great Prince, Sleep, sleep in peace,
  Reliev'd from Vice, and Mortal care:
Whilst we, that pine in Life's disease,
  Our fading Joys, less happy are:
Translated thus, from Earth to Heaven,
  Thy blissful Transports hourly grow,
Whilst we by Passions toss'd and driven,
  Live wretched in this Vale of woe:
But if our State, some glimpse of Comfort shew,
We're only blest, since so much Worth must die,
To have the skill, in sacred Verse, still to preserve thy
    Memory.

A

A Dialogue *Sung at a Play, by a Eunuch Boy, and a* Girl.

She. FLY, fly from my sight, fly far away,
My scorn thou'lt only purchase by thy stay,
Away, away, away fond Fool away.
He. Dear, dear Angel no,
Here on this place i'll rooted grow,
Those pretty, pretty Eyes,
Has charm'd me so,
I Cannot, cannot stir, I cannot, cannot go.
She. Thou Silly, silly creature, be advis'd,
And do not, do not stay to be despis'd;
By all my Actions, thou may'st see,
My Heart can spare no room for thee.
He. Why, why dost thou hate me, ah, confess
Thou sweet disposer of my Joys?
Why I can Kiss, and I can play,
And tell a thousand pretty tales;
Can Sing, can sing the livelong day,
If any other Talent fails.
She. Boast not thy Musick, for I fear,
Thy singing Gift, has cost thee dear;
Each warbling Linnet on the Tree
Has far a better Fate than thee:
For they Life's happy pleasures prove,
As they can sing, so they can Love.
He. Why so can I,
She. No, no, no poor Boy:
He. Why, why cannot I?
She. The reason is, I only guess
There's something in thy Face and Voice,
That thou'rt not made like other Boys,
No, no poor Boy.
He. Pray do but try, do but try, *&c.*
I know no reason, no reason why?
She. You know, you know, you know you Lye.

The

Pleasant and Divertive.

The Bonny Milk-Maid. *Sung in my Play of* Don Quixote.

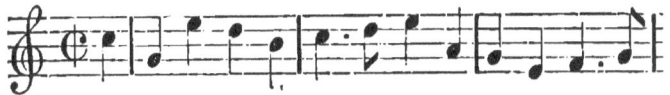

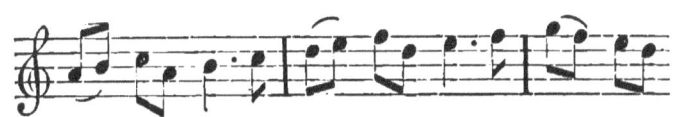

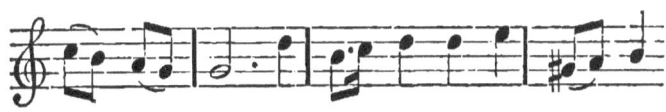

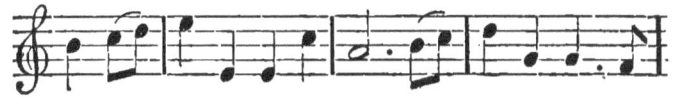

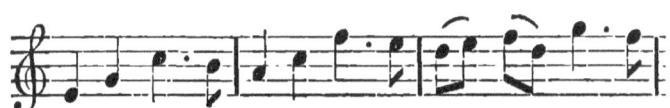

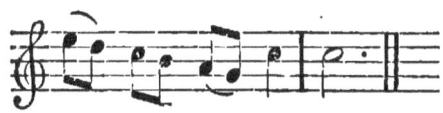

Ye

YE Nymphs and *Sylvian* Gods,
That love green Fields and Woods;
   When Spring newly blown,
   Her self does adorn,
With Flowers and blooming buds:
   Come sing in the praise,
   Whilst Flocks do graze,
In yonders pleasant Vale;
   Of those that choose,
   Their Sleep to lose,
   And in cold Dews,
   With clouted Shoes,
Do carry the Milking Pail.
The Goddess of the Morn,
With blushes they adorn;
   And take the fresh Air,
   Whilst Linnets prepare,
A consort on each green Thorn:
   The Blackbird and Thrush,
   On every bush,
And the charming Nightingale;
   In merry vein,
   Their throats do strain,
   To entertain,
   The jolly train,
That carry the Milking Pail.
When cold bleak Winds do roar,
And Flowers can spring no more;
   The Fields that were seen,
   So pleasant and green,
By Winter all candid o'er:
   Oh how the Town Lass,
   Looks with her white Face,
And her Lips of deadly pale;
   But it is not so,
   With those that go,
   Thro' Frost and Snow,
   With Cheeks that glow,
To carry the Milking Pail.

The

The Miss of Courtly mould,
Adorn'd with Pearl and Gold;
  With washes and Paint,
  Her Skin does so taint,
She's wither'd before she's Old :
  Whilst she in Commode,
  Puts on a Cart load,
And with Cushions plumps her tail ;
  What Joys are found,
  In Russet Gown,
  Young, plump and round,
  And sweet and sound,
That carry the Milking Pail.
The Girls of *Venus* Game,
That ventures Health and Fame ;
  In practising feats,
  With Colds and with Heats,
Make lovers grow Blind and Lame :
  If Men were so Wise,
  To value the prise,
Of the Wares most fit for Sale ;
  What store of *Beaus*,
  Would daub their Cloaths
  To save a Nose,
  By following those,
That carry the Milking Pail.
The Country Lad is free,
From fears and Jealousie ;
  When upon the Green,
  He is often seen,
With his Lass upon his Knee ;
  With Kisses most sweet,
  He does her greet,
And swears she'll ne'er grow stale ;
  Whilst the *London* Lass,
  In e'ery place,
  With her brazen Face,
  Despises the grace,
Of those with the Milking Pail.

SONGS *Compleat,*

A Rapture on Albion *and* Cælia.

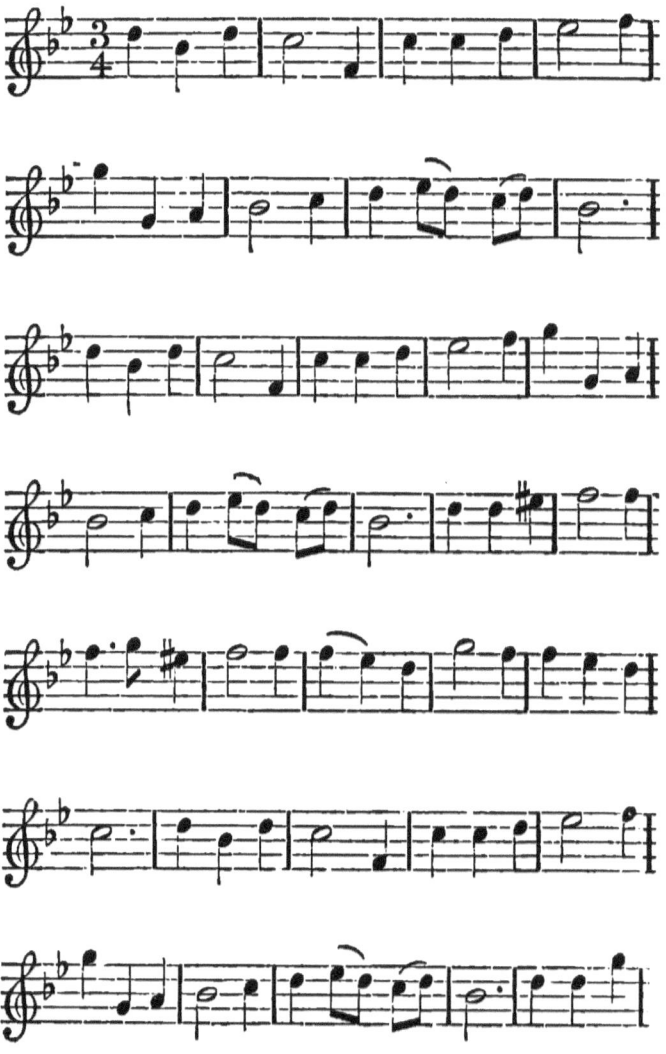

Pleasant and Divertive.

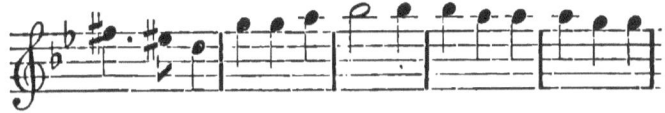
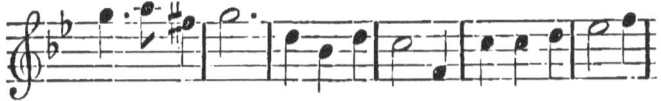
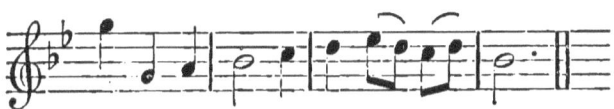

Raptures attending dwellers Divine,
  Can ne'er be transcending *Albion's* and mine;
Fame's noble story Charms her fair Isle,
And I as much Glory in *Cælia's* smile;
Victory rears her conquering Cross,
Whilst *France* in Tears bewails her sad loss.

Raptures attending dwellers Divine,
Can ne'er be transcending *Albion's* and mine;
Conquest Triumphant too, comes from the Sea,
Thus *Fate* blesses *Albion*, and *Cælia* me.
Raptures attending dwellers Divine,
Can ne'er be transcending *Albion's* and mine.

On the Glorious Victory lately won by that Wond'rous Hero Prince Eugene, *over the* Turkish *Army.*

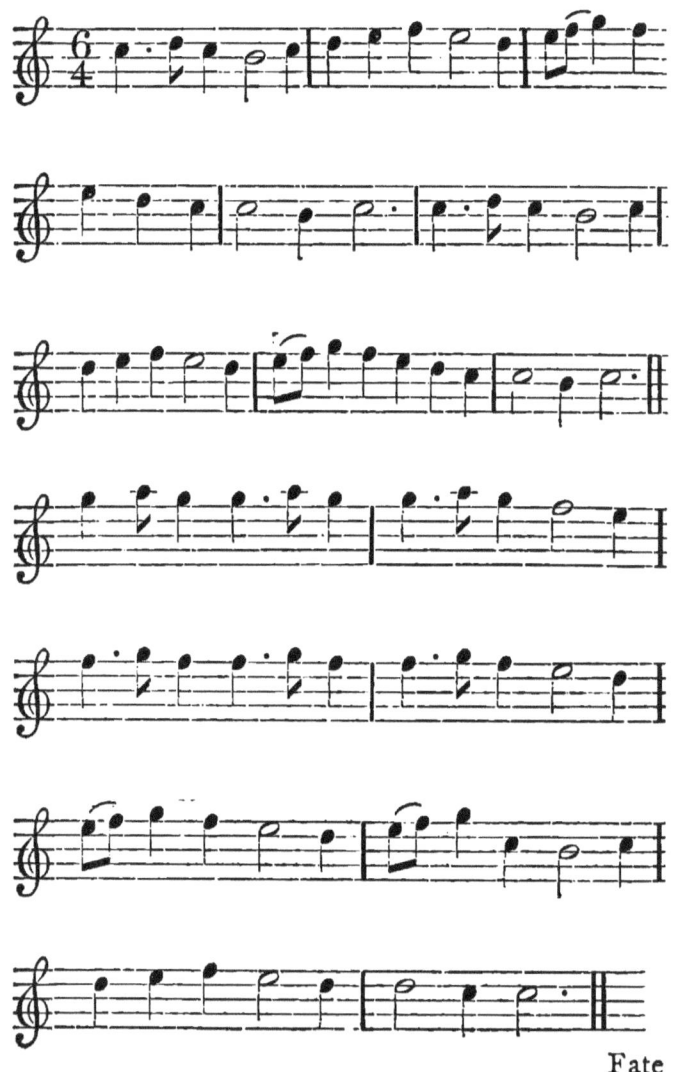

Fate

Pleasant and Divertive.

FATE had design'd this worst of all Ages,
    For *Christian* Valour a glorious doom ;
This the *Grand Signior*'s prowess inrages,
    Who thought a Million would soon o'ercome :
Mahomet sent the great *Mufti* a Vision,
How all the *Germans* bemoan'd their Condition,
        Squadrons were scanted,
        Officers wanted,
    Only *Eugene* for *Christendom.*

Two Hundred thousand made the *Turks* Army,
    Three quarters more then in Fight prevail ;
Not so the *Germans* who could alarm ye,
    Only with Valour when forces fail :
Now the Grand *Vizier* his Musselmen treating,
Swore the poor handfuls were scarce worth his beating,
        But not performing,
        Brave *Eugene* storming,
    All ran away from proud Horse-tails.

Now soars the Cross, and now flys the Cressent,
    Thousands now wait the Victorious prize ;
Now bloody Wounds and groans are incessant,
    Now the bold *Vizier* dispairing dies :
Farewel the Grandure of *Ottoman* power,
Thinking the brightness of *Christians* to lower
        Brave *Eugene's* story,
        Blooms with fresh Glory,
    Whilst *Christendom* old Faith enjoys.

A Dialogue between Teague *an* Irish *Priest and the Arch-bishop of* Paris, *on the taking of* Tournay, *and the State of the* French *affairs. The Words made to an* Irish *Tune.*

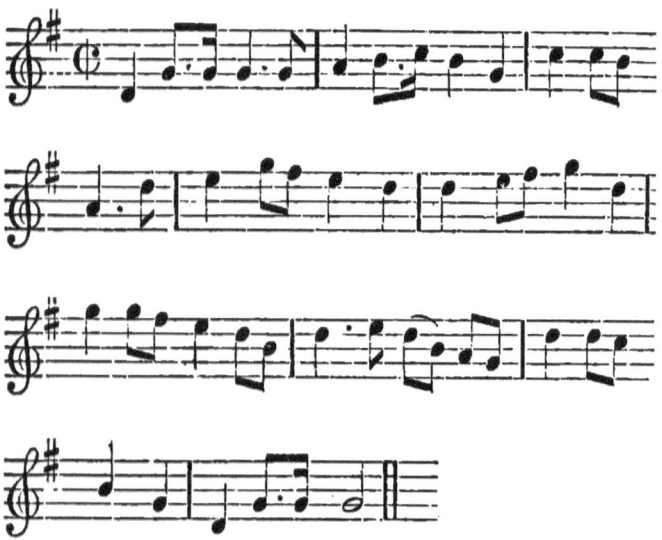

Teague.

HARK *Lewis* groans, good Fador wat ailsh him,
  None of our loud *Te-Deums* availsh him;
Creesh shave my Showl by Trumpets and Drumming,
The Raison's plain now great *Marlborough* is coming:
  Yough hone o hone.

Bishop.

Leave off your howle you seemple Bogtrotter,
Vat can me do in tings of dis nature;
Get you to Mass and dose matters handle,
To Curse him back vid your bell Book and Candle:
  Ah Jernie bleiw.

Teague

Teague.

Patrick our Shaint successes delaying,
Curshing will do no more good than Praying;
Dreadful *Eugene* the Deevil sure carrys,
Now *Tournay*'s taken he'll soon come to *Paris*:
   Yogh hone o hone.

Bishop.

If dey go on as now dey'r beginning,
Routing our Troops and Towns daily winning;
If in dey'r Lines our Army lyes Sleeping,
Adiew de Gold we so long have been heaping:
   Ah Jernie bleiw.

Teague.

Dis by my Showl's de fruit of Ambition,
Wee'r by his Pride in woful condition;
He must be making Kings of *Welch* Princes,
A plague upon't he has quite lost his Shences:
   Yogh hone o hone.

Bishop.

Dis comes of Plots with *Sweden* combining,
And of proposing Peace and not signing;
Dey'r Gen'rals now such Anger discover,
Dey'l sure demand both *Versails* and de *Louvre*:
   Ah Jernie bleiw.

Teague.

Burgundy's Mad dat Fool has undon us,
Savoy's the same who now seems to shun us;
Berwick is sent out to seek his undoing,
Tallard strong Ale for *Villiars* is Brewing:
   Yogh hone o hone.

Advice to the City, a famous SONG, *set to a Tune of Signior* Opdar, *so remarkable, that I had the Honour to Sing it with King* CHARLES *at* Windsor; *He holding one part of the Paper with Me.*

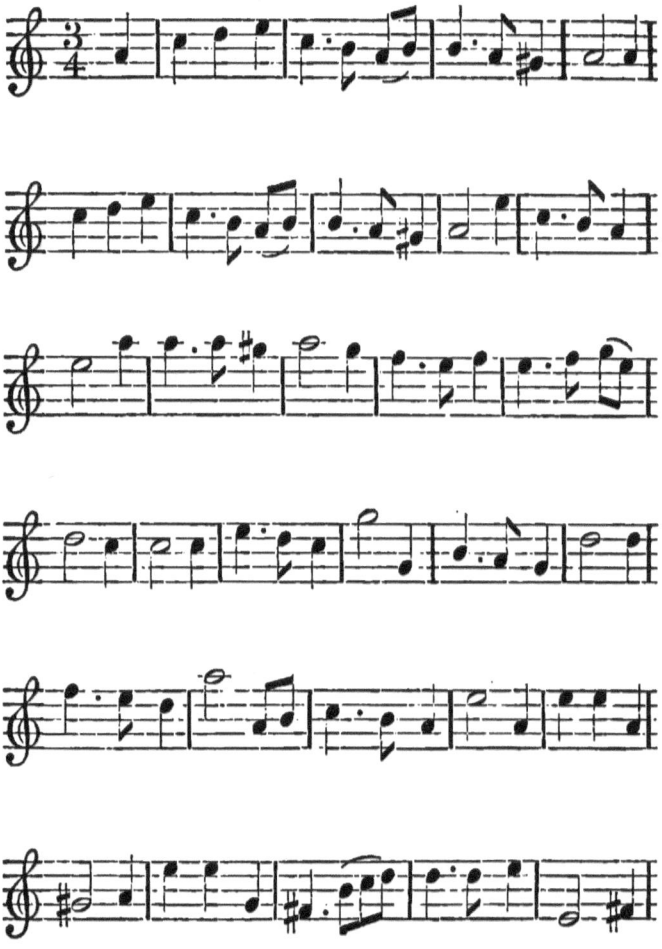

Pleasant and Divertive.

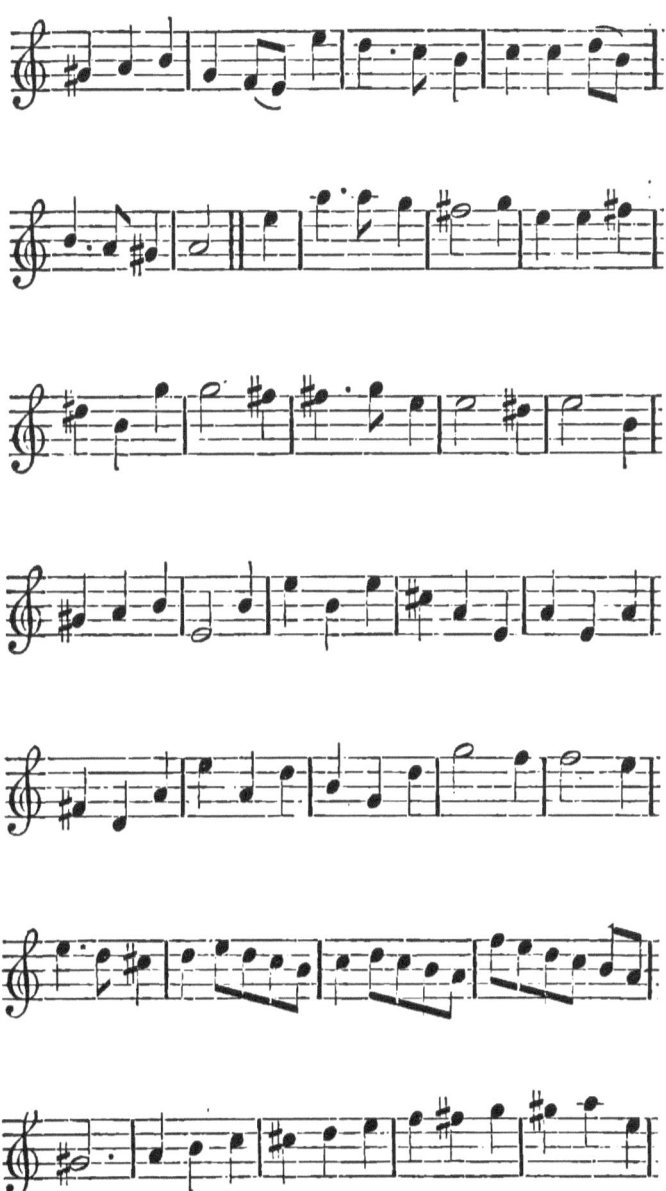

248 SONGS *Compleat,*

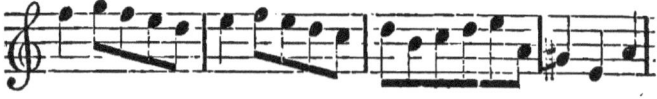

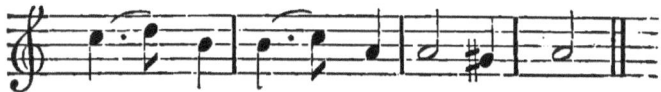

Emember ye *Whiggs* what was formerly done,
Remember your Mischiefs in *Forty* and *One*;
When Friend oppos'd Friend, and Father the Son,
Then, then the Old Cause, went rarely on ;
The Cap sat aloft, and low was the Crown,
The Rabble got up, and the Nobles went down :
    Lay Elders in Tubs,
    Rul'd *Bishops* in Robes,
    Who mourn'd the sad Fate,
    And dreadful disaster,
    Of their Royal Master,
    By Rebels betray'd.
Then London *be wise and baffle their Power,*
And let them play the old game no more;
Hang, hang up the Sherriffs *those Baboons in pow'r,*
Those popular Thieves, those Rats of the Tower ;
Whose Canting tale the Rable believes in a hurry,
And never sorry, merrily they still go on ;
Fie for shame, we're too tame, since they claim
The combat, Tan ta ra ra ra, tan ta ra ra,
Dub, a dub, a let the Drum beat, the strong Militia
    Guards the Throne.

When Faction possesses the popular voice,
The cause is supply'd still with nonsence and noise,
And *Tony*, their Speaker, the Rable leads on,
He knows if we prosper that he must run ;
Carolina must be his next station of ease,
And *London* be rid of her worst disease ;
                            From

Pleasant and Divertive. 249

> From Plots and from Spies,
> From Treason and Lies,
>   We shall ever be free;
> And the Law shall be able,
> To punish a Rebel,
>   As cunning as he:

Then London, &c.

Rebellion ne'er wanted a Loyal pretence,
These Villains swear all's for the good of their Prince;
Oppose our Elections, to shew what they dare,
And loosing their Charter Arrest the Mayor;
Fool *Je—ks* was the first o' th' Cuckoldly crew,
With *Ell—s* and *Jea—kll* and *Hub—lnd* the *Jew;*
   Fam'd Sparks of the Town,
   For Wealth and Renown,
      Give the Devil his due,
   And such as we fear,
   Had their Soveraign been their,
      Had Arrested him too:
Then London, &c.

The Mouse *Trap. Made to a comical Tune in the Country* Wake.

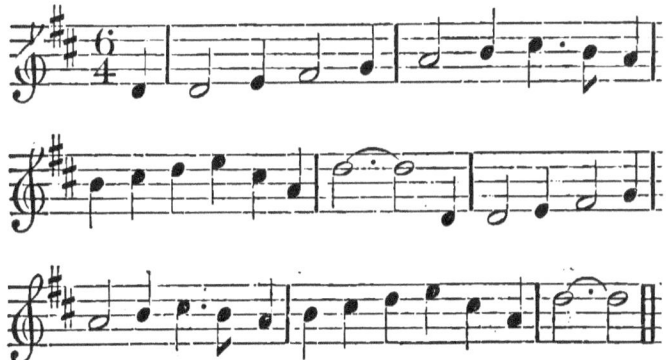

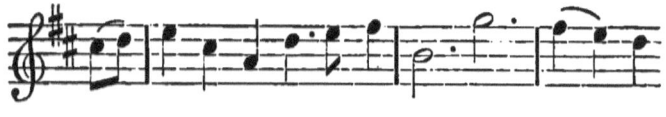
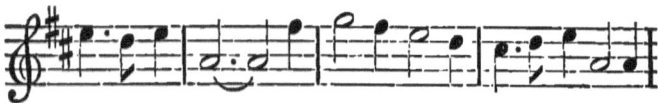
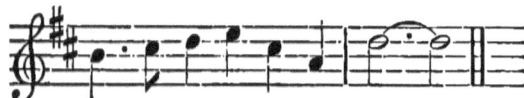

OF all the simple things we do,
    To rub over a Whimsical Life ;
There's no one Folly is so true,
    As that very bad Bargain a Wife ;
We'er just like a Mouse in a Trap,
    Or Vermin caught in a Gin ;
We Sweat and Fret, and try to Escape,
    And Curse the sad Hour we came in.

I Gam'd and Drank, and play'd the Fool,
    And a Thousand Mad frolicks more ;
I Rov'd and Rang'd, despis'd all Rule,
    But I never was Married before ;
This was the worst Plague could ensue,
    I'm Mew'd in a smoky House ;
I us'd to Tope a Bottle or two,
    But now 'tis small Beer with my Spouse.

My darling Freedom crown'd my joys,
    And I never was vext in my way ;
If now I cross her Will her Voice,
    Makes my Lodging too hot for my stay ;
Like a Fox that is hamper'd in vain,
    I fret out my Heart and Soul ;
Walk to and fro the length of my Chain,
    Then forc'd to Creep into my Hole.

A Scotch Song, Sung by Mr. Leveridge.

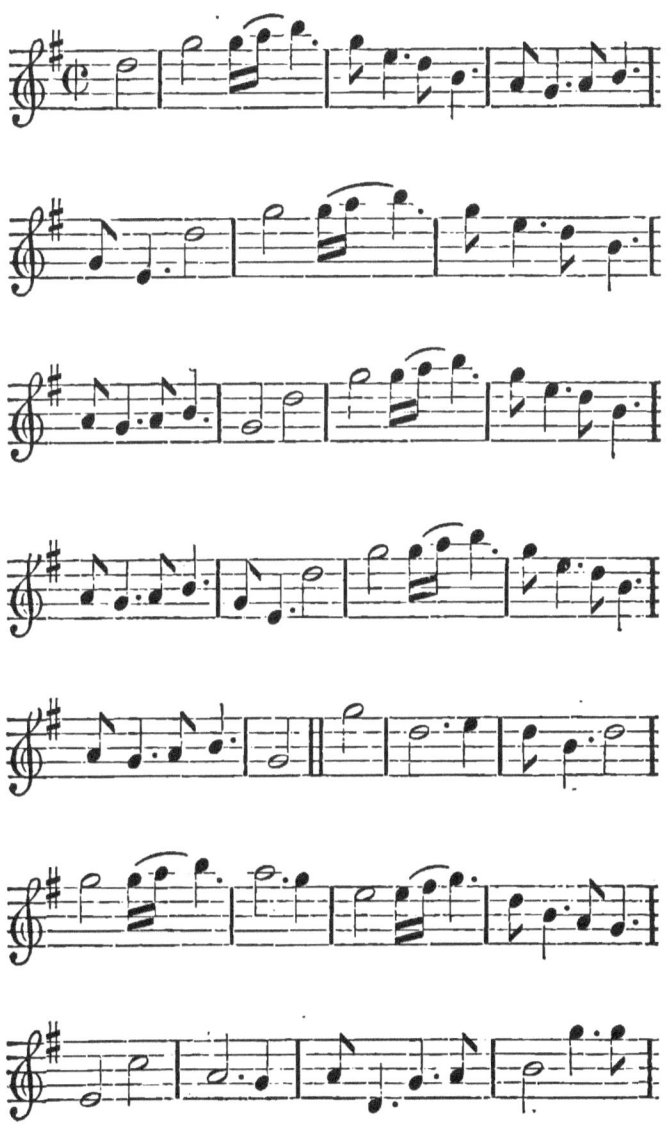

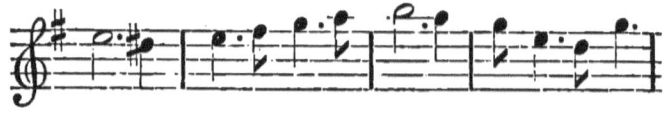

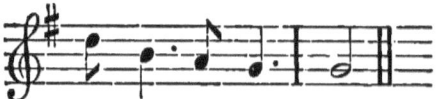

Fareweel my Bonny, bonny witty, pretty *Moggy*,
    And aw the Rosie Lasses, Milking on the Down,
Adiew the flow'ry Meadows, late so dear to *Jockey*,
    The sports and merry glee of *Edinborough* Town:
Since *French* and *Spanish* loons, stand at Bay,
And Valiant Lads of *Britain* hold 'em play,
My Reap-huke, I mun throw quite away;
And Fight too like a Man,
Among 'em for our Royal Queen *Ann*.

Each Carl of *Irish* mettle battles like a Dragon,
    The *German* waddles, and straddles to the Drum;
The *Italian* and the butter bowzy *Hogan Mogan*,
    Gud feth then *Scottish Jockey* may not ligg at home;
For since their ganging to Hunt renown,
And swear they'll quickly ding the *Mounsieur* down;
Ise follow for a pluck at his Crown,
To shew that *Scotland* can,
Excel 'em for our Royal Queen *Ann*.

2d *Movement*.

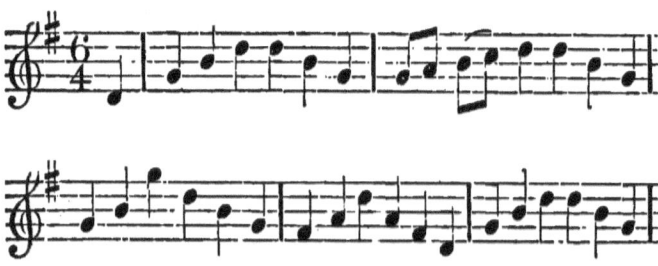

Pleasant and Divertive.

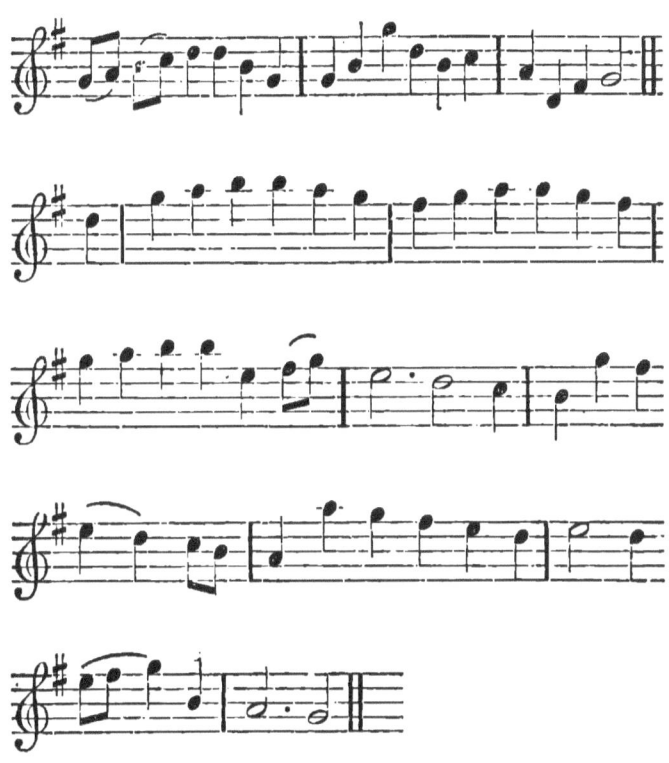

THEN welcome from *Vigo*,
   And Cudgeling *Don Diego*,
With bouger Rascallion,
And Plund'ring the Galleoons;
Each brisk Valiant fellow,
Fought at *Rodondellow*,
And those who did meet,
With the *Newfound-Land* Fleet;
Then for late Successes,
Which *Europe* Confesses,
At Land by our galliant Commanders;
The *Dutch* in strong Beer,
Shou'd be Drunk for one Year,
With their General's Health, in *Flanders*.

The

The Scotch *Cuckold*: *A New* Song *to a Northern Tune.*

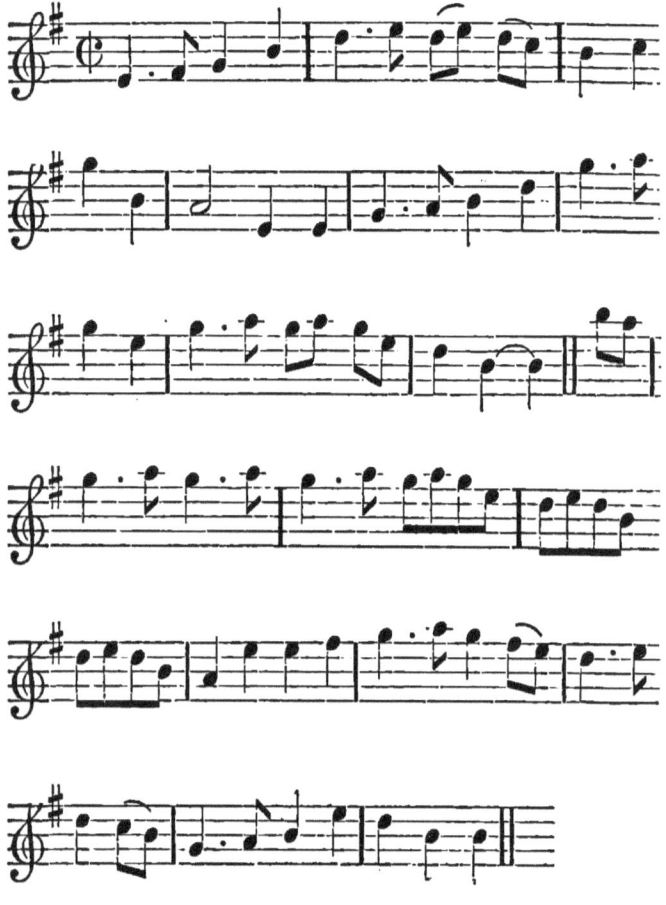

Twanty Years and mear at *Edinborrow Jockey* liv'd Unmarry'd,
At last he would to *London* gang, and there the silly Loon miscarry'd;

Whily

Pleasant and Divertive. 255

Whily *Kate* the Brown, the Plump,
   The Frowzy Browzy,
   Hoyty Toyty,
Covent-Garden Harridan,
Soon made poor *Jockey's* Head to Ake,
And spoyl'd him for a merry Man.

Wae is me he cry'd, that ever I should change my free Condition,
The Quean my Wife will gad abroad, whilst I meet e'ry where Derision ;
   I may sigh and Pine and Whine,
      And run about,
      The Town about,
   Each Hour crying Welladay,
With roaring Boys she diverts her time,
And all the Week makes Holliday.

The First Song *in the Third Act, Sung by* Altisidora *to Don* Quixote.

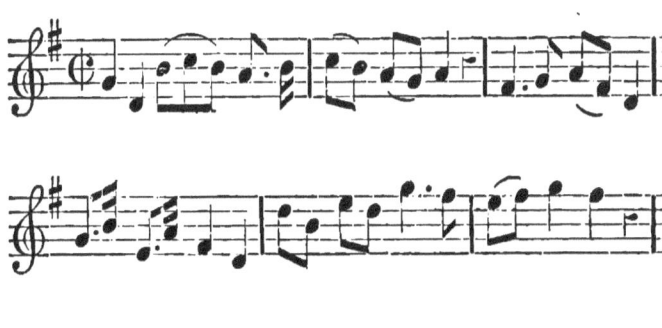

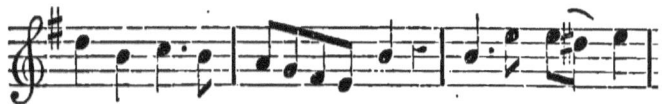

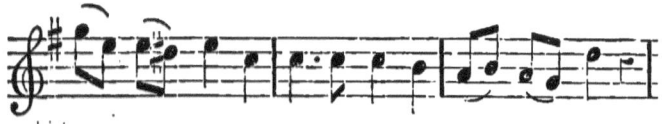

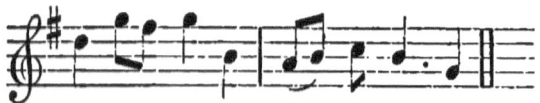

D<i>Amon</i> turn your Eyes to me,
   Wither simply wou'd you, wou'd you lead 'em;
Can you, can you think another she,
   Has more Charms, has more Charms than I to feed 'em:
He that leaves a Rosie, rosie Cheek,
   Lips Vermillion like a Ruby;
Blindly coarser fare to seek,
   Pox, pox upon him for a Booby.

If a smile the Lover's joy,
   Can allure, i'll do't divinely;
Or d'ye love a Sleepy Eye,
   Here is one can Oagle finely,
Charms wou'd make another Man,
   Gaze an age, I'll shew to win ye;
And when I've shewn all I can,
   If you go, the Devil's in ye.

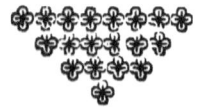

The

The Poet's *Lyrical Address to the* QUEEN. *With Remarks on the present Affairs, and the Happy* UNION; *brought to perfection by Her Majesty, being on Force on* May *the First,* 1717. *To be Said, or Sung to a Humourous Tune call'd Green Sleeves, and is also Set to other Musick, by One of our Best Masters.*

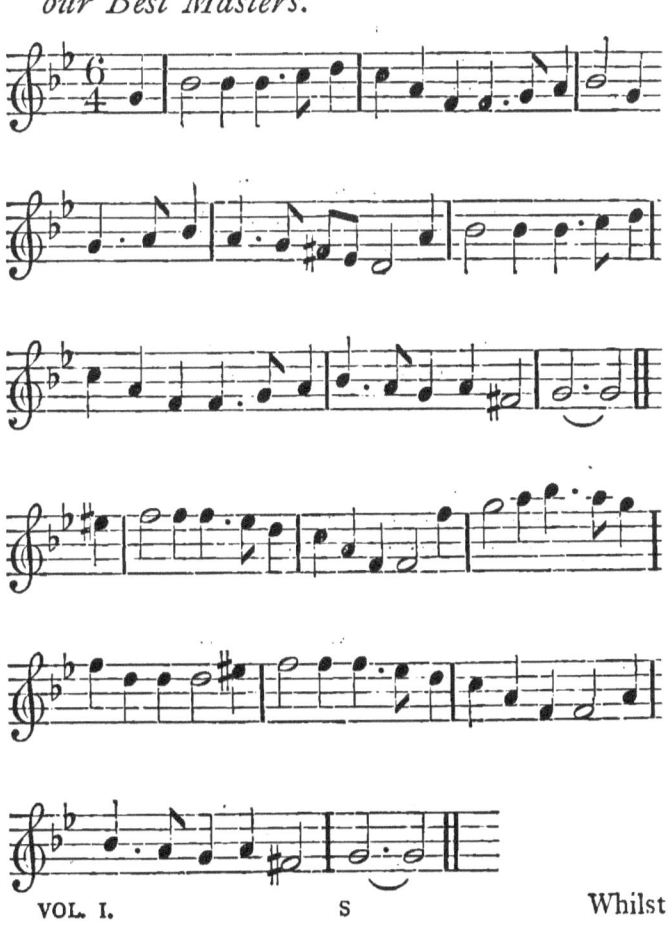

VOL. I.   S   Whilst

Whilst favour'd Bishops new Sleeves put on,
    And Toleration has each *Non Con*;
And Courtiers get places of Gracious Queen *Ann*,
    All bustling in every Station:

A Son of *Phœbus*, whose Muse oft sings
Our Nation's Glory, with other Things,
A stanch Loyal Lover of Queens, and of Kings,
    To make this Address takes Occasion:

Oh long and bright may your Glory shine,
Great Patroness of the Tuneful Nine,
Who all, like the Vision of *Pharoah's* Lean Kine,
    Late mourn'd on a sad Desolation:

But now they flourish in Golden Days,
And Bounty showrs on *Apollo's* Race,
Let me too be happy in Soveraign Grace,
    Now *Britain* is made a blest Nation.

Great *Marlborough*, who for the Field prepares,
And Loads of Lawrel through *Flanders* bears;
Yet are not in weight like his Annual Cares,
    To crown his late Deeds is contriving.

Then, whether Mounsieur can well maintain
What to half *Europe's* against the Grain,
His Grandson young *Philip*, to King it in *Spain*,
    You'll find at our Forces arriving.

For tho' we late into Feuds did grow,
Some for the *High-Church*, and some the *Low*,
We now must unite to drive out such a Foe
    By Aids, to support the Invasion.

Dull *Baden*, Fate, has casheer'd at last,
Had brave *Eugene* on the *Rhine* been plac'd,
One Hour had atton'd for an Age that has past,
    And given for new Trophies Occasion.
                                            The

Pleasant and Divertive.

The Crown's Succession is past all fear,
Great *Britain*'s Kingdoms have fix'd an Heir,
And Princess *Sophia* runs glib in Church-Prayer,
    Defying all Chances hereafter :

France must forgive the *Welsh* Prince's Score,
For him to bring new Pretensions o'er;
Now politick *Scotland* has shut her Back-door,
    I think is a thing worthy Laughter.

Since Happy *Union*, all Hearts commands
The Plads, and Bonnets, and Cloak, and Bands,
With long pleated Cassock must join and shake Hands,
    Most Friendly in every Station.

Oh *Scotland*, *Scotland*, old Faults we wave,
Thank Royal *Ann* for the Prize She gave,
Prove Loyal, and truly we know you are brave,
    Then *Britain* will be a blest Nation.

Rejoice then, *Caledonian* Sons,
Sound loud your Trumpets, and fire your Guns,
Whilst Dutyful Thanks the swift Season out-runs,
    In Volumes of Loyal Addresses.

Let *Edinborough* with Praise abound,
The Kirk dole Sanctified Hymns around,
Whilst *Pauls* with its Organ in ravishing Sound,
    Cælestial Devotion expresses.

Tell both the *Poles* how our Glorious *Ann*,
A Labour several Kings began,
Yet fail'd to effect, has concluded, and done,
    T' Eternize her wonderful Story.

With *Albany* a blest *Union* made,
Increas'd our Power, improv'd their Trade,
And taken from Mounsieur the Means to invade,
    Eclipsing his dazling Vainglory.

Some say that *Belgia* mislikes our Dish,
The *Union* relishes not their Wish,
Who lately by provident catching our Fish,
   Defray'd all Dragooning Expences.

For fear vile Int'rest the League should spoil,
Since Malice Butter can turn to Oil,
And Honour don't grow in a plashy, cold Soil,
   Let Prudence take care of Defences.

Th' *Hibernian* Wits, who no Statesmen are,
Depend upon the new Viceroy's Care,
And now, mighty Queen, as a finishing Prayer,
   Long Live in your Royal Vocations;

And when you e'er a State Game begin,
May then your Trumps come all pouring in,
For never had Gamester a harder to win,
   Then who has *United* these Nations.

A Song.

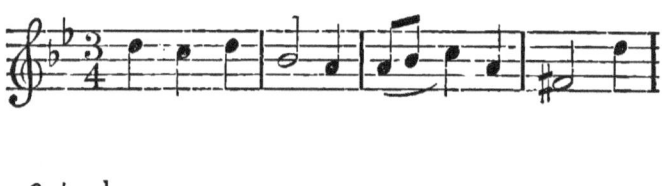

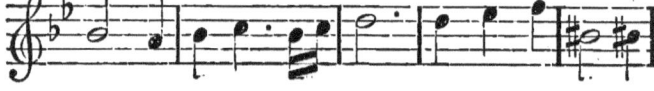

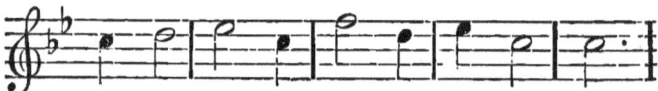

Pleasant and Divertive. 261

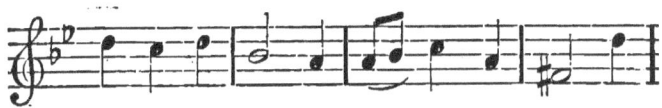

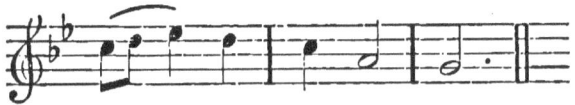

Bright was the Morning, cool was the Air,
   Serene was all the Sky;
When on the Waves I left my dear,
   The Center of my joy:
Heaven and Nature smiling were,
   And nothing sad but I.

Each Rosie Field did Odours spread,
   All Fragrant was the shore;
Each River God rose from his Bed,
   And sigh'd and own'd her power:
Curling their Waves they deck'd their heads,
   As proud of what they bore.

So when the fair *Egyptian* Queen,
   Her Heroe went to see;
Cidnus swell'd o'er his Banks in pride,
   As much in Love as he:
Cidnus swell'd, &c.

Glide on ye waters, bear these lines,
   And tell her how distress'd;
Bear all my sighs ye gentle winds,
   And waft 'em to her Breast:
Tell her if e'er she prove unkind,
   I never shall have rest.

The

The DISAPPOINTMENT.

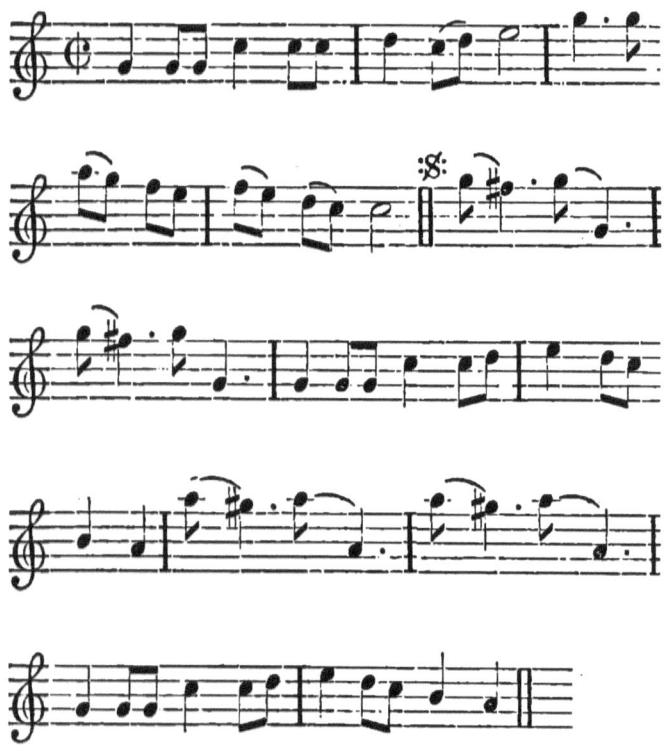

THE Clock had struck, faith I cannot tell what,
But Morning was come as Grey as a Cat;
Cocks and Hens from their Roosts did fly,
Grunting Hogs too had left their stye;
    When in a Vale,
    Carrying a Pail,
Sissly her new Lover met, Dapper *Harry;*
    First they Kiss'd,
    Then shook Fist,
Then talk'd as Fools do that just were to Marry.
                                  Zooks

Pleasant and Divertive.

Zooks cry'd *Hall*, I can't but think,
Now we are come to Wedlock brink ;
How pure a stock 'twill be how fine,
When you put your good mark to mine ;
    Siss at that,
    Glowing hot,
Buss'd him as if she'd have burnt him to Tinder ;
    Thus they Woo,
    But see how,
Damn'd Fate contriv'd now the Bargain to hinder.

Sissly had got a Cold I suppose,
And 'twixt her Fingers was blowing her Nose ;
Harry, that Linnen too wanted I doubt,
Lent her his Glove, to serve for a Clout ;
    Scraping low,
    Manners to show,
And tell her how much he was her adorer :
    Pray mark the Joke,
    Leather thong broke,
And Breeches fell down to his Ancles before her.

Sissly who saw him thus distrest,
Pulls of her Garter of woolen List ;
And with a sly and leering look,
Gave it to mend up what was broke ;
    Fumbling he,
    Could not see,
What he discover'd, tho' e'er he had ty'd all :
    For just before,
    Shirt was tore,
And as the Devil would have't she had spy'd all.

She gave him then so cold a Look,
Discontent it plainly spoke ;
And running from him near a Mile,
He overtook her at a stile ;
    Too much hast,
    Milk down cast,
And topsy turvy she fell on her Pole with't :
                            He

He seeing that,
Runs with's Hat,
But could not Cover her C—— for his soul with't.

Have you not seen at Noon of Day,
The Sun his glorious Face display;
So *Sissly* shone with Beauty's Rays,
Reflecting from her Postern grace;
    Till at last
    Strugling past,
Wide sprawling Legs were again set in order:
    But poor *Hall*,
    Since her fall,
Stood just like one was found guilty of Murder.

The God of Love, or else old Nick,
Sure had design'd this Devilish trick,
To make the Bridegroom and the Bride;
With themselves dissatisfy'd;
    She grown coy,
    Call'd him Boy,
He getting from her cry'd Zoons you'r a rouzer:
    Foh, she cry'd,
    By things spy'd,
She had as live a meer Baby should espouse her.

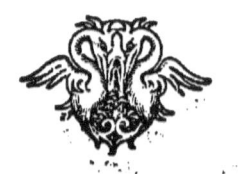

Pleasant and Divertive. 265

THE
SONGS
AND
DIALOGUES

In the First and Second Part of Massaniello. *The First* SONG *Set by Mr.* Daniel Purcell.

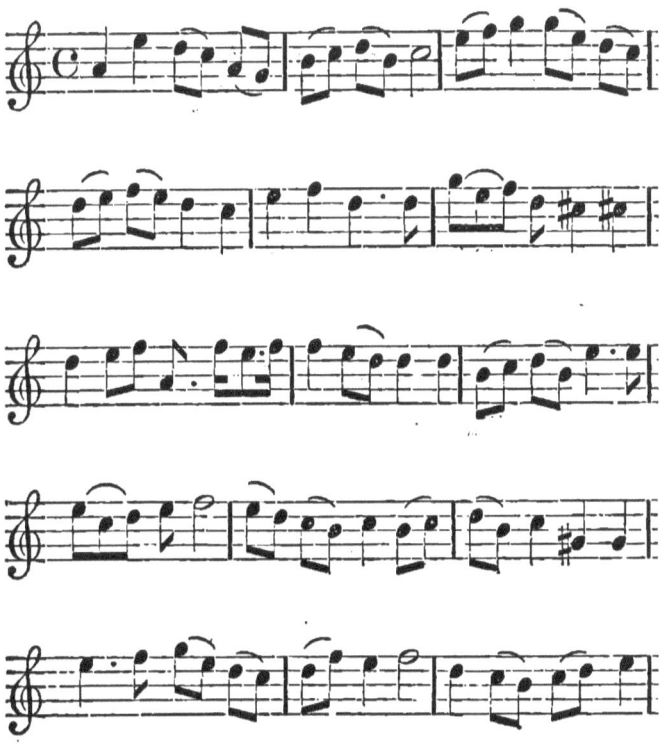

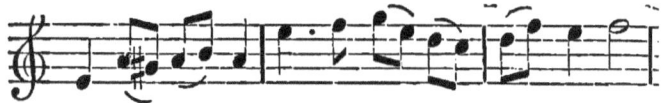

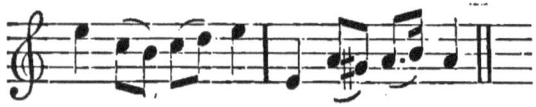

YOung *Philander* woo'd me long,
  I was peevish and forbid him;
Nor would hear his loving Song,
  And yet now I wish, I wish I had him:
For each Morn I view my Glass,
  I perceive the Whim is going;
For when Wrinkles streak the Face,
  We may bid farewel to Wooing.
For when Wrinkles streak the Face,
  We may bid farewel to Wooing.

Use your time ye Virgins fair,
  Choose before your days are Evil;
Fifteen is a Season rare,
  Five and Forty is the Devil:
Just when Ripe consent to do't,
  Hug no more the lonely Pillow;
Women like some other Fruit,
  Loose their relish when too Mellow.

The

The Fisherman's SONG, *In the First Part, of* Massaniello. *Set by Mr*. Leveridge.

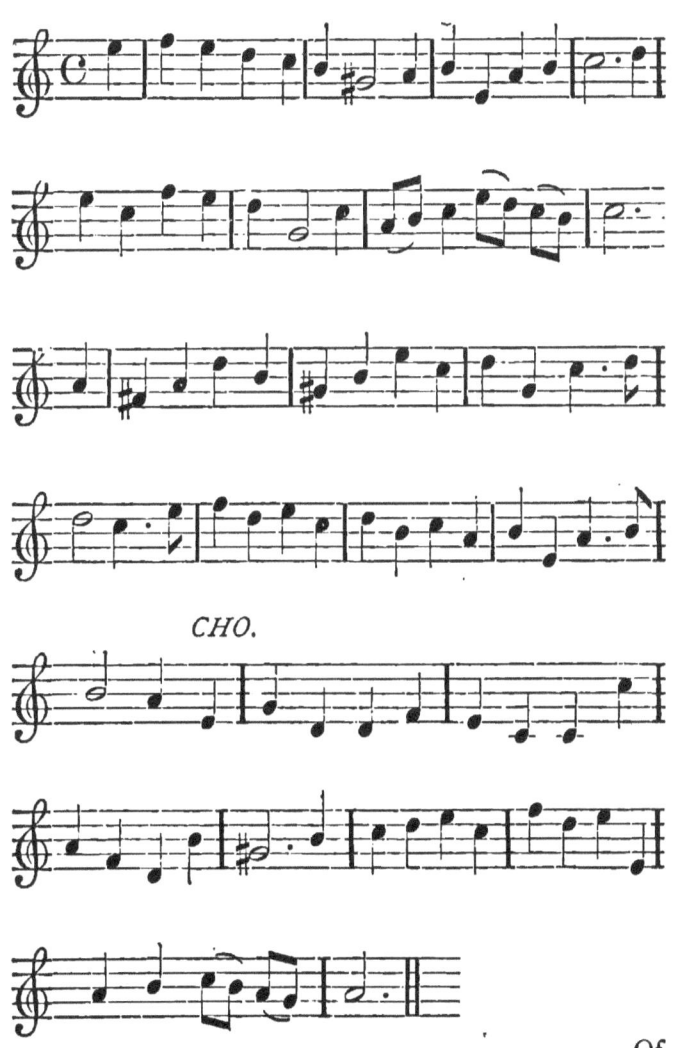

OF all the World's Enjoyments,
   That ever valu'd were;
There's none of our Employments,
   With Fishing can Compare:
      Some Preach, some Write,
      Some Swear, some Fight,
All Golden Lucre courting,
   But Fishing still bears off the Bell;
For Profit or for Sporting.
   Then who a Jolly Fisherman, a Fisherman will be?
      His Throat must wet,
      Just like his Net,
   To keep out Cold at Sea.

The Country Squire loves Running,
   A Pack of well-mouth'd Hounds;
Another fancies Gunning
   For wild Ducks in his Grounds:
      This Hunts, that Fowls,
      This Hawks, *Dick* Bowls,
No greater Pleasure wishing,
   But *Tom* that tells what Sport excells,
Gives all the Praise to Fishing,
   Then who, &c.

A good *Westphalia Gammon*,
   Is counted dainty Fare;
But what is't to a *Salmon*,
   Just taken from the Ware:
      Wheat Ears and *Quailes*,
      Cocks, *Snipes*, and *Rayles*;
Are priz'd while Season's lasting,
   But all must stoop to Crawfish Soop,
Or I've no skill in tasting.
   Then who, &c.

Keen Hunters always take too
   Their prey with too much pains;
Nay often break a Neck too,
   A Pennance for no Brains:

They

Pleasant and Divertive.

    They Run, they Leap,
    Now high, now deep,
Whilst he that Fishing chooses ;
  With ease may do't, nay more to boot,
  May entertain the Muses.
    Then who, &c.
And tho' some envious wranglers,
  To jeer us will make bold ;
And Laugh at Patient Anglers,
  Who stand so long i' th' Cold :
    They wait on Miss,
    We wait on this,
And think it easie Labour ;
  And if you'd know, Fish profits too,
  Consult our *Holland* Neighbour.
    Then who, &c.

A New Song, *Made in honour of his Grace the Duke of* Marlborough, *and the General Officers, upon the Glorious success of this last* Campaign. *Set by Mr.* J. Weldon.

BEat the Drum, Beat, beat the Drum,
    Let Martial Trumpets sound ;
The jolly Bowl prepare,
  With fragrant Roses Crown'd :
The Grand *Leviathan* of *France* is Tumbling down,
Tumbling down, is tumbling, tumbling down ;
Lawrel wreaths for Glorious pains,
Once more great *Marlborough*, great *Marlborough* Gains :
Thus whilst Conquer'd, whilst conquer'd *Flanders* falls,
Proud *Orleans*, from *Turin's* Walls,
Is like a Vapour gone.
The *Mounsieur's* mawl'd by Sea and Land,
Then take six Bumpers in a Hand ;
To each brave *Brittish* Son,
They, they the Work have done,
They, they the Work have done.

A

A DIALOGUE *between a Town Sharper and his Hostess, Sung by Mr.* Leveridge *and Mr.* Pate ; *in the first Part. Set by Mr.* Daniel Purcell.

Sharp.

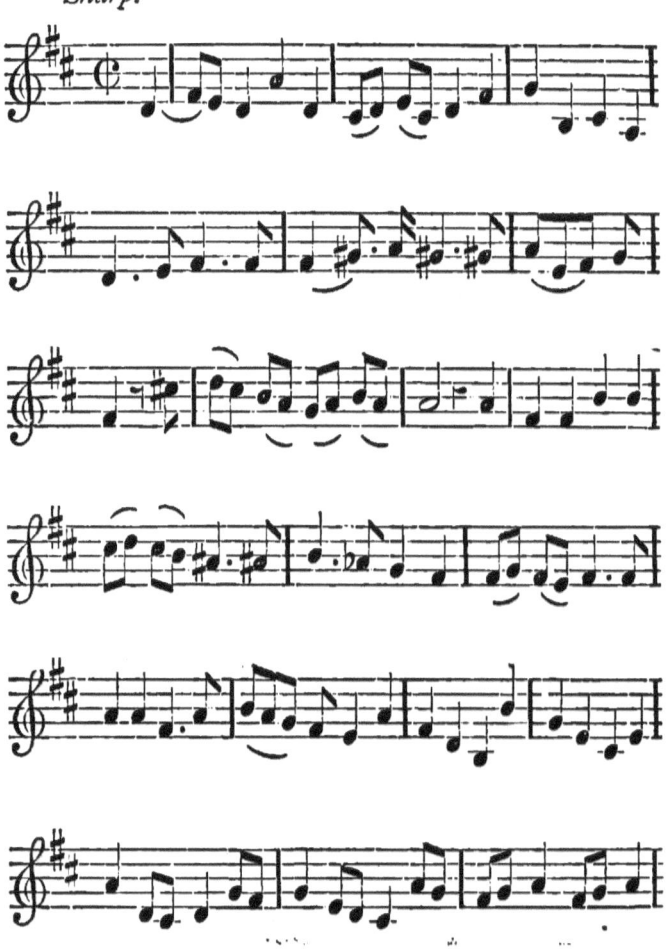

Pleasant and Divertive.

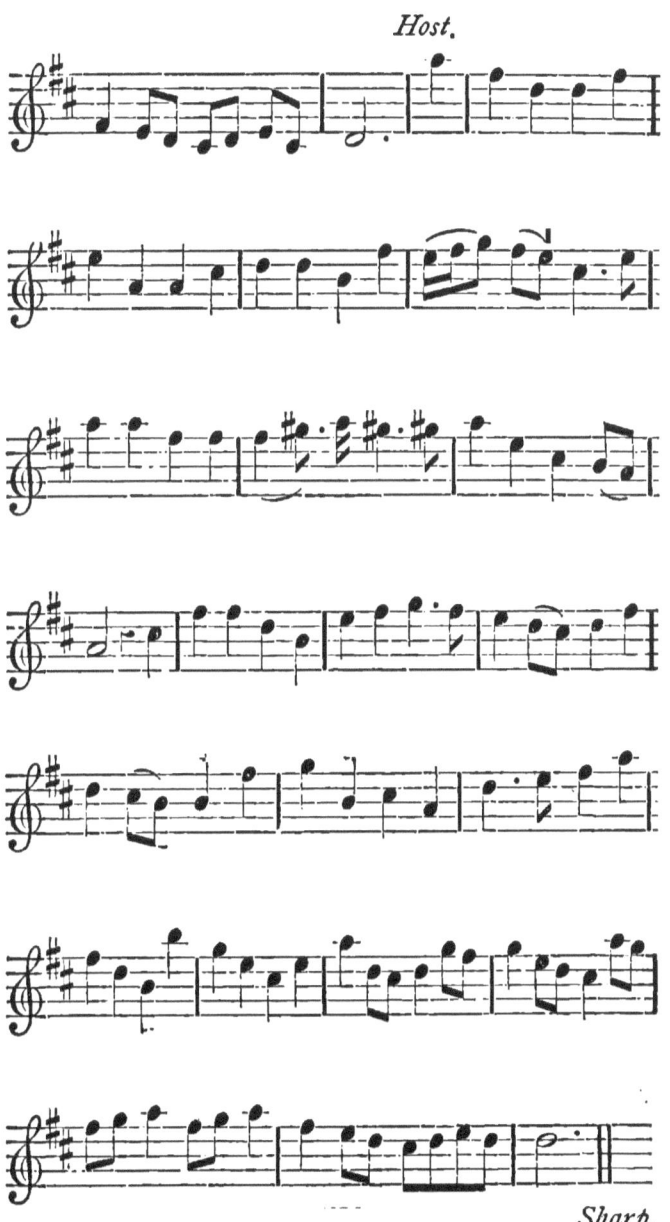

Sharp.

Sharp. WHilst wretched Fools sneak up and down,
    Play hide and seek about the Town;
Deprest by Debts, and Fortune's Frown,
    By Duns to keep in awe:
When ever my occasions call,
And 'mongst my Creditors I fall;
I've one fine Song that Pays 'em all,
    Fa, la, &c.

Host. Good Morrow Sir, I'm glad to see,
Your Humour is so brisk and free;
I hope the better 'tis for me,
    If you your Purse will draw:
Y'have been two Years at Bed and Board,
And I, Lord help me, took your Word;
But now must have what here is scor'd,
    For all your *Fa, la, la, la,* &c.

Sharp. My Purse sweet Hostess is but lank,
But I have something else in Bank;
And you at Home I'll kindly thank,
    With charming sweet *Sol fa:*
We'll sit and Chaunt from Morn to Noon,
No Nightingale in *May* or *June;*
Did ever Sing so fine a Tune,
    As *Fa, la, la, la, la, la,* &c.

Host. You take me for an Ideot sure,
Will this fine Tune my Debt secure;
Or Pay my Baker and my Brewer,
    Or keep me from the Law:
To buy your Shirts there's Money lent,
Besides in Meat and Drink more spent;
And can you think I pay my Rent,
    With *Fa, la, la, la, la,* &c.

Sharp. I'll teach thee such a pretty Song,
Shall please the Rich, Poor, Old, and Young;
Get thee a Husband Stout and Strong,
    Some Country Rich Jack-Daw:
        Nay

Pleasant and Divertive.

    Nay, more I'll bring to quit my Scores,
    A crew of Toping Sons of Whores,
    Shall Drink all Night and charm the Hours,
        With *Fa, la, la, la, la, la,* &c.

Host. Ye cunning Rogue this weedling talk,
    You fancy will rub out my Chalk;
    But I your sly design will baulk,
        When you to Jayl I draw:
    Your boasted Song's a foolish thing,
    For do but you the Money bring;
    You'll find I can already Sing,
        Fa la, la, la, la, la, &c.

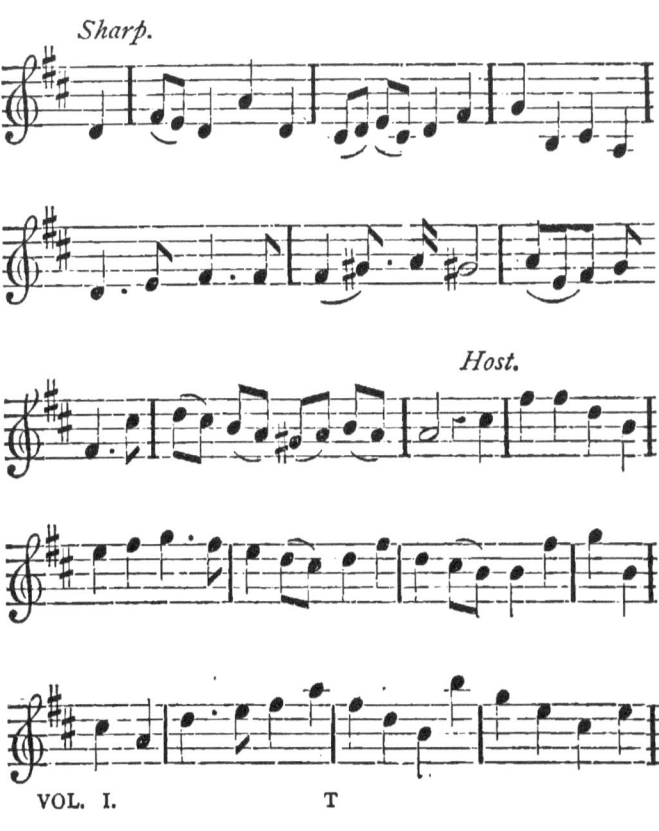

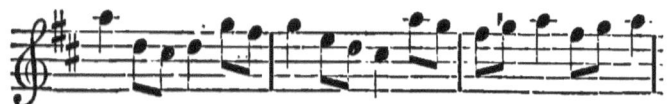

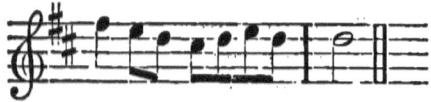

Sharp. Well since Dame Fortune is my Foe,
   And that I must to Prison go;
Let's have a Neat frisk or so,
   And then rub on the Law:
Host. Well since you're on the merry Pin,
   And make so slight the Counter-Gin;
I'll do't, and let the Tune begin,
   With *Fa, la,* &c.

They DANCE.

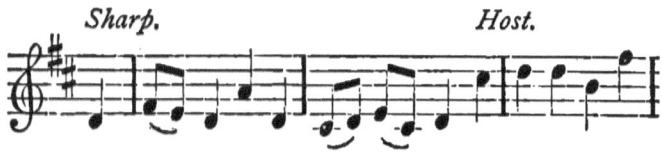

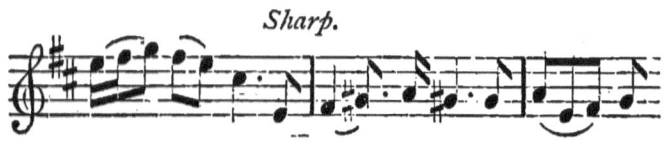

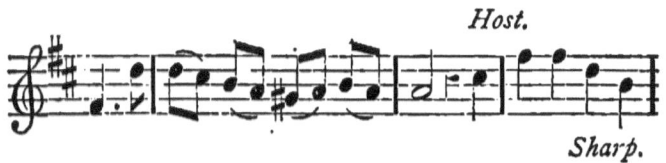

Pleasant and Divertive.

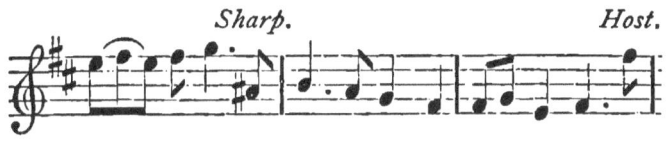

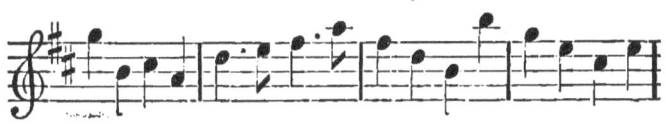

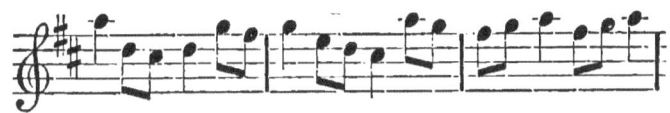

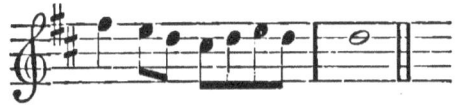

Sharp. Has not my Dance ill Humour Charm'd,
Host. I must confess my Blood is warm'd :
Sharp. And Heart I hope by Love alarm'd,
    To Laugh *Ha, ha, ha, ha :*
Host. You think you've catch'd me now I smile,
Sharp. No that i'll do at Night dear Child ;
Host. Well I'll the Bayliffs stop a while,
    To try your *Fa, la, la,* &c.

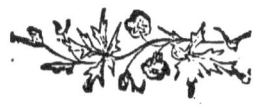

The Winchester *Wedding ; or* Ralph *of* Redding, *and black* Bess *of the* Green.

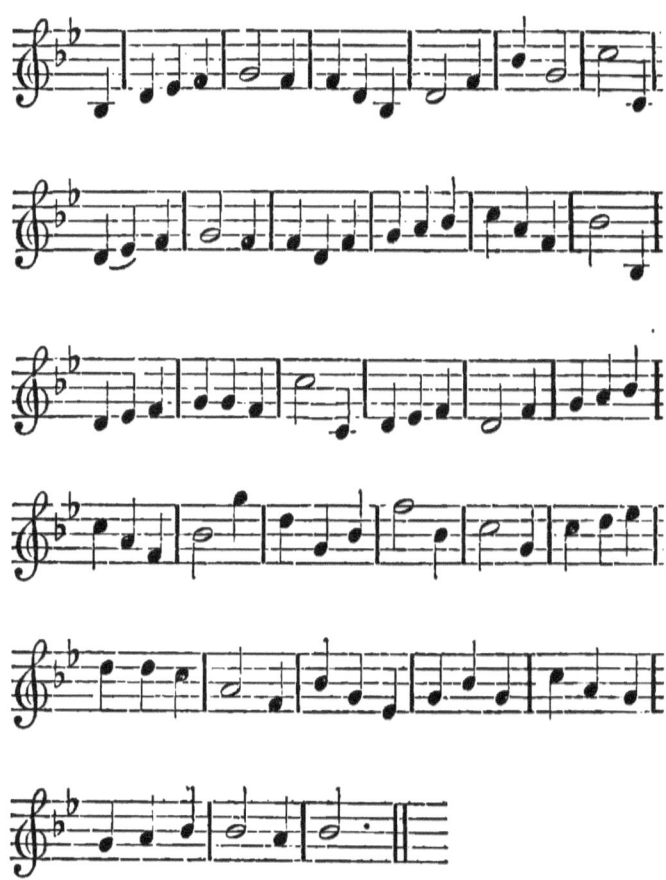

A T *Winchester* was a Wedding,
　　The like was never seen,
Twixt lusty *Ralph* of *Redding*,
　　And bonny black *Bess* of the *Green :*

The

Pleasant and Divertive.

The Fidllers were Crouding before,
　Each Lass was as fine as a Queen;
There was a Hundred and more,
　For all the Country came in:
Brisk *Robin* led *Rose* so fair,
　She look'd like a Lilly o'th' Vale;
And Ruddy Fac'd *Harry* led *Mary*,
　And *Roger* led bouncing *Nell*.

With *Tommy* came smiling *Katy*,
　He help'd her over the Stile;
And swore there was none so pretty,
　In forty, and forty long Mile:
Kit gave a Green-Gown to *Betty*,
　And lent her his Hand to rise;
But *Jenny* was jeer'd by *Watty*,
　For looking blue under the Eyes:
Thus merrily Chatting all,
　They pass'd to the *Bride-house* along;
With *Johnny* and pretty fac'd *Nanny*,
　The fairest of all the throng.

The Bride came out to meet 'em,
　Afraid the Dinner was spoil'd;
And usher'd 'em in to treat 'em,
　With *Bak'd*, and *Roasted*, and *Boil'd*:
The Lads were so frolick and jolly,
　For each had his Love by his side;
But *Willy* was Melancholy,
　For he had a Mind to the Bride:
Then *Philip* begins her Health,
　And turns a Beer Glass on his Thumb;
But *Jenkin* was reckon'd for Drinking,
　The best in *Christendom*.

And now they had Din'd, advancing
　Into the midst of the *Hall*;
The Fidlers struck up for Dancing,
　And *Jeremy* led up the *Brawl*:
　　　　　　　　　　　　　But

But *Margery* kept a quarter,
   A Lass that was proud of her Pelf,
Cause *Arthur* had stolen her Garter,
   And swore he would tie it himself:
She struggl'd, and blush'd, and frown'd,
   And ready with Anger to cry;
'Cause *Arthur* with tying her Garter,
   Had slip'd his Hand too high.

And now for throwing the Stocking,
   The Bride away was led;
The Bridegroom got Drunk and was knocking,
   For Candles to light 'em to Bed:
But *Robin* that found him Silly,
   Most friendly took him aside;
The while that his *Wife* with *Willy*,
   Was playing at *Hoopers-hide*:
And now the warm *Game* begins,
   The *Critical Minute* was come;
And chatting, and Billing, and Kissing,
   Went merrily round the Room.

Pert *Stephen* was kind to *Betty*,
   And blith as a Bird in the Spring;
And *Tommy* was so to *Katy*,
   And Wedded her with a *Rush Ring*:
Sukey that Danc'd with the *Cushion*,
   An Hour from the Room had been gone;
And *Barnaby* knew by her Blushing,
   That some other Dance had been done:
And thus of Fifty fair Maids,
   That came to the Wedding with Men;
Scarce Five of the Fifty was left ye,
   That so did return again.

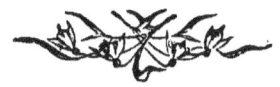

A Song, *Sung by a* Fop *newly come from* France.

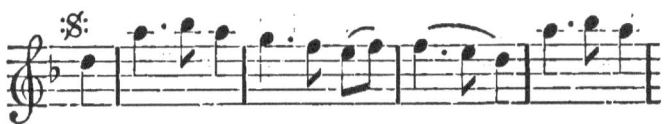
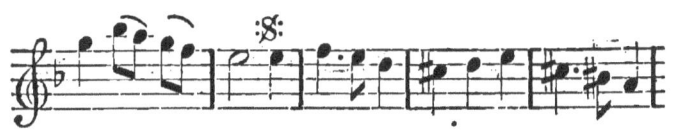
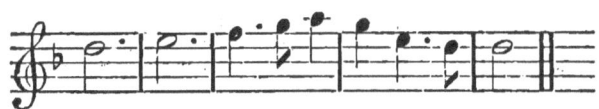

AH! *Phillis* why are you less *tender*,
    To my despairing *Amore!*
Your Heart you have promis'd to *tender*,
    Do not deny the *Retour:*
My Passion I cannot *defender*,
    No, no Torments encrease *tous les Jour.*

To forget your kind Slave is *cruelle*,
    Can you expect my *Devoir;*
Since *Phillis* is grown *infidelle*,
    And wounds me at every *Revoir!*
Those Eyes which were once *agreeable*,
    Now, now are Fountains of black *Des espoire.*

Adieu to my false *Esperance*,
    Adieu *les Plaisirs des beaux Jours;*
My *Phillis* appears at *distance*,
    And slights my unfeigned *Efforts:*
To return to her Vows *impossible*,
    No, no adieu to the Cheats of *Amours.*

A SONG.

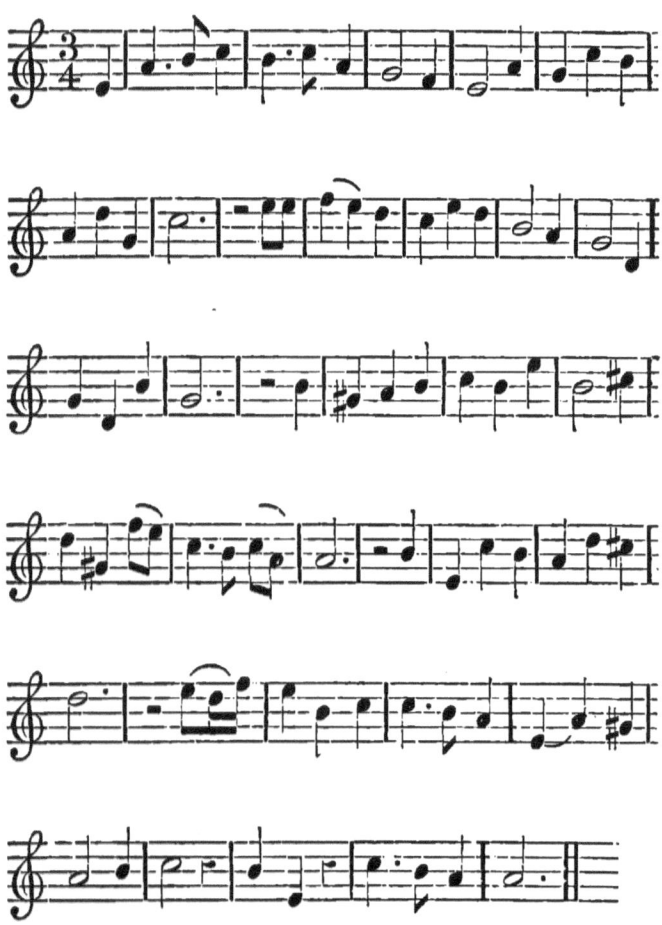

Great *Jove* once made Love like a Bull, (a Bull)
With *Leda* a Swan was in Vogue;
And to persevere in that Rule, (that Rule)
He now does Descend like a Dog:

For

Pleasant and Divertive.

For when I to *Celia* would speak,
   And on her Breast sigh what I mean;
My Heart-Strings are ready to break,
   For their I find Mounsieur *Le Chien*, (*Le Chien*,)
Le Chien, Mounsieur, Mounsieur *Le Chien*).

For knowledge of Modish Intrigues,
   Or managing well an Amour;
I defie any one with two Legs,
   But here I am Rivall'd by four:
Distracted all Night with my Wrongs,
   I cry, Cruel Gods! what d'ye mean!
That what to my Merit belongs,
   You bestow upon Mounsieur *Le Chien*.

For Feature, or Niceness in Dress,
   Compare with him surely I can;
Nor vainly my self should express,
   To say, I am much more a Man;
To th' Government firm too as he,
   The former I cunningly mean;
And if he Religious can be,
   I've as much sure as Mounsieur *Le Chien*.

But what need I publish my Parts,
   Or Idly my Passion relate;
Since Fancy that Captivates Hearts,
   Resolves not to alter my Fate:
I may Sing, Caper, Ogle, and Speak,
   And make a long Court, *Ausi bien*,
And yet with one Passionate Lick,
   I'm out-Rivall'd by Mounsieur *Le Chien*.

A

282   SONGS *Compleat*,

A SONG.

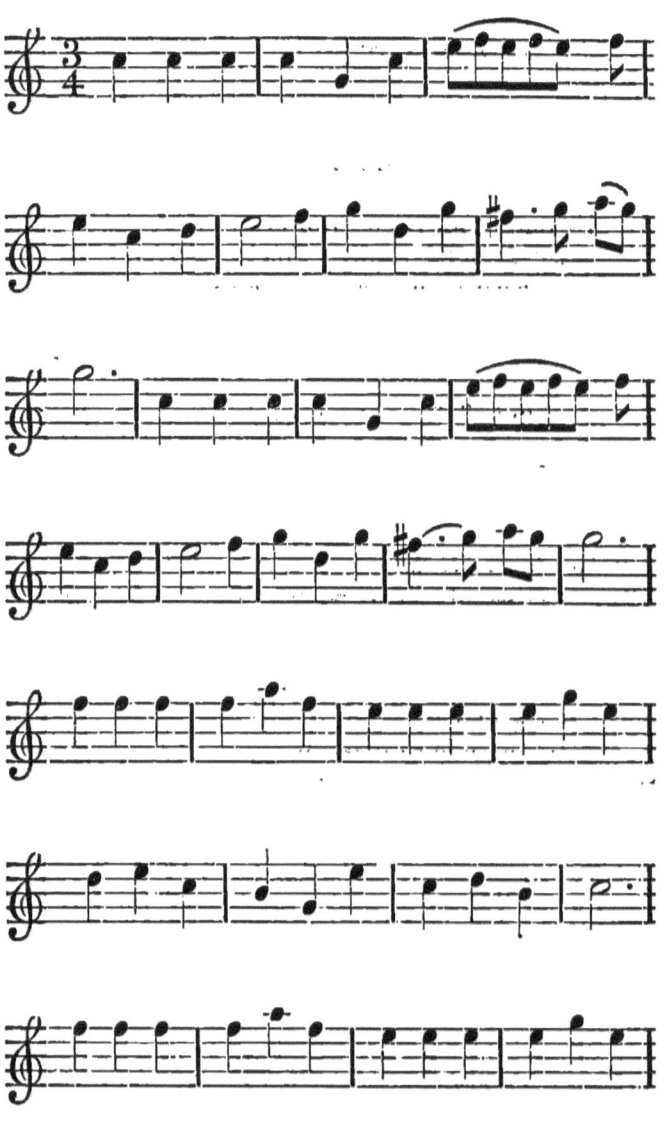

Pleasant and Divertive.

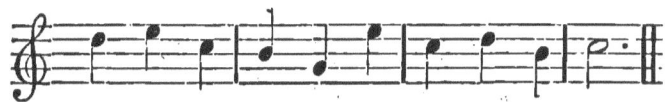

D EAR Pinckaninny, if half a Guinny,
    To Love will win ye,
    I lay it here down;
We must be Thrifty,
'Twill serve to shift ye,
And I know Fifty,
    Will do't for a Crown.

Dunns come so boldly,
King's Money so slowly,
That by all things Holy,
    'Tis all I can say;
Yet I'm so rapt in,
The Snare that I'm trapt in,
As I'm a true Captain,
    Give more than my Pay.

Good Captain Thunder,
Go mind your Plunder,
Ods———ns I wonder,
    You dare be so bold;
Thus to be making,
A Treaty so sneaking,
Or Dream too of taking,
    My Fort with small Gold.

Other Town Misses,
May gape at Ten Pieces,
But who me possesses,
    Full Twenty shall Pay;
To all poor Rogues in Buff,
Thus, thus I strut and huff,
So Captain kick and cuff,
    March on your way.

A

A two Part Song: *Being part of an* Ode, *Made to Entertain the Nobility and Gentry of the County of* York. *Set by Mr.* Henry Purcell.

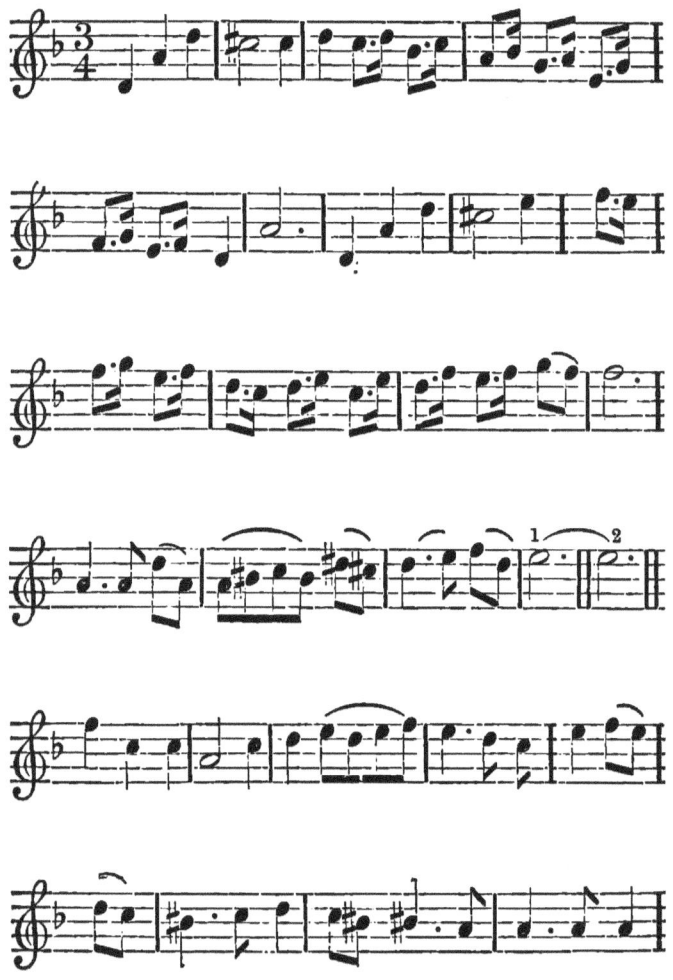

Pleasant and Divertive. 285

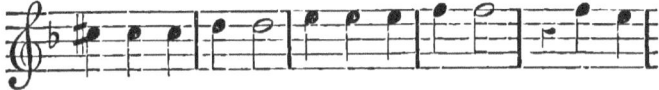

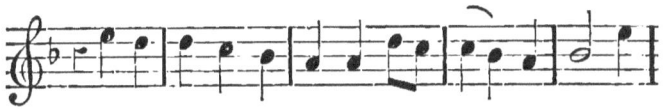

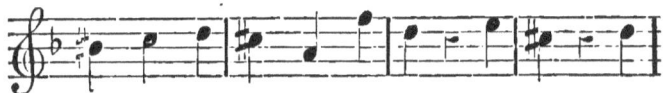

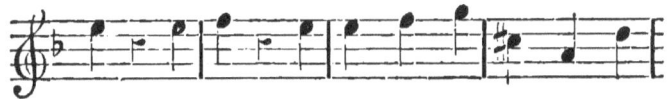

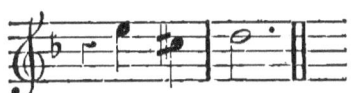

AND in each track of Glory, since,
And in each track of Glory, since;
For their lov'd Country, or their Prince.
Princes that hate, that hate *Rome's* Tyranny,
And joyn the Nations right, with their own Royalty:
None were more ready, none were more ready,
None, none, none, none, none were more ready
    In Distress to Save;
No none were more Loyal, none, ‖ : : ‖ : : ‖ : : ‖ : : ‖ : : ‖ :
    None were more Loyal, none, none more Brave.

A

A Prophetick SONNET, *On the Ensuing Campaign : Made to encourage the Officers and Soldiers. To a pretty Trumpet-Tune.*

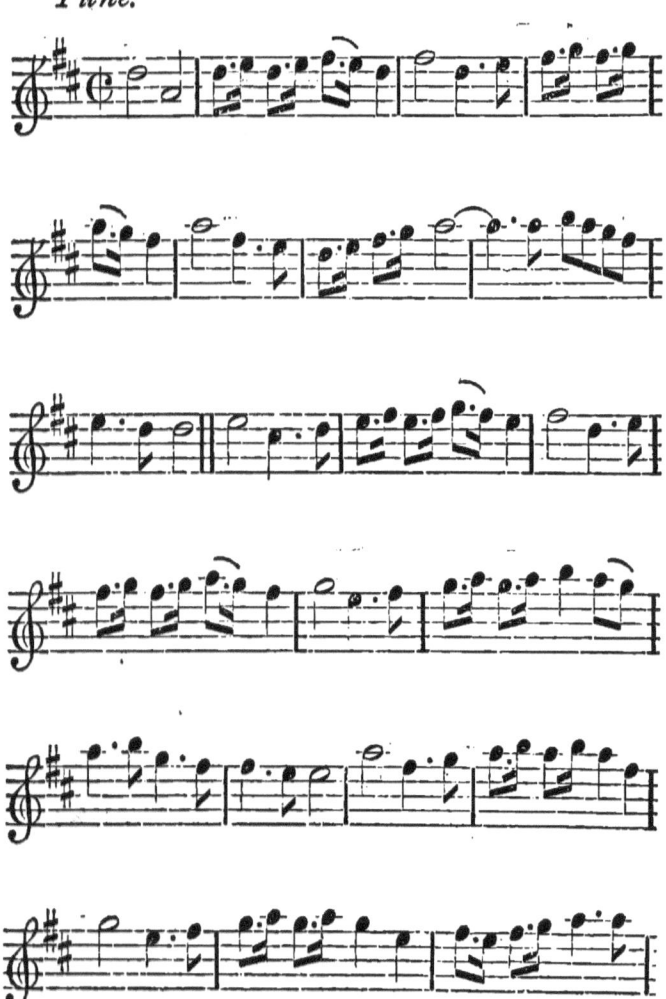

Pleasant and Divertive. 287

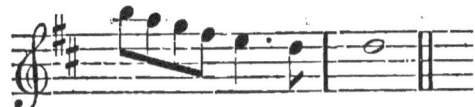

NOW, now Winter is retreating,
Hark, hark the Martial Drum is beating;
Fate smiles upon the Glorious Year,
Predestin'd for Proud *France* to fear :
Flanders shall shake with *Marlborough's* Thunders,
Spain too where *Staremberg* did Wonders,
Spight of some late unlucky blunders ;
And the taking of *Girrone* March,
March, begin the Seige of *Arras*,
Then, then lead on your way to *Paris ;*
Mounsieur you'll confound,
And *Philip* must in course go down.

Cease, cease *Brittish* Men your jangling,
Great harms befall us by your wrangling ;
Rank feuds encourage still the Foe,
You else might quickly overthrow :
Joyn all, let Royal *Anna* charm ye,
Use means to pay the Fleet and Army ;
No pow'r of bragging *France* will harm ye,
   Tho' *Te Deums* never cease ;
Tho' tho' with Boyish crowds they threaten,
All know their *Marshalls* can be beaten ;
   Conquests will increase,
And soon we shall command a Peace.

Second Movement.

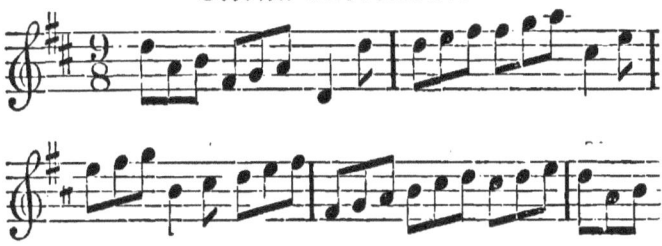

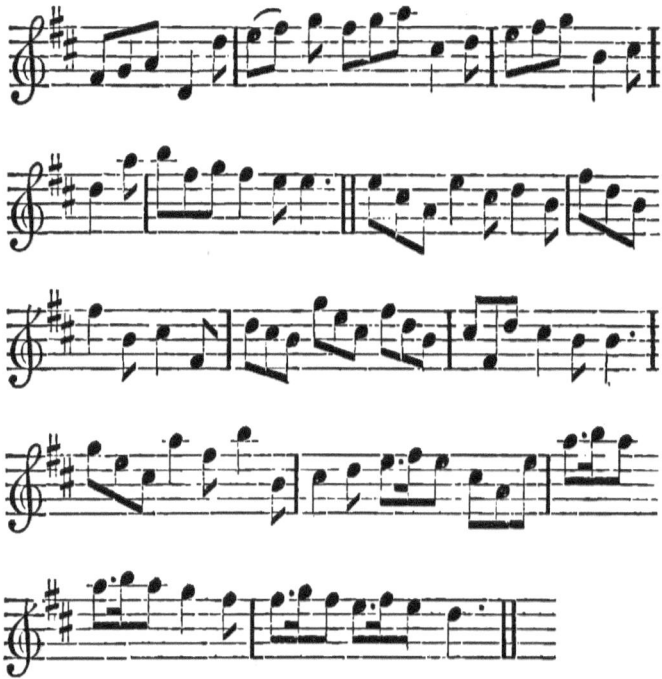

But if we squable and brawl,
And daily to difference fall;
  If Jarr in our Votes,
  As Ranters, and Canters,
And Thy *Church*, and my *Church*,
  We're ready for Cutting of Throats;
Then as plainly will be seen,
    Our losses begins with shame,
And teaze the Gracious *Queen:*
Ah, how will *France* delight in't,
Who'll go to *Spain*, to Fight in't,
    Lifters and Shifters,
Press Masters may follow and seize in vain,
    No good luck follows Waring,
    Where the Natives are Jarring;   (again.
Then happily let us agree, and have at the *Mounsieur*
                                                    A

Pleasant and Divertive. 289

A Song.

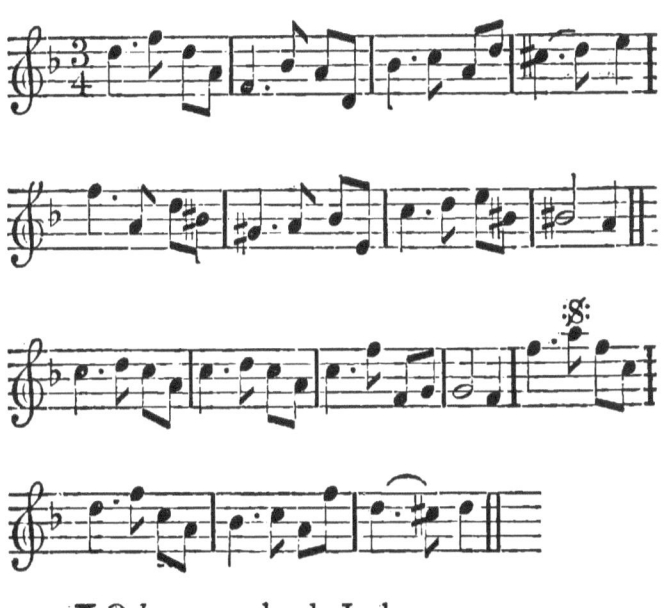

Jockey was a dawdy Lad,
  And *Jemmy* swarth and Tawney;
They my Heart no Captive made,
  For that was Prize to *Sawney:*
Jockey Woes, and Sighs and Sues,
  And *Jemmy* offers Money;
Weel I see they both love me,
  But I love only *Sawney.*

Jockey high his Voice can raise,
  And *Jemmy* tunes the Viol;
But when *Sawney* Pipes sweet Lays,
  My heart kens no denial:
One he Sings, and to'ther Strings,
  Tho' sweet, yet only teaze me;
Sawney's Flute, can only do't,
  And Pipe a Tune to please me.

A Catch for Three Voices, Set by *Mr.* Hen. Purcell. *Translated from the* Latin *of* Buchanan.

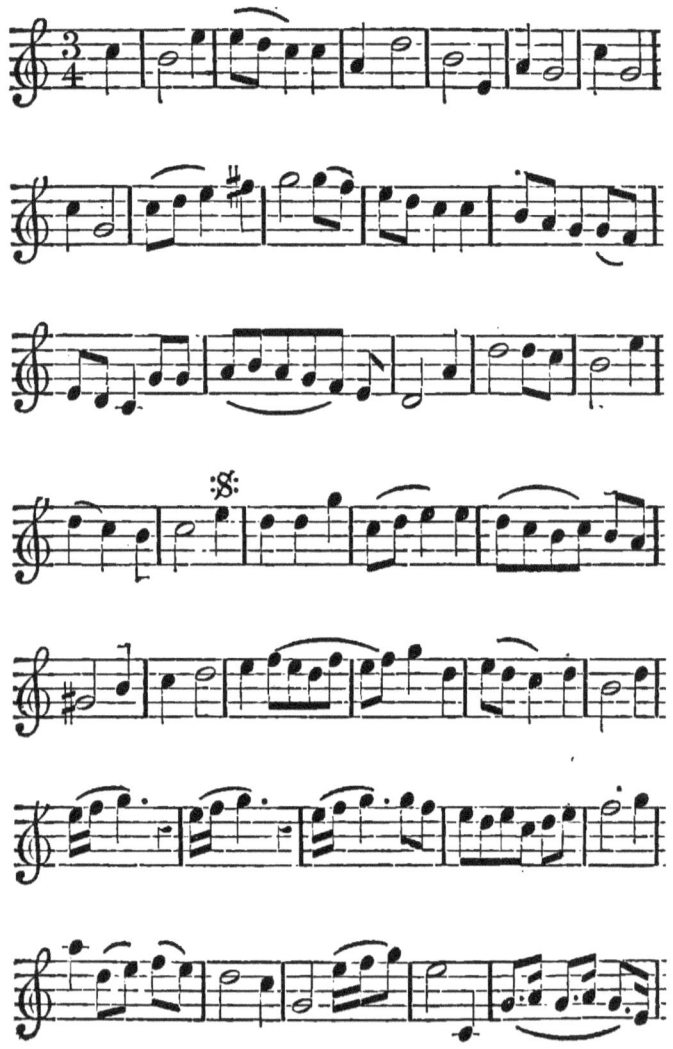

Pleasant and Divertive.

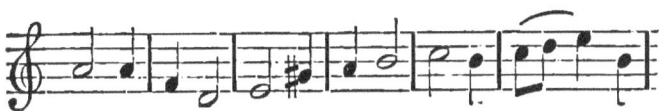

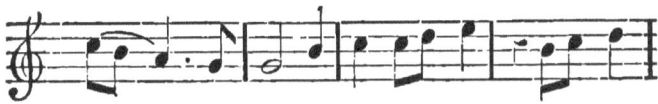

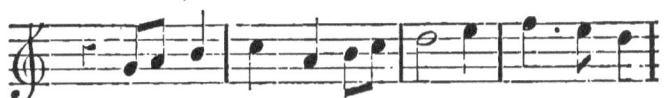

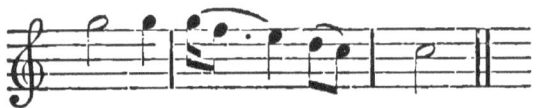

YOung *Collin*, cleaving of a Beam,
    At ev'ry Thumping, thumping blow cry'd hem;
And told his Wife, and told his Wife,
And told his Wife who the Cause would know,
That Hem made the Wedge much further go:
Plump *Joan*, when at Night to Bed they came,
And both were Playing at that same;
Cry'd Hem, hem, hem prithee, prithee, prithee
    Collin do,
If ever thou lov'dst me, Dear hem now;
He laughing answer'd no, no, no,
Some Work will Split, will split with half a blow;
Besides now I Bore, now I bore, now I bore,
Now, now, now I bore,
I Hem when I Cleave, but now I Bore.

A SONG.

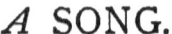

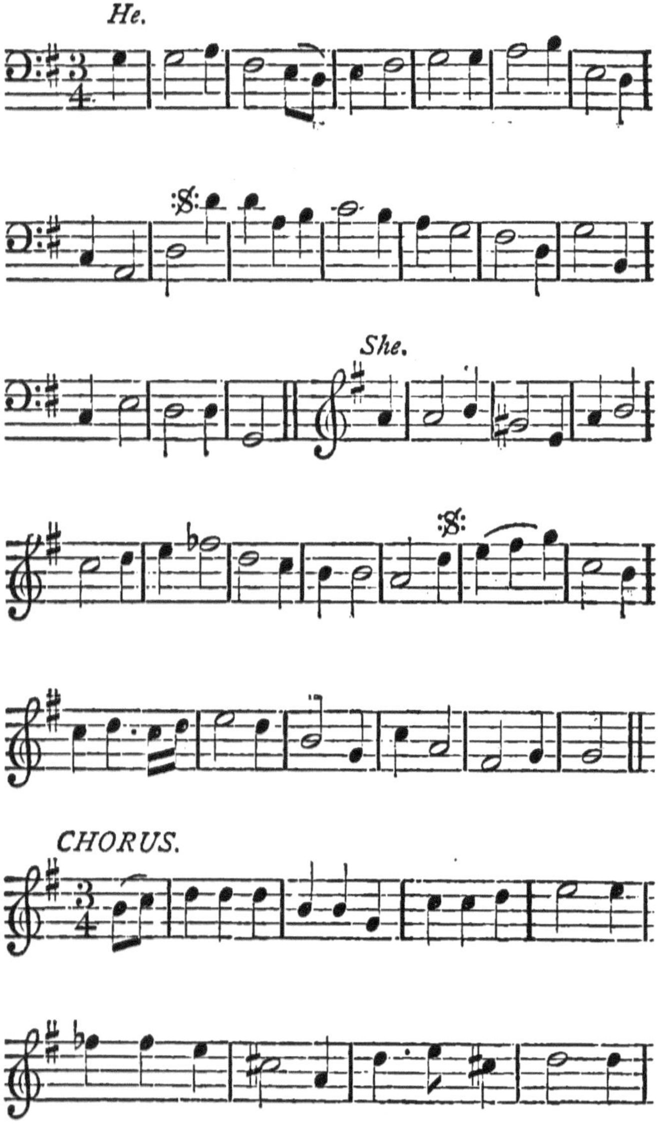

Pleasant and Divertive. 293

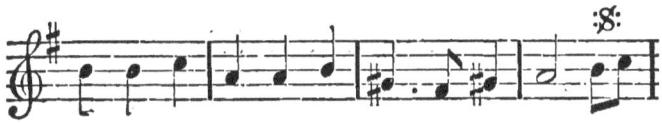

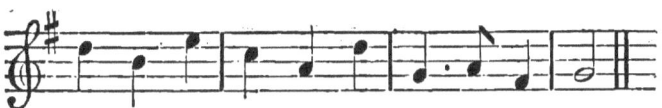

John. Come *Jug*, my Honey, let's to bed,
It is no Sin, sin we are wed;
For when I am near thee by desire,
I burn like any Coal of Fire.

Jug. To quench thy Flames I'll soon agree,
Thou art the Sun, and I the Sea;
All Night within my Arms shalt be,
And rise each Morn as fresh as he.

CHO. *Come on then, and couple together,*
Come all, the Old and the Young,
The Short and the Tall;
The richer than Crœsus,
And poorer than Job,
For 'tis Wedding and Bedding,
That Peoples the Globe.

John. My Heart and all's at thy command,
And tho' I've never a Foot of Land,
Yet six fat Ewes, and one milch Cow,
I think, my *Jug*, is Wealth enow.

Jug. A Wheel, six Platters and a Spoon,
A Jacket edg'd with blue Galloon;
My Coat, my Smock is thine, and shall
And something under best of all.

CHO. *Come on then,* &c.

A

A Scotch SONG.

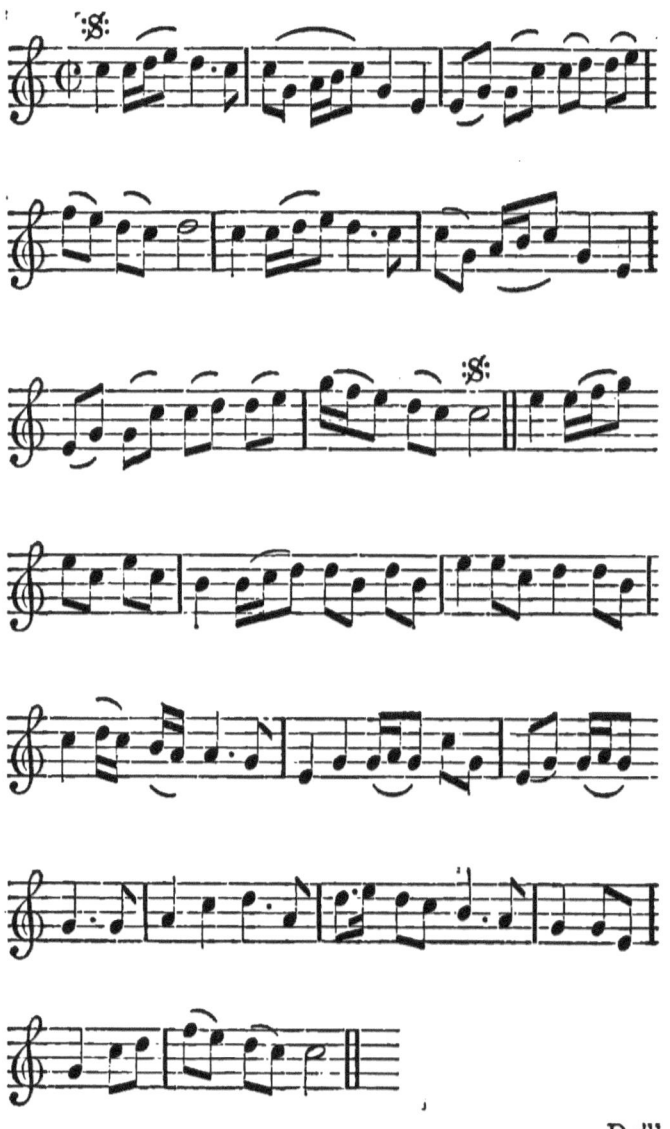

De'll

Pleasant and Divertive.   295

D E'll take the War, that hurry'd *Willy* from me,
    Who to love me, just had sworn,
They made him Captain sure to undoe me,
    Woe is me, he'll ne'er return ;
A thousand Loons abroad will Fight him,
    He from thousands ne'er will run ;
Day and Night I did invite,
    To stay safe from the Sword and Gun:

  I us'd alluring Graces,
   With muckle kind Embraces,
Now sighing, then Crying, Tears dropping fall ;
   And had he my soft Arms,
   Preferr'd to Wars alarms :
By Love grown Mad, without the Man of Gad,
I fear in my fit, I had grented all.

I Wash'd and Patch'd to make me look provoking,
    Snares that they told me wou'd catch the Men ;
And on my Head a huge Commode sat cocking,
    Which made me shew as Tall agen :
For a new Gown too, I paid muckle Money,
    Which with golden Flowers did shine ;
My Love well might think me gay and Bonny,
    No *Scotch* Lass was e'er so Fine.

   My Petticoat I Spotted,
    Fring too with Thread I Knotted,
Lace Shoes, and Silk Hose, Garter full over Knee ;
    But oh ! the fatal thought,
    To *Willy* these are nought,
Who rid to Towns, and Riffled with Dragoons,
When he silly Loon might have Plunder'd me.

A

296　　Songs *Compleat,*

A SONG.

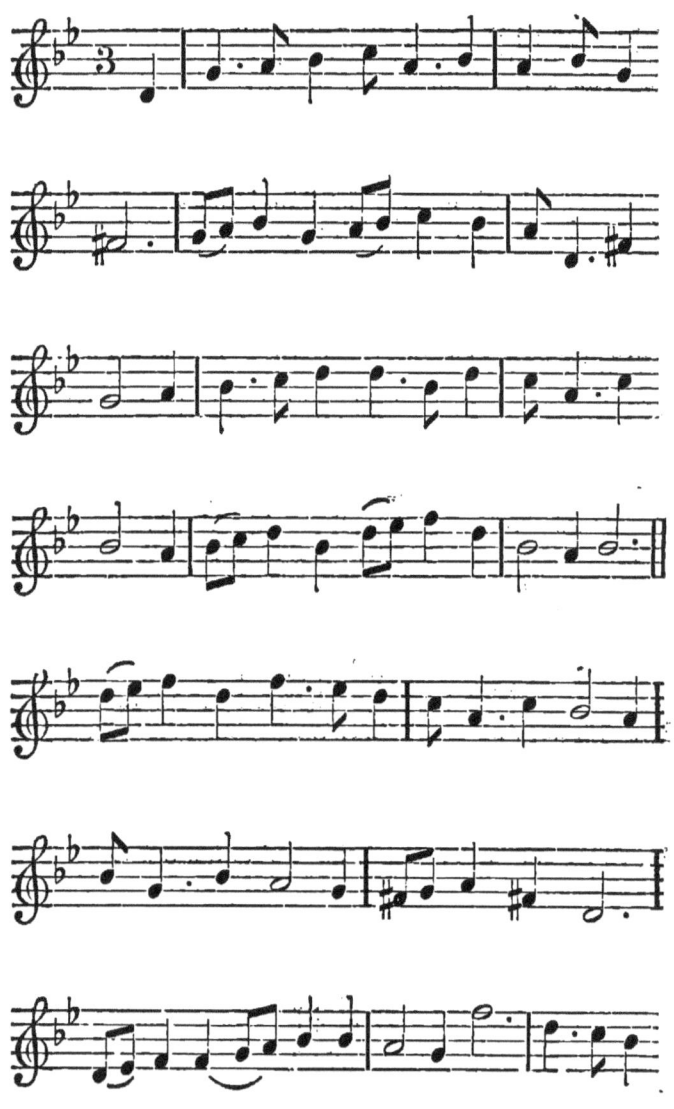

Pleasant and Divertive. 297

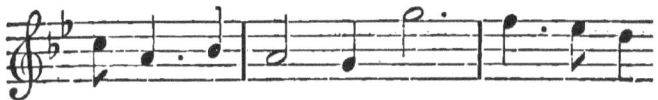

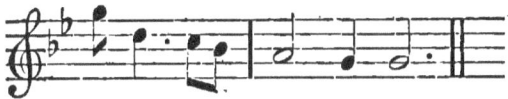

HOW vile are the Sordid Intrigues of the Town,
   Cheating and Lying continually sway;
From Bully and Punk, to the Politick Gown,
   In Plotting and Sotting, they waste the Day :
All their Discourse is of Foreign Affairs,
The *French* and the Wars is always the cry;
   Marriage alas is declining,
   Nay, tho' a poor Virgin lies pining,
Ah Curse of this Jarring, what luck have I.

I hop'd a rich Trader by Ogling Charms,
   Into my Conjugal Fetters to bring;
I planted my snare too, for one lov'd Arms,
   But found his design was another thing:
From the Court Province, down to the dull Cites,
Both Cully and Wits of Marriage are shy;
   Marriage alas is declining,
   Nay, tho a poor Virgin lies pining,
Ah pox of the *Mounsieur*, what luck have I.

Hampton

Hampton Court, *a new Song.* *To a pretty new Tune, made by a Person of Quality.*

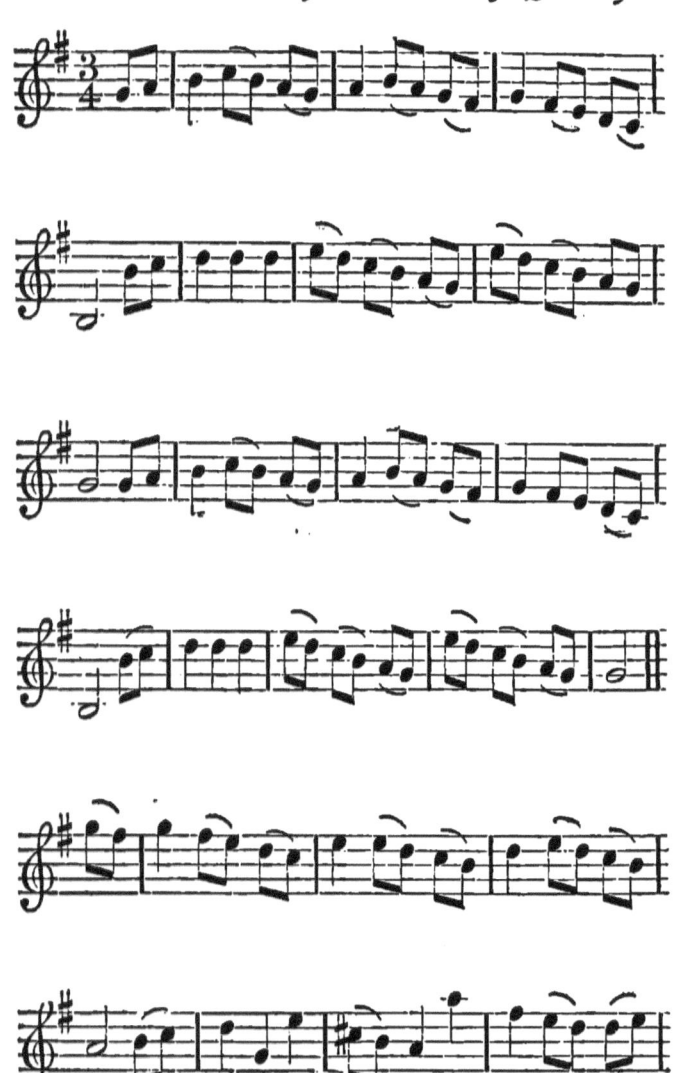

Pleasant and Divertive.

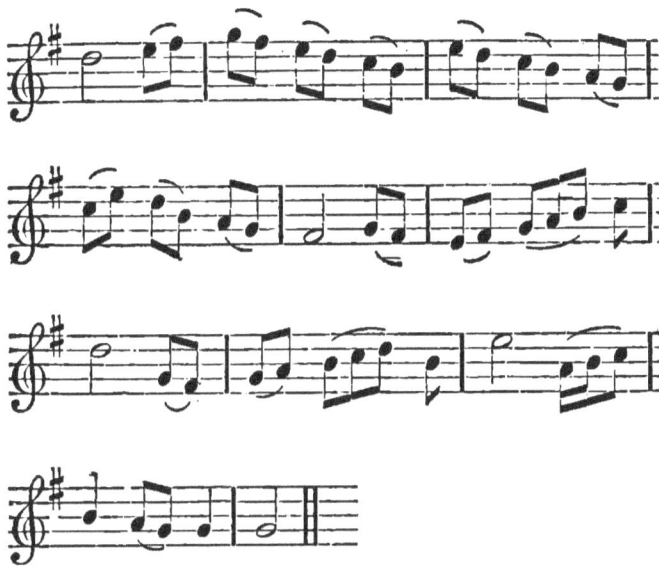

WHere divine *Gloriana*, her Palace late rear'd,
And the choicest delights, Art and Nature prepar'd,
On the bank of sweet *Thames*, gently gliding along ;
The Love-sick *Philander* sate down and thus Sang :
More happy than yet any place was before,
Thou dear blest resemblance of her I adore ;
All Eyes are delighted with prospect of thee,
Thou charm'st ev'ry Sense, thou charm'st ev'ry Sense,
Ah ! just so does she.

As the River's clear Waves *Zephyr* softly does rowl,
So her breath moves the Passions, that flow in my Soul ;
As the Trees by the Sun, feel a nourishing joy ;
So my Heart is refresh'd by a glance from her Eye :
The Birds pretty Notes, we still hear when she speaks ;
And the sweetest of Gardens, still blooms in her Cheeks ;
Had I that dear bliss, for no other I'd sue ;
Who enjoys this sweet *Eve*, who enjoys this sweet *Eve*,
Has all Paradise too.

A

A Song on the Victory over the Turks.

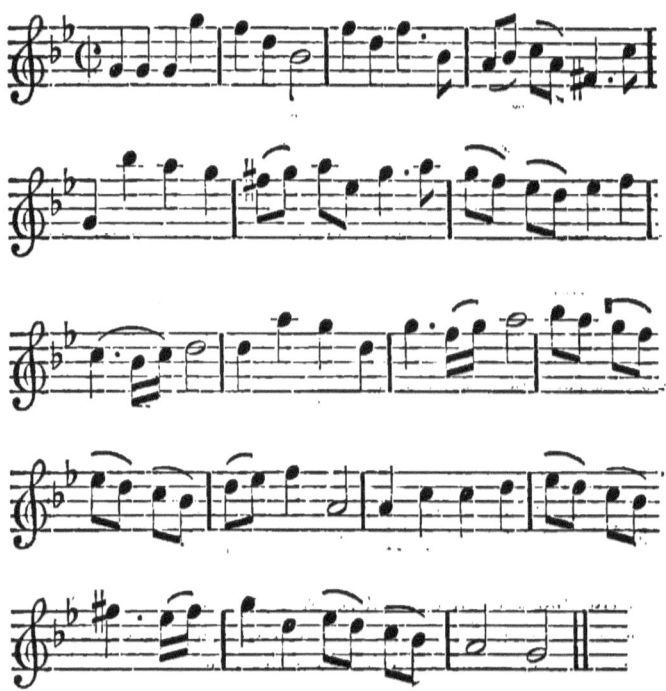

Ark the thundring *Cannons* roar,
Ecchoing from the *German* shore,
And the joyful News comes o'er;
  The *Turks* are all confounded?
Lorrain comes, they run, they run,
Charge your Horse thro' the grand half Moon,
We'll Quarter give to none,
  Since *Staremberg* is wounded.

Close your rank, and each brave soul
Take a lusty flowing bowl,
A grand carouse to the *Royal Pole*,
  The Empires brave defender;

No

Pleasant and Divertive.

No Man leave his post by stealth,
Plunder the *Grand Visier*'s wealth,
But drink a Helmet full to th' Health,
    Of the second *Alexander*.

Mahomet was a sober dog,
A *Small-beer*, drowzy, senseless *Rogue*,
The juice of the Grape so much in vogue,
    To forbid to those adore him;
Had he but allow'd the *Vine*,
Given 'em leave to carouse in *Wine*,
The *Turk* had safely past the *Rhine*,
    And conquer'd all before him.

With dull *Tea* they fought in vain,
Hopeless Vict'ry to obtain,
Where sprightly *Wine* fills ev'ry Vein;
    Success must needs attend him;
Our *Brains* (like our Cannons) warm,
With often firing feels no harm,
While the Sober sot flies the alarm,
    No *Laurel* can befriend him.

Christians thus with conquest crown'd :
Conquest with the *Glass* goes round,
Weak *Coffee* can't keep its ground,
    Against the force of *Claret* :
Whilst we give them thus the Foil,
And the *Pagan Troops* recoyl,
The Valiant *Poles* divide the spoil,
    And in brisk *Nectar* share it.

Infidels are now o'ercome,
But the most Christian Turk's at home,
VVatching the fate of *Christendom*,
    But all his hopes are shallow;
Since the *Poles* have led the Dance,
Let English *Cæsar* now advance,
And if he sends a Fleet to *France*,
    He's a VVig that will not follow.

An ODE *to* Cynthia *walking on* Richmond-Hill. *Set by Mr.* Henry Purcell.

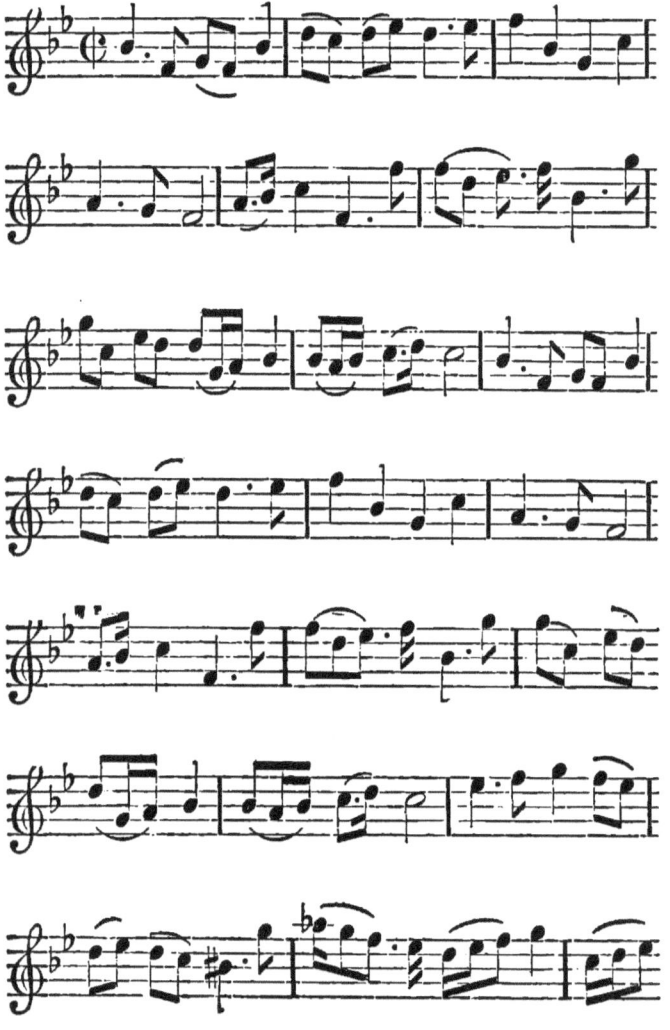

Pleasant and Divertive.   303

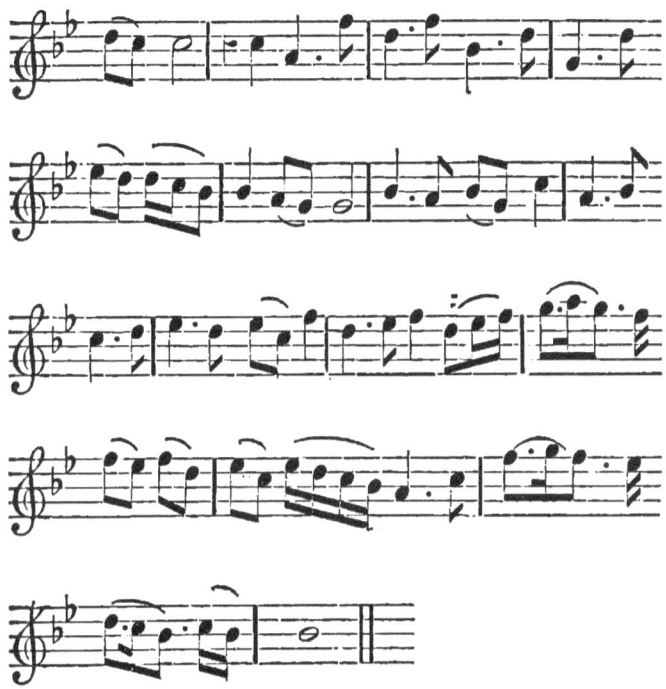

ON the Brow of *Richmond* Hill,
Which *Europe* scarce can parallel,
Ev'ry Eye such Wonders fill,
　　To view the Prospect round ;
By whose fair Fruitful side,
The Silver *Thames* does softly glide,
Meadows dress'd in Summers Pride,
　　With verdant Beauties crown'd :
Lovely *Cynthia* passing by,
With brighter Glories blest my Eye,
Ah ! then in vain, in vain said I,
　　The Fields and Flowers do shine :
Nature in this Charming Place,
Created Pleasure in Excess,
But all are Poor to *Cynthia*'s Face,
　　Whose Features are Divine.

　　　　　　　　　　　　See

SONGS *Compleat*,

See the Beautious River run,
See every Billow Rowling on,
Trees and flowers Court the Sun,
  In yonder shady Wood,
But when *Cynthia* does appear,
To bless my Eyes with all that's fair,
Ah! what Beauty can compare
  To Charming Flesh and Blood;
Nature all her Rural Joys,
At large exposes to our Eyes,
But Hills and Valleys, Air and Skyes
  Henceforth let fools admire;
Cynthia that my Life may be,
Crown'd with true felicity,
Let my Prospect still be thee
  No other I'll desire.

A Scotch SONG.

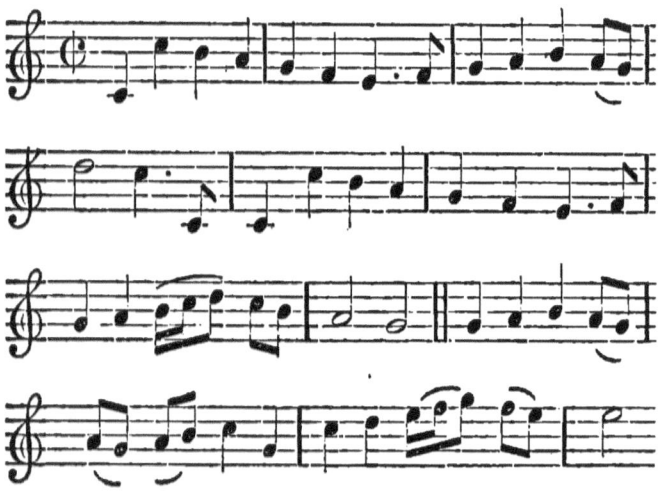

Pleasant and Divertive.

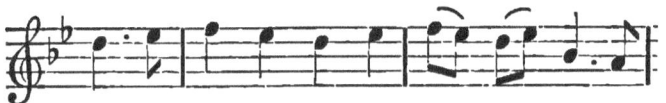

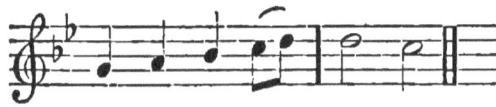

Lads and Lasses Blith and Gay,
  Hear what my Song discloses,
As I one Morning sleeping lay,
  Upon a bank of Roses:
Willy ganging out his Gate,
  By geud luck chanc'd to spy me;
And pulling Bonnet from his Pate,
  He softly lay down by me.

Willy tho' I muckle priz'd,
  Yet now I wou'd not know him;
But made a Frown my Face disguis'd,
  And from me strove to throw him:
Fondly he still nearer prest,
  Upon my Bosom lying;
His beating Heart too thump'd so fast,
  I thought the Loon was dying.

But resolving to deny,
  An angry Passion feigning;
I often roughly push'd him by,
  With words full of disdaining:
Willy baulk'd no favour wins,
  Went off so discontented;
But I geud faith for all my Sins,
  Ne'er half so much Repented.

A Scotch SONG.

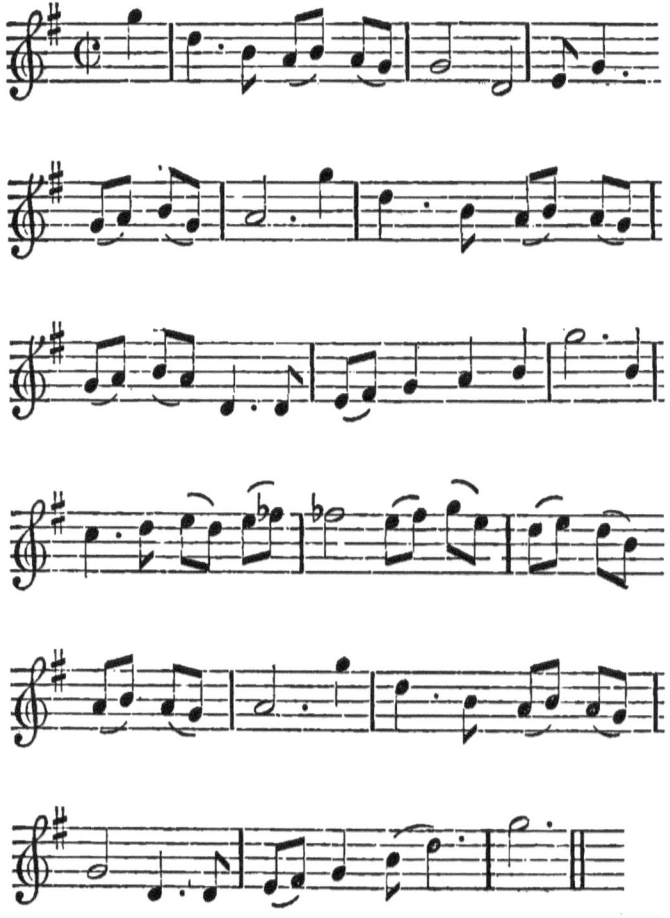

IN *January* last, on *Munnonday* at Morn,
As I along the Fields did pass to view the Winter's Corn;
I leaked me behind, and I saw come over the Knough,
Yan glenting in an Apron with bonny brent Brow.

I

Pleasant and Divertive.

I bid gud morrow fair Maid, and she right courteouslie,
Bekt lew and fine, kind Sir, she said, gud day àgen to
   ye ;
I spear'd o her, fair Maid quo I, how far intend ye now ?
Quo she, I mean a Mile or twa, to yonder bonny brow.

Fair Maid, I'm weel contented to have sike Company,
For I am ganging out the Gate that ya intend ta be ;
When we had walk'd a Mile or twa, Ize said to her,
   my Doe,
May I not dight your Apron fine, kiss your bonny brow.

Nea, gud Sir, you are far misteen, for I am nean o'those,
I hope ya ha more Breeding then to dight a Womans
   Cloaths ;
For I've a better chosen than any sike as you,
Who boldly may my Apron dight and kiss ma bonny
   brow.

Na, if ya are contracted, I have ne mar to say,
Rather than be rejected, I will give o'er the play ;
And I will chose yen o me own that shall not on me
   rew,
Will boldly let me dight her Apron, kiss her bonny
   brow.

Sir, Ize see ya are proud-hearted, and leath to be said
   nay,
You need not tall ha started, for eight that Ize ded say ;
You know Wemun for Modestie, ne at the first time boo,
But, gif we like your Company, we are as kind as you.

The Nurses Song.

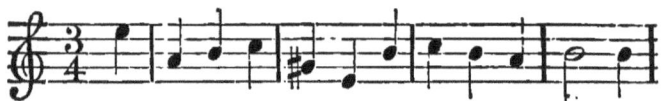
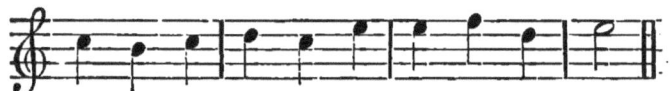
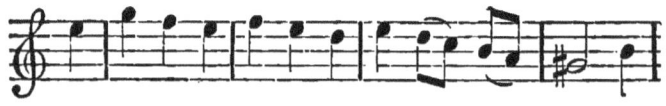
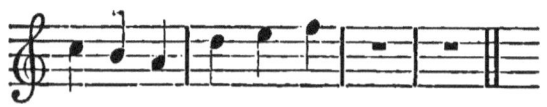

MY dear Cock adoodle,
   My Jewel, my Joy;
My Darling, my Honey,
   My Pretty sweet Boy:
Before I do Rock thee,
   With soft Lul-la-by;
Give me thy sweet Lips,
   To be Kiss, kiss, kiss, kiss, kiss, kiss.

Thy Charming high Fore-head,
   Thy Eyes too like Sloes;
Thy fine Dimple Chin,
   And thy right *Roman* Nose:

Pleasant and Divertive.

With some pretty marks,
   That lie under thy Cloaths;
Sure thou'lt be a rare one,
   To Kiss, kiss, &c.

To make thee grow quickly,
   I'll do what I can :
I'll Feed thee, I'll Stroak thee,
   I'll make thee a Man :
Ah ! then how the Lasses,
   Moll, Betty and *Nan;*
By thee will run Mad,
   To be Kiss, kiss, &c.

And when in due Season,
   My *Billy* shall Wed ;
And Lead a young Lady,
   From Church to the Bed :
A Welfare the loosing,
   Of her Maiden-Head ;
If *Billy* come near her,
   To Kiss, kiss, &c.

Then Welfare high Fore-head,
   And Eyes black as Sloes ;
And Welfare the Dimple,
   And Welfare the Nose :
And all pretty Marks,
   That lie under the Cloaths ;
For none is more hopeful,
   To Kiss, kiss, &c.

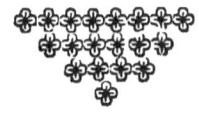

A

A New SONG.
Set by Mr. J. Clarke.

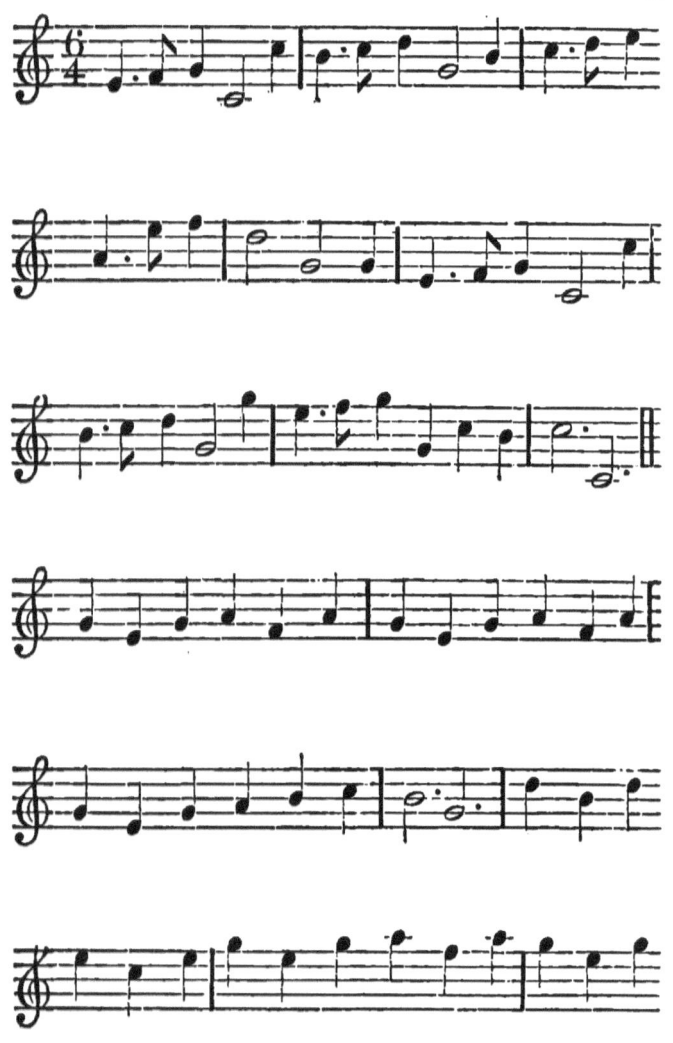

Pleasant and Divertive.

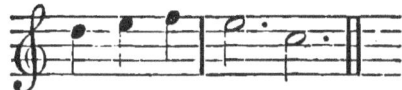

Hark the Cock crow'd, 'tis Day all abroad,
  And looks like a jolly fair morning;
Up *Roger* and *James*, and drive out your Teams,
  Up quickly to carry the Corn in:
Davy the drowzy and *Barnaby* bowzy,
  At Breakfast we'll flout and we'll jear boys;
Sluggards shall chatter with Small-beer and Water,
  Whilst you shall tope off the March beer, Boys.

Lasses that Snore for shame give it o'er,
  Mouth open the Flies will be blowing;
To get us stout Hum when *Christmas* is come,
  Away where the Barly is Mowing:
In your Smock sleeves too, go bind up the Sheaves too,
  With nimble young *Rowland* and *Harry;*
Then when work's over, at Night give each Lover,
  A Hugg and a Buss in the Dairy.

Two for the Mow, and two for the Plow,
  Is then the next labour comes after;
I'm sure I hired four, but if you want more,
  I'll send you my Wife and my Daughter:
Roger the trusty, tell *Rachel* the lusty,
  The Barn's a brave place to steal Garters;
'Twixt her and you then, contrive up the Mow then,
  And take it at Night for your Quarters.

A

312   SONGS *Compleat*,

A SONG.

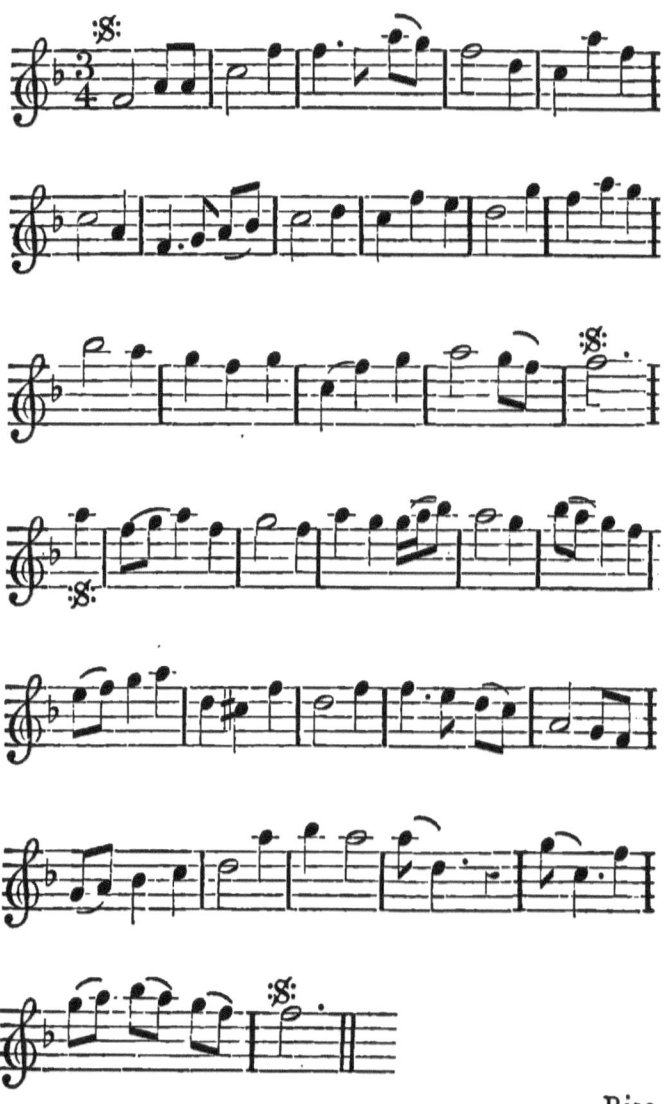

Rise

Pleasant and Divertive.

RISE Bonny *Kate*, the Sun's got up high,
    The Fidlers have play'd their last merry Tune;
Let's give 'em a George and bid 'em god b'w'y,
    And gang to the Wells before 'tis noon.

There to thy Health ize drink my three quarts,
    Then raffle among the Beauties divine;
Where tho' some young Fops may chance to lose hearts,
    Assure thy self *Jockey's* shall still be thine.

When we come home we'll kiss and we'll bill,
    And Feast on each other as well as our meat;
Then saddle our Nags and away to Box-hill,
    And there, there, there, consummate the Treat.

And when at Bowls I chance to be broke,
    Smile thou, and for losses I care not a pin;
I'll push on my Fortune at Night at the Oak,
    And quickly, quickly, quickly, recov'r all agen.

For thy diversion coud'st thou but think,
    Why here all degrees cold Bumpers take off;
Or why all this croud come hither to drink,
    In spight of the Spleen twou'd make thee laugh.

Courtiers and Plough-men, States-men and Citts,
    The Men of the Sword, and Men of the Laws;
The Virgin, the Punck, the Fools, and the Wits,
    All tope off their Cups for a different Cause.

New Marry'd Brides their Spouses to please,
    Each Morning quaff largely in hopes to conceive;
The Bully too drinks to wash off his Disease,
    Still fearing the Fall of the Leaf.

Old musty Wives take Nine in a hand,
    The Maiden takes five too, that's vex'd with her Greens;
In hopes they'll have pow'r to prepare her for Man,
    When ever she comes to her Teens.

A

A SONG.

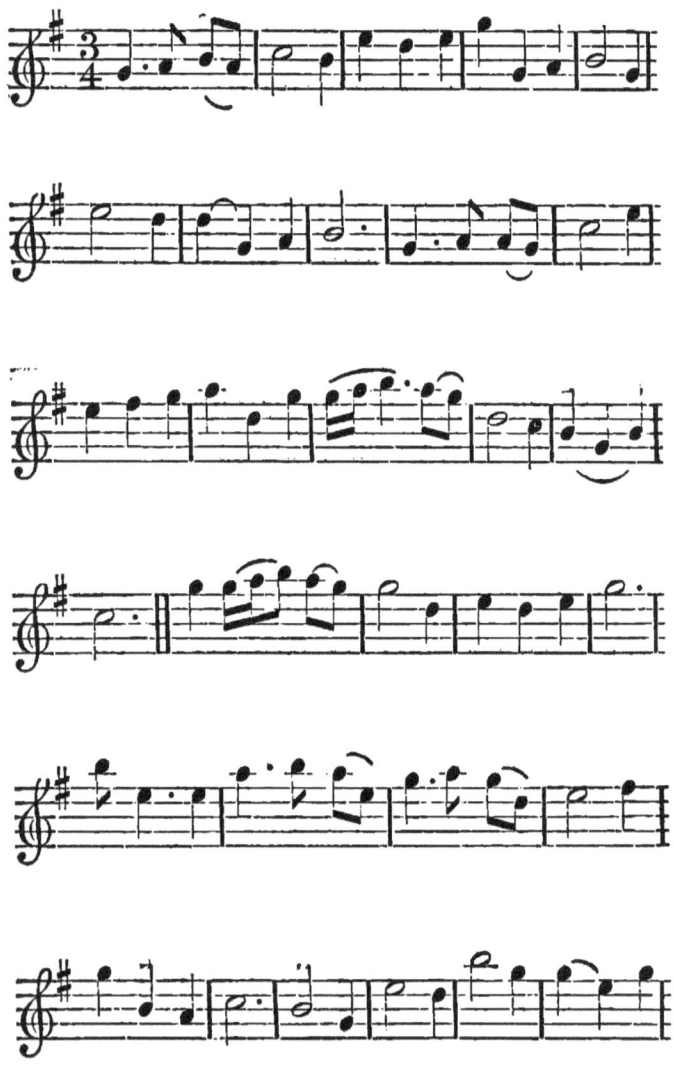

Pleasant and Divertive. 315

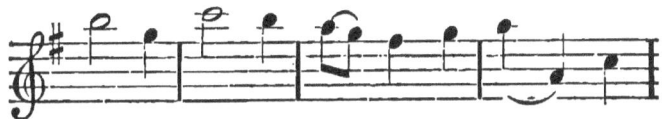

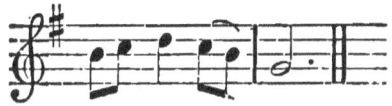

ROyal and fair, great *Willy's* dear Blessing,
    The Charming Regent of the Swains ;
Heavy with Care, thus sadly expressing
    Her Grief, sat weeping on the Plains :
Why did my Fate exalt me so high,
If fading State must deprive me of Joy ;
    Since *Willy* is gone,
    Ah ! How vainly shines the Sun,
    'Till Fates decree, the Winds and Sea,
    Waft, waft him to me.

Large are my Flocks, and flowry my Pastures,
    Worth Treasures vast of Silver and Gold ;
Where ravenous Wolves too fain would be Masters,
    Devour all my Lambs, and break down my Fold :
Willy, while here, secur'd me from fear,
All the *Wild* Herd stood in awe of my Dear ;
    But poor helpless I,
    Mourning Sigh and hourly Cry,
    Let Fates decree, the Winds and Sea,
    Waft *Willy* to me.

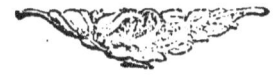

A SONG.

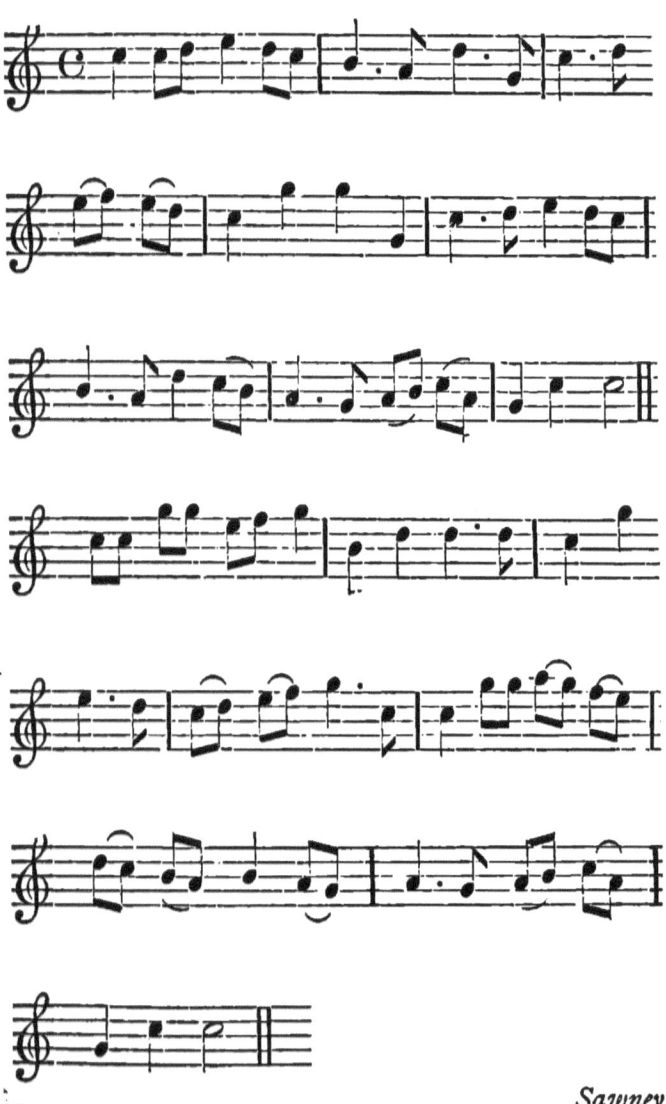

Sawney

Pleasant and Divertive.

SAwney was tall and of Noble Race,
    And lov'd me better than any eane ;
But now he ligs by another Lass,
    And *Sawney* will ne'er be my love agen :
I gave him fine *Scotch* Sarke and Band,
I put 'em on with mine own hand ;
I gave him House, and I gave him Land,
    Yet *Sawney* will ne'er be my Love agen.

I robb'd the Groves of all their store,
    And Nosegays made to give *Sawney* one ;
He kiss'd my Breast and feign would do mere,
    Geud feth me thought he was a bonny one :
He squeez'd my fingers, grasp'd my knee,
And carv'd my Name on each green Tree,
And sigh'd and languish'd to lig by me,
    Yet now he wo'not be my Love agen.

My Bongrace and my Sun-burnt-face,
    He prais'd, and also my Russet Gown ;
But now he doats on the Copper Lace,
    Of some leud Quean of *London* Town :
He gangs and gives her Curds and Cream,
Whilst I poor Soul sit sighing at heam,
And near joy *Sawney* unless in a Dream,
    For now he ne'er will be my Love again.

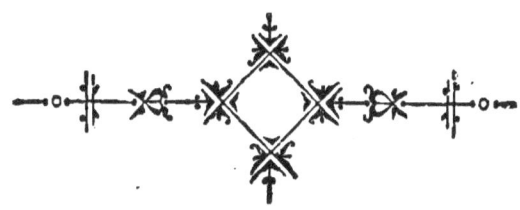

A

A SONG.

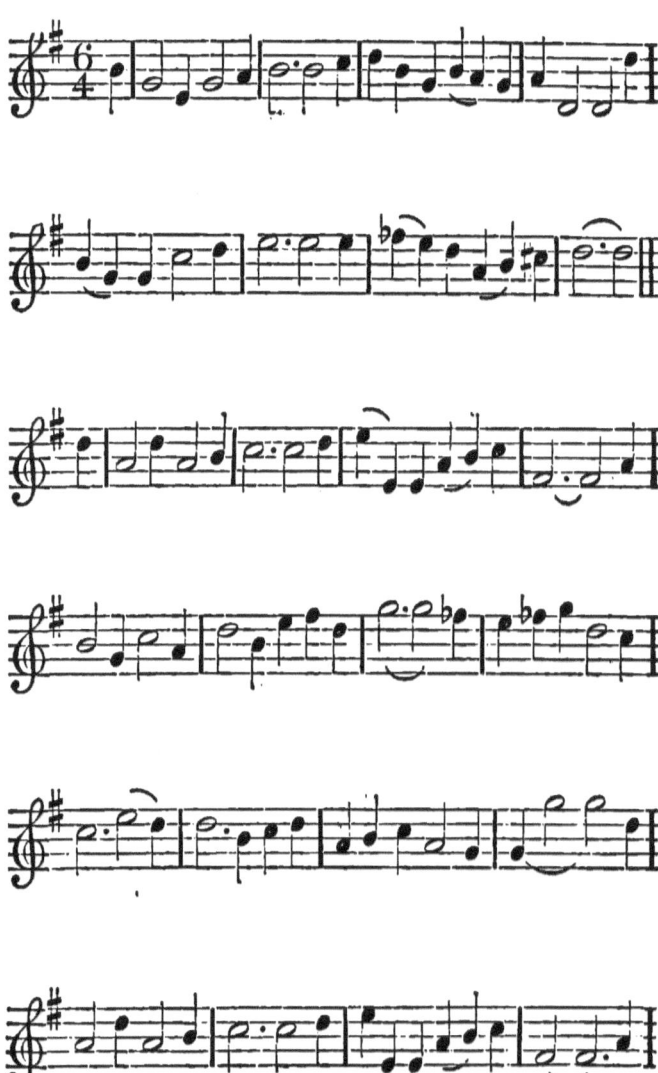

Pleasant and Divertive. 319

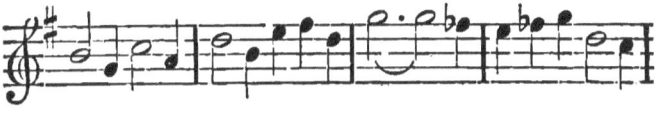

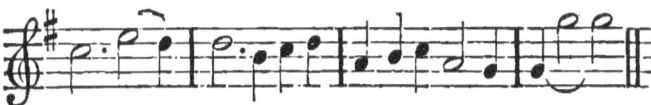

'Twas when the Sheep were Shearing,
    And under the Barly Mow;
Dick gave to *Doll* a Fairing,
    As she had milk'd her Cow:
Quoth he, I fain wou'd Wed thee,
    And tho' I cannot Wooe;
I've Hey Pish, Hey Cock, Hey, and hey for a Boy;
    Sing, shall I come Kiss thee now,
Sing, ah! shall I come, shall I come Kiss thee now?
    I long Sweet-heart to Bed thee,
And merrily Buckle too,
With Hey Pish, Hey Cock, Hey, and hey for a Boy;
    Sing, shall I come Kiss thee now,
Sing ah! shall I come, shall I come Kiss thee now?

Doll seem'd not to regard him,
    As if she did not care;
Yet Simper'd when she heard him,
    Like any Miller's Mare:
And cunningly to prove him,
    And Value her Maiden-head,
Cry'd fie, nay Pish, nay fie, and prithee stand by,
    For I am too young to Wed;
She said, she ne'er cou'd Love him,
    Nor any Man close in Bed;
Then fie Pish, fie, nay Pish, nay prithee stand by,
    For I am too young to Wed.

Like one that's struck with Thunder,
    Stood *Dickey* to hear her talk;
All hopes to get her under,
    This sad resolve did baulk:

At

At last he swore, grown bolder,
  He'd hire some common Shrew;
For hey pish, hey fie, hey for a Boy,
  Sing, shall I come Kiss thee now?
In Loving Arms did fold her,
  E'er Sneak, and Cringe, and Cry;
With hey pish, hey fie, hey for a Boy,
  Sing, shall I come Kiss thee now.

Convinc'd of her Coy folly,
  And stubborn Female will;
Poor *Doll* grew Melancholy,
  The Grist went by her Mill:
I hope, she cry'd, you're wiser,
  Then credit what I have said;
Tho' I do cry nay fie, and pish, and prithee stand by,
  That I am too young to Wed;
Bring you the Church adviser,
  And dress up the Bridal Bed;
Then try, tho' I cry, fie and pish, and prithee stand by,
  If I am too young to Wed.

A Song.

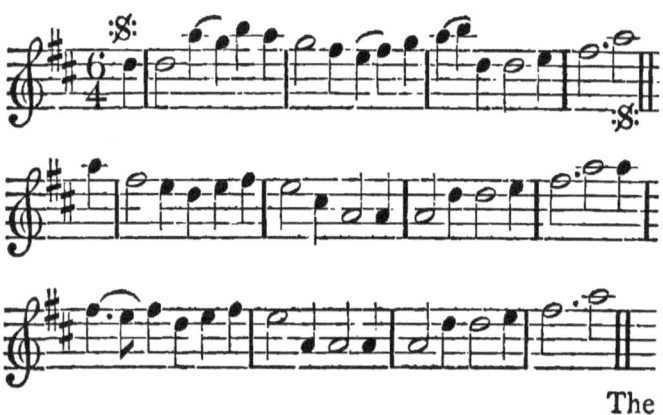

The

Pleasant and Divertive.

THE Sun had loos'd his weary Team,
    And turn'd his Steeds a grazing ;
Ten Fathoms deep in *Neptunes* Stream,
    His *Thetis* was embracing :
The Stars they tripp'd in the Firmament,
    Like Milkmaids on a *May-day ;*
Or Country Lasses a Mumming sent,
    Or School Boys on a Play-day.

Apace came on the grey-ey'd Morn,
    The Herds in Fields were lowing ;
And 'mongst the Poultry in the Barn,
    The Ploughman's Cock sate crowing :
When *Roger* dreaming of Golden Joys,
    Was wak'd by a bawling Rout, Sir ;
For *Cisly* told him, he needs must rise,
    His *Juggy* was crying out, Sir.

Not half so quickly the Cups go round,
    At the tapping a good Ale Firkin ;
As *Roger*, Hosen and Shoon had found,
    And Button'd his Leather Jerkin :
Gray Mare was saddl'd with wondrous speed,
    With Pillion on Buttock right Sir ;
And thus he to an old Midwife ride,
    To bring the poor Kid to light, Sir.

Up, up dear Mother, then *Roger* crys,
    The Fruit of my Labour's now come ;
In *Juggy's* Belly it sprawling lies,
    And cannot get out till you come :
I'll help it, crys the old Hag, ne'er doubt,
    Thy *Jug* shall be well again, Boy ;
I'll get the Urchin as safely out,
    As ever it did get in, Boy.

The Mare now bustles with all her feet,
    No whipping or Spurs were wanting ;
At last into the good House they get,
    And Mew, soon cry'd the bantling :

A Female Chit so small was born,
  They put it into a Flagon;
And must be Christen'd that very Morn,
  For fear it should die a *Pagan*.

Now *Roger* struts about the Hall,
  As great as the Prince of *Conde;*
The Midwife crys, her Parts are small,
  But they will grow larger one day:
What tho' her Thighs and Legs lie close,
  And little as any Spider;
They will when up to her teens she grows,
  By grace of the Lord lie wider.

And now the merry Spic'd-bowls went round,
  The Gossips were void of shame too;
In butter'd Ale the Priest half drown'd,
  Demands the Infant's Name too;
Some call'd it *Phill*, some *Florida*,
  But *Kate* was allow'd the best hin't;
For she would have it *Cunicula*,
  Cause there was a pretty Jest in't.

Thus *Cunny* of *Winchester* was known
  And famous in *Kent* and *Dover;*
And highly rated in *London* Town,
  And courted the Kingdom over:
The Charms of *Cunny* by Sea and Land,
  Subdues each human Creature;
And will our stubborn Hearts command,
  Whilst there is a Man in Nature.

Pleasant and Divertive. 323

A SONG

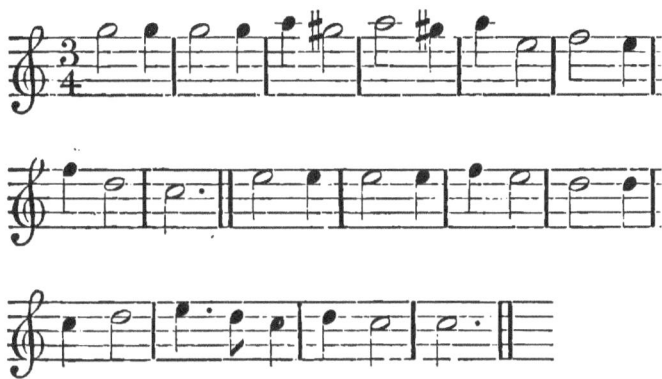

Oy to the Bridegroom! fill the Sky
With pleasing sounds of welcome Joy:
Joy to the Bride, may lasting Bliss,
And every Day still prove like this.
    Joy to the, &c.

Never were Marriage Joys Divine,
But where two constant Hearts Combine;
He that proves false, himself doth cheat,
Like sick Men tasts, but cannot eat.
    He that, &c.

What is a Maiden-head? ah what?
Of which weak Fools so often prate?
'Tis the young Virgin's Pride and Boast,
Yet never was found but when 'twas lost.
    'Tis the, &c.

Fill me a Glass then to the brink,
And its Confusion here I'll drink;
And he that baulks the Health I nam'd,
May he die young, and then be D——
    And he that, &c.

A SONG.

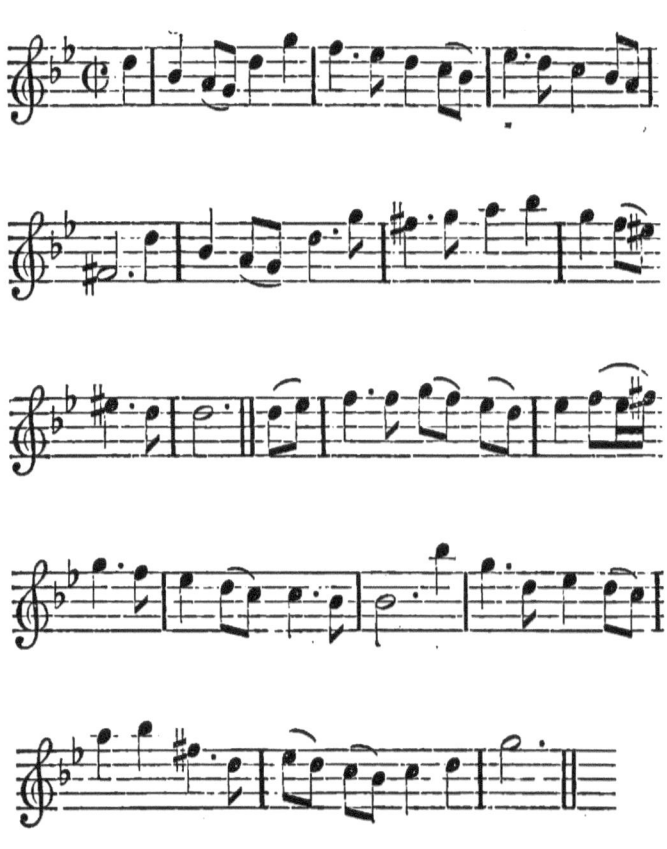

THE Night her blackest Sable wore,
    And gloomy were the Skies;
And glitt'ring Stars there were no more,
    Than those in *Stella's* Eyes:
When at her Father's Gate I knock'd,
    Where I had often been,
And Shrowded only with her Smock,
    The fair one let me in.

Fast

Fast lock'd within her close Embrace,
  She trembling lay asham'd ;
Her swelling Breast, and glowing Face,
  And every touch inflam'd :
My eager Passion I obey'd,
  Resolv'd the Fort to win ;
And her fond Heart was soon betray'd,
  To yield and let me in.

Then ! then ! beyond expressing,
  Immortal was the Joy ;
I knew no greater blessing,
  So great a God was I :
And she transported with delight,
  Oft pray'd me come again ;
And kindly vow'd that every Night,
  She'd rise and let me in.

But, oh ! at last she prov'd with Bern,
  And sighing sat and dull ;
And I that was as much concern'd,
  Look'd then just like a Fool :
Her lovely Eyes with tears run o'er,
  Repenting her rash Sin ;
She sigh'd and curs'd the fatal hour,
  That e'er She let me in.

But who could cruelly deceive,
  Or from such Beauty part ;
I lov'd her so, I could not leave
  The Charmer of my Heart :
But Wedded and conceal'd the Crime,
  Thus all was well again ;
And now she thanks the blessed Hour,
  That e'er she let me in.

A

326 SONGS *Compleat*,

A Scotch SONG.

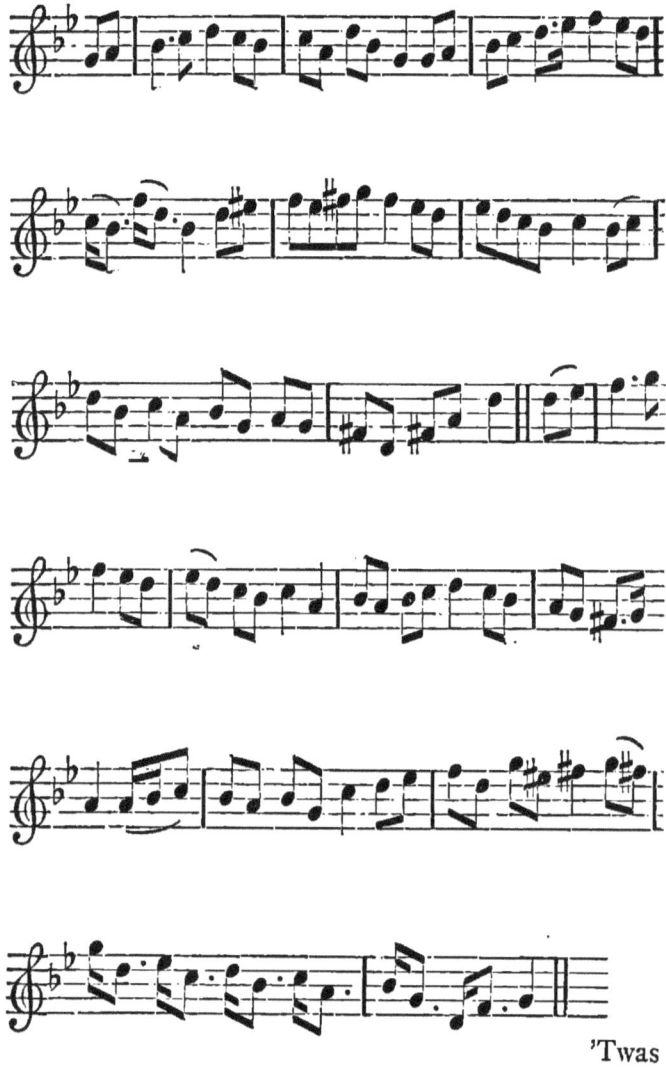

'Twas

Pleasant and Divertive.

'TWas within a Furlong of *Edinborough* Town,
In the Rosie time of year when the Grass was
down;
Bonny *Jockey* Blith and Gay,
Said to *Jenny* making Hay,
Let's sit a little (Dear) and prattle,
'Tis a sultry Day:
He long had Courted the Black-Brow'd Maid,
But *Jockey* was a Wag and would ne'er consent to Wed;
Which made her pish and phoo, and cry out it will not do,
I cannot, cannot, cannot, wonnot, monnot Buckle too.

He told her Marriage was grown a meer Joke,
And that no one Wedded now, but the Scoundrel Folk;
Yet my dear, thou shouldest prevail,
But I know not what I ail,
I shall dream of Clogs, and silly Dogs,
With Bottles at their Tail;
But I'll give thee Gloves, and a Bongrace to wear,
And a pretty Filly-Foal, to ride out and take the Air;
If thou ne'er will pish nor phoo, and cry it ne'er shall do,
I cannot, cannot, *&c.*

That you'll give me Trinkets, cry'd she, I believe,
But ah! what in return must your poor *Jenny* give,
When my Maiden Treasure's gone,
I must gang to *London* Town,
And Roar, and Rant, and Patch and Paint,
And Kiss for half a Crown:
Each Drunken Bully oblige for Pay,
And earn an hated Living in an odious Fulsom way;
No, no, it ne'er shall do, for a Wife I'll be to you,
Or I cannot, cannot, *&c.*

A SONG.

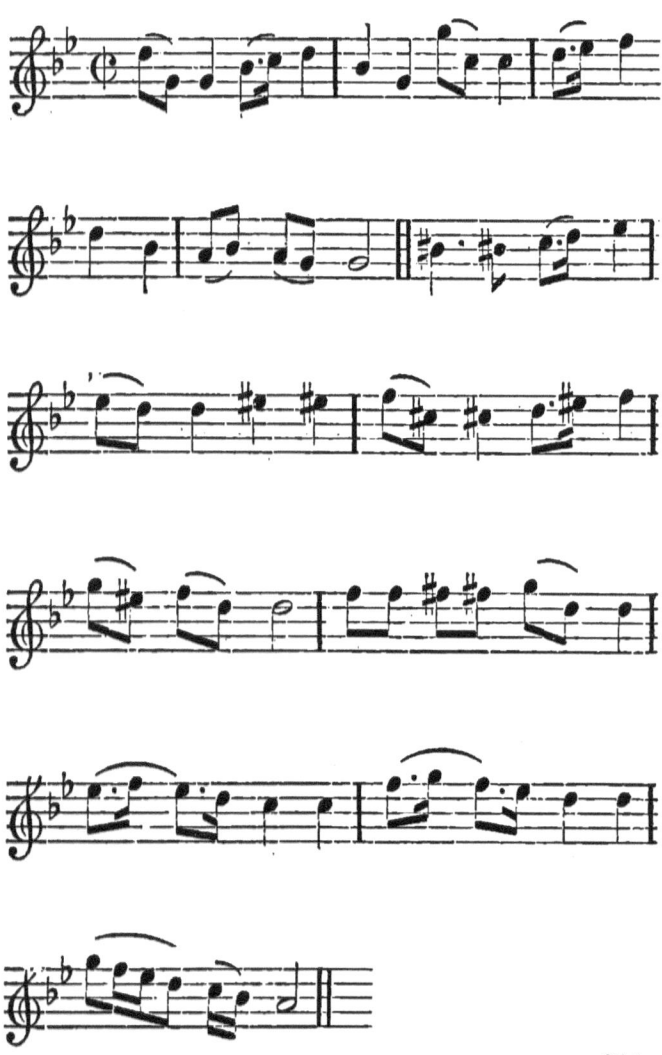

Chloe

Pleasant and Divertive.

CHloe found *Amyntas* lying,
  All in Tears upon the Plain :
Sighing to himself and crying,
  Wretched I to love in vain !
Kiss me, kiss me, Dear, before my Dying ;
  Kiss me once and ease my pain.

Sighing to himself and crying,
  Wretched I to love in vain ;
Ever scorning and denying,
  To reward your faithful Swain :
Kiss me, Dear, before my Dying,
  Kiss me once and ease my pain.

Ever scorning and denying,
  To reward your faithful Swain ;
Chloe, laughing at his crying,
  Told him that he Lov'd in vain ;
Kiss me, Dear, before my Dying,
  Kiss me once and ease my pain.

Chloe laughing at his crying,
  Told him that he lov'd in vain ;
But repenting and Complying,
  When He Kiss'd, She Kiss'd again :
Kiss'd him up before his Dying,
  Kiss'd him up, and eas'd his pain.

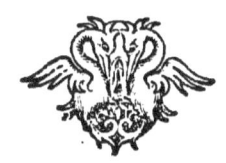

A

A New Scotch SONG, *or a Game at* Pam.

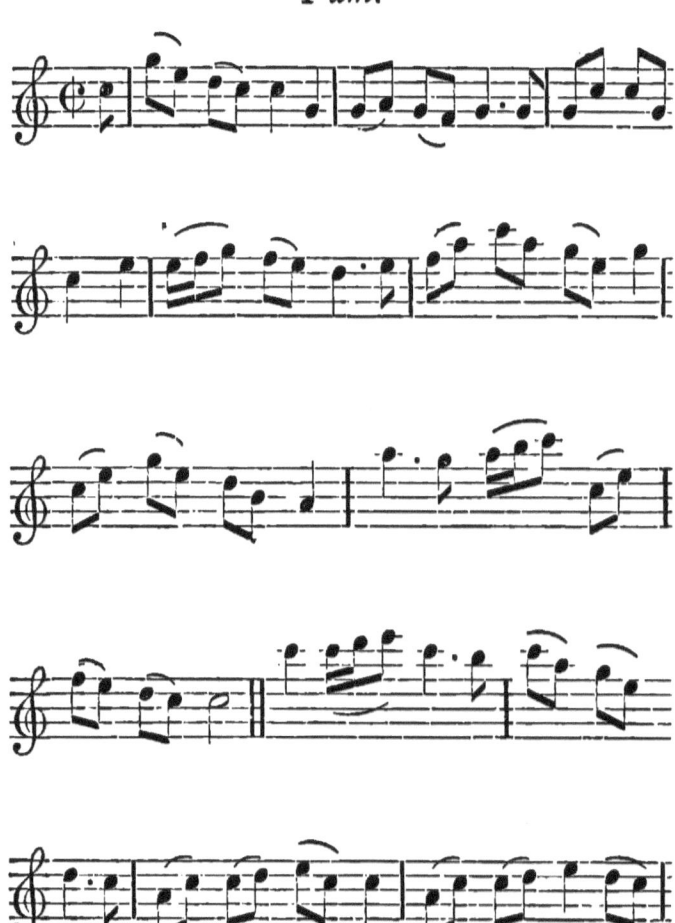

Pleasant and Divertive. 331

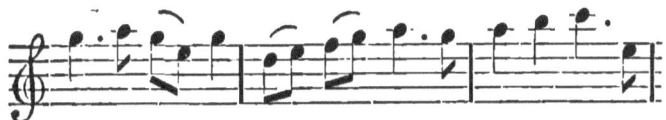

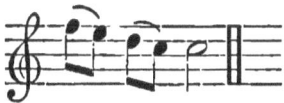

WHEN *Phillida* with *Jockey* play'd at *Pam*,
The bonny Lad nea whit cou'd heed his Game;
But sighing in his doleful dumps,
Leuk'd at her and lost his Trumps,
Ah! a blither sport was *Jockey's* chief Aim:
  Those bright Eyes,
    The Loon Heart wounded cries,
Ah welladay, dear *Phillida*,
Joy, and yet destroy me,
I'se ne'er win by Mournival or blaze,
Or conquering Knave whilst on my Queen I gaze.

Thus *Phillida* with Beauty, Wit, and Art,
His Money won, who had before his Heart;
  Until the laughing God of Love,
  Pack'd the Cards and made 'em prove,
All combin'd to take poor *Jockey's* weak part:
  No kind Knave,
    The Charmer now cou'd have,
Her Lover too, Recover'd too,
More than lost before too,
Till to please them love chang'd the wrangling Game,
To Wedlock Joys, and *Jockey* was her *Pam*.

A

A SONG.

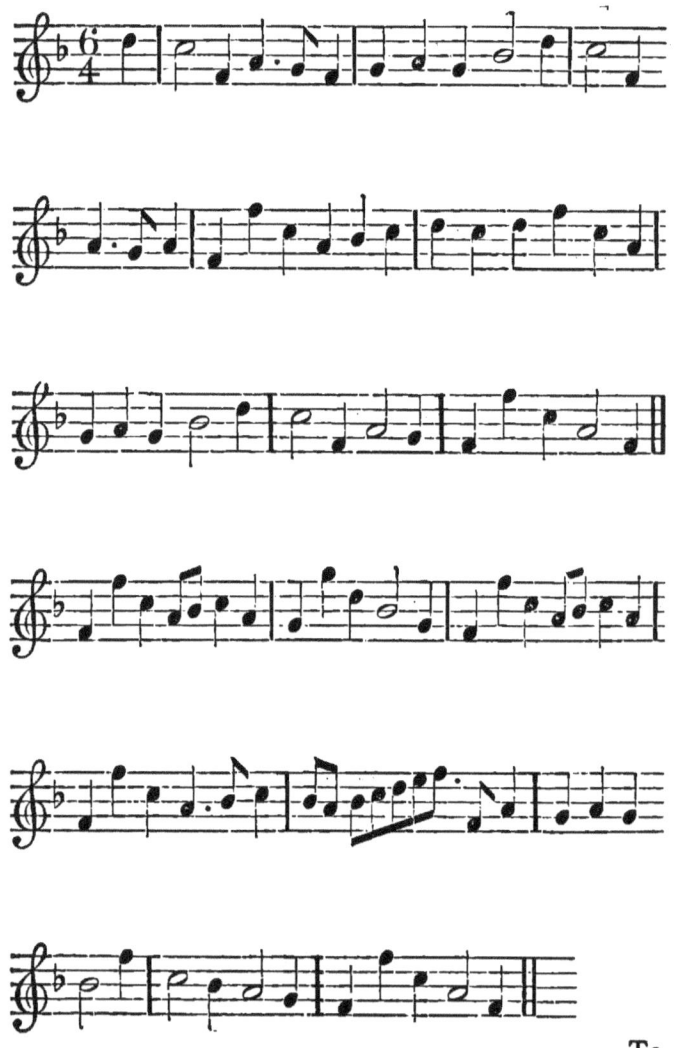

To

Pleasant and Divertive.

TO Horse, brave boys of *Newmarket*, to Horse,
    You'll lose the Match by longer delaying ;
The Gelding just now was led over the Course,
    I think the Devil's in you for staying :
Run, and endeavour all to bubble the Sporters,
Bets may recover all lost at the Groom-Porters ;
Follow, follow, follow, follow, come down to the Ditch,
Take the odds and then you'll be rich.

For I'll have the brown Bay, if the blew bonnet ride,
    And hold a thousand Pounds of his side, Sir ;
Dragon would scow'r it, but *Dragon* grows old ;
He cannot endure it, he cannot, he wonnot now
    run it,
    As lately he could :
Age, age, does hinder the Speed, Sir.

Now, now, now they come on, and see,
    See the Horse lead the way still ;
Three lengths before at the turning the Lands,
    Five hundred Pounds upon the brown Bay still :
Pox on the Devil, I fear we have lost,
    For the Dog, the *Blue Bonnet*, has run it,
    A Plague light upon it,
The wrong side the Post ;
Odszounds, was ever such Fortune.

A SONG.

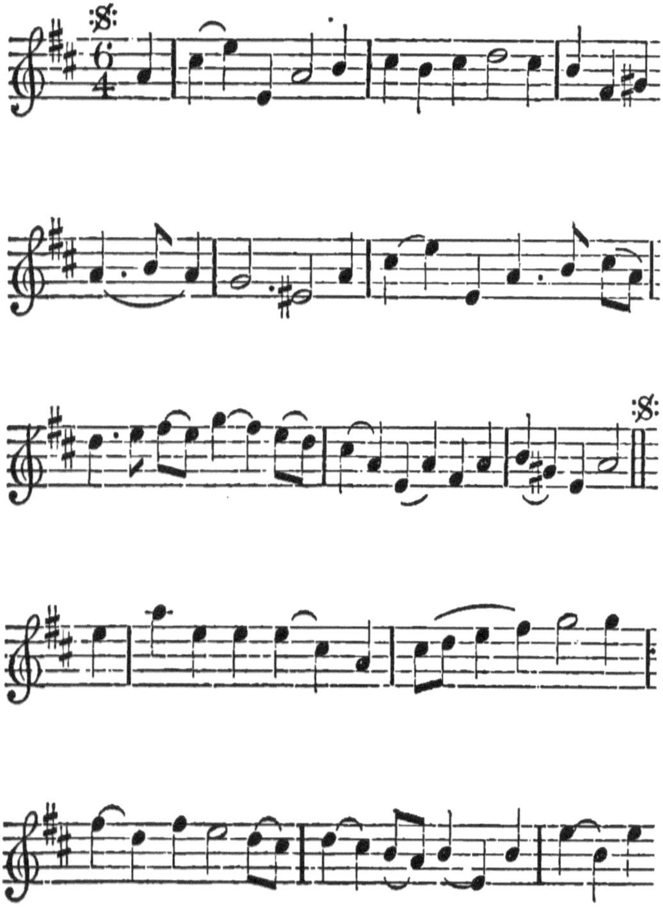

Pleasant and Divertive. 335

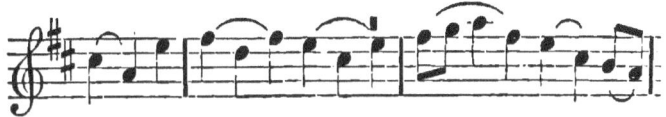

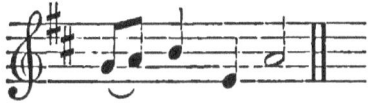

WHEN first *Amyntas* su'd for a Kiss,
  My innocent Heart was tender;
That tho' I push'd him away from the bliss,
  My Eyes declar'd my Heart was won;
I fain an artful Coyness wou'd use,
  Before I the Fort did Surrender:
But Love wou'd suffer no more such abuse,
  And soon, alas! my cheat was known:
He'd sit all day, and laugh and play,
A thousand pretty things would say;
My hand he'd squeez, and press my knees,
Till farther on he got by degrees.

My Heart, just like a Vessel at Sea,
Wou'd toss when *Amyntas* was near me;
But ah! so cunning a Pilot was he,
  Thro' Doubts and Fears he'd still sail on:
I thought in him no danger cou'd be,
Too wisely he knows how to steer me;
And soon, alas! was brought to agree,
  To tast of Joys before unknown:
Well might he boast his Pain not lost,
For soon he found the Golden Coast;
Enjoy'd the Oar, and 'tach'd the shore,
Where never Merchant went before.

A Mock to the foregoing SONG : *When first* Amyntas *su'd for a Kiss*, &c.

A *Minta* one Night had occasion to P————ss,
    Joan reach'd her the Pot that stood by her;
I in the next Chamber could hear it to hiss,
    The Sluice was small, but Stream was strong:
My Soul was melting, thinking of bliss,
    And raving I lay with desire;
        But nought could be done,
        For alas she P————d on,
Nor car'd for Pangs I suffer'd long:
    Joan next made hast,
    In the self same Case;
To fix the Pot close to her own A————;
        Then Floods did come,
        One might have swom,
And puff a Whirl-wind flew from her B————.

Says *Joan*, by these strange Blasts that do rise,
    I guess that the Night will grow windy;
For when such Showers do fall from the Skies,
    To clear the Air the North-wind blows;
Ye nasty Quean, her Lady replies,
    That Tempest broke out from behind ye;
And though it was decently kept from my Eyes,
    The troubled Air offends my Nose:
        Says *Joan* 'ods-heart,
        You have P————d a Quart,
And now you make ado for a F————t;
        'Tis still your mind,
        To squeeze behind,
But never fell Shower from me without wind.

Orations, Poems, Prologues, *and* Epilogues, *on several Occasions.*

A Poetical Oration,
Written in Queen ANN's *Reign, in Honour of the Ladies, intended for a New Comedy call'd, a* Wife worth a Kingdom : *And Spoken by me on the Publick* THEATRE *in* DRURY LANE, June *the 7th,* 1714.

IN this wise Town two Games precedence get,
   The Game of Politicks, the Game of Wit ;
The first, the Heads profound, with Art pursue,
But since with State Affairs, I've nought to do,
I leave that Winning for the Lord knows who :
The Game of Wit suits more my own Affair,
Time was an Author in an Elbow Chair,
Sate on the Stage as Judge, find fault, who dare ?
But now ('tis hard) that things should alter so,
Poor I stand here, with Posture humbly low :
To beg each Tyrant Critick, not to be my Foe,
In my own Person sue, to change the mood,
Which truly I should blush for, if I could :
Yet Parent *Thespis,* oft harangu'd the Throng,
And to *Augustus,* tuneful *Ovid* sung ;
Nor did fam'd *Shakespear* Buskin'd here, his noble
   Genius wrong,
In honour of bright Beauty then I come,
To entertain the Fair, now thus presume ;
Smile you, and dart an influencing Ray,
I shall perform as once, when Young and Gay :
Oh Heaven ! that Ray's enough to fix Renown,
On envious Carpers now I dare look down ;

Y'have

Y'have wrought a *Miracle* upon my *Tongue*,
From charming Eyes, first Elocution sprung :
I, that through Imperfection, Fear, or Shame,
Could never utter to Great *CHARLES* my Name ;
Oh pow'r of Beauty ! now my Soul can raise,
To speak a long *Oration*, in your Praise :
The Play too will I hope, meet some Esteem,
One thing I'm sure of, 'tis a glorious Theam ;
A Wife, in full perfection of the sort,
It reaches the bright *Zenith* of the Court :
Puts ye in mind of Sacred Majesty,
Who wears that Title, in most high degree ;
For search the spacious *Globe*, there will be seen,
Never a better Wife, never so good a Queen :
You Ladies the next Prize your own may call,
Since with her Lustre guilt, you glitter all,
Transfixt in that bright Sphere, and ne'er to fall ;
So when the dazling Soveraign of the Night,
Decks the Horizon with her glorious Light :
Th' attending Planets round her brightly burn,
And by Example glitter in their turn ;
So much that part, now to another thing,
A brace of Fops too here I nicely bring,
One has a Trick to Lisp, and one to Sing :
Full of themselves, think half the World adore 'em,
And that all Womankind must fall before 'em ;
When simple Creatures the good Housewife hear,
Values a sneaking look, a subtle Tear,
A Feast of Oaths, and Vows, cook'd up with Art,
With a neat Dish of Lyes for a Desert ;
No more than a grand Courtier, high in Grace,
A Complimenting Friend, that wants a Place :
Yet must dear Self-conceit, frail Nature share,
How many frowzy Pates, Humps, Scrubs, alas there are,
Who vainly think themselves like these, the Victors of the Fair.
With them some other Comick parts you'll view,
Pleasant I think, would you would be so too ;

'Tis

'Tis then on generous Favour I rely,
And since the Winter of my time draws nigh :
That can't such Fruits and Flowers to treat ye bring,
As us'd to deck my Summer, and my Spring ;
Accept with Candor now this mean repast,
Add one Indulgence more to Crown the rest,
With this regard, that it may be your last.

An ORATION

Address'd to the KING, *the* PRINCE *and* PRINCESS : *And on the glorious Advantage of* UNION *and* AMITY, *Written and spoken by me on the Publick* Theatre *in* DRURY LANE, June *the* 3d, 1714.

WHEN the new World, all Laws divine withstood,
And Heaven to purge it of that Impious brood,
Showr'd down it's Vengeance in th' o'erwhelming Flood,
Submissive Duty in the few were spar'd,
Whose constant Prayers and Vows were daily heard ;
Found gracious means to quel Celestial Rage,
And Time and Nature form'd a Golden Age :
Then *Bards* and *Prophets*, that from Heroes sprung,
A Sacred Genius all Inspiring sung ;
So since Indulgent Heaven has once again,
Decreed our future Blessings to maintain,
In a long Series of great *George*'s Reign.
Amongst the rest that sound his Praise with Joy,
Proud that I can so well my Verse employ,
With Loyal grateful duty Charm'd am I :

I that my comick Prose and Lyrick Rhime,
Had quite resign'd to the decays of Time ;
Now prune my drooping Wings that flagg'd before,
By his great Theam inspir'd, aloft I soar.
And with new Vigour court the *Muse* once more :
The *Muse* that Sings, how *Britain* in distress,
Has in her Royal Guardian found redress ;
Sees a fam'd Heroe, in her awful Lord,
Ready in shining Arms to weild his Sword,
In brave defence of Right, by Providence restor'd :
    And as in Fable, when the *Brutes* made War,
When stubborn Factions with Intestine Jar ;
Rashly resolv'd each other to oppose,
Tumultuous crowds about Succession rose :
But when they would a lawless Heir impose,
The Soveraign Lion, the bold Parties aw'd,
Controul'd his Foes at home, and those abroad ;
Proclaim'd his Right, prov'd his vindictive Power,
And made the growling Herd, all tremble at his Roar:
    The Paralell is plain, and clear the Case,
Nor must the *Muse* cease here her noble Chace,
This hunt of Fame, fix'd in the Royal Race.
The *Prince* is next, and by Eternal doom,
Fated for Greatness in the Years to come,
Whose florent Spring, now bears delightful Bloom :
Upon that glorious Subject how my Song,
Could here dilate, but oh ! my trembling Tongue,
Desponding faulters, when I Thought renew,
And still a brighter Glory in the *Princess* view ;
Oh let that gracious Planet ! whose blest Charms,
Still new Creates the Subject that she warms :
Forgive a Reverence, that transports so far,
To call her *Britain*'s most indulgent Star ;
Sent from the Pow'r that guards our grand Affairs,
That no more Strifes be for Pretending Heirs :
Let her be ever blest who doles such Joy,
And blasts aspiring Hopes that would destroy ;
Fill'd with Seraphick Love does timely breed,
And bears a Race of Angels to succeed :
                                                 Thus

Thus as some desart Land, whose wild distress,
Seems wanting Providential Care to bless;
Where the coy *Sun* ne'er darts a genial Ray,
But cold bleak Frosts blasts each returning Day;
Prayers of some fav'rite Votaries Shipwreck'd there,
Having with pious Toyl exacted heavenly Care,
And chang'd rough Seasons to serene and fair.
Great Goddess Nature proves her kindly force,
Turns to proliffick Heat their steril Course;
Relieves all Wants caus'd by Celestial doom,
Gives Fruit and Grain to crown the Years to come,
And now fresh. budds and plants appear, and
    princely Roses bloom.
So beauteous *Albion* wouldst thou happy be,
Happy thy Natives all, could they agree;
But baneful Feuds prevent that valued Lot,
And hateful Jarrs about the Lord knows what:
Right and Religion, the great Cause they feign,
Yet tho' that specious Maxim some maintain,
There is a sly and subtile Devil called Gain;
That oft unstedfast Nature does surprize,
And turns to mischievous the Grave and Wise:
Else we're all guided by calm Reason's Rules,
Tory and *Whig* were only Terms for Fools.
  Oh sacred Union! could thy Charm command,
The Erring stubborn Factions of the Land;
We need not shrink for fear of Foreign harms,
Or value *Southern* Heats, or *Northern* Storms:
But arm'd with Amity, Victorious be,
Securely Proud, we're circl'd round with Sea.
  And now methinks I see the Dove appear,
Soaring with Argent Plumes, to settle here;
A virdant Olive branch, he bears t'express,
The Emblem of soft Union, Love and Peace;
The joyful Natives all with general Joy,
That for their Country's Aid, their Force employ,
Resolve to banish Discord, with a *Vive le Roy.*

The

The Singers *Defence;* A POEM.

The Author answers his Friend, who blames him for not Singing when desir'd: He contradicts the Third Satyr of HORACE, *beginning with* Omnibus hoc vitium est Cantoribus, *&c. He defends* TIGELLIUS, *and proves that* HORACE *had no actual Skill in Vocal* MUSICK.

IF this strange Vice in all good Singers were,
   As the admir'd *Horace* does declare ;
That if, *when ask'd* tho' blest with Health and Ease,*
Their choicest Friends, they still deny to Please:
And yet unask'd, will rudely Sing so long,
To tire each Friend, with each repeated Song:
I strongly then, should take his Satyr's part,
Lash the Performers, and despise their Art ;
But having studied long enough to be
A small Proficient in that Faculty :
I found, when I that rigid Version met,
'Twas more from Prejudice, than Judgment writ ;
And *Horace* was in his Reproof more free,
Because *Tigellius* was his Enemy :
Whose frequent Vices caus'd that fierce Assault,
And all the rest are lash'd for one Man's fault ;
   Satyr should never take from Malice Aid,
For, with due Reverence to *Horace* paid ;
Who rails at Faults, through Pers'nal Prejudice,
Shews more his own, than shame another's Vice :
   Tigellius, as his Character is plain,
Was of a Humour most absurd and vain,
Fantastick in his Garb, unsettled in his Brain :
And if (as once great *Cæsar* he deny'd)
When ask'd to Sing, 'twere the effect of Pride ;

---

* Horace's *own Words.*

Lictors

Lictors and *Fasces* should have bluntly taught
The Fool to know th' Obedience, that he ought :
But if *Augustus*, his Commands did lay,
When the Genius was not able to Obey ;
As oft with Singers it will happen so,
According as their Joys or Troubles grow ;
'Twas no Offence then to excuse his Art,
The Soul untun'd, makes Discord in each part :
And Monarchs can no more give Vocal Breath,
Than they can hinder when Fate Summons Death.
   A Pleasure lov'd by one, is lik'd by more,
Suppose Sir, I have Sung too much before ;
Made my self Hoarse, and even rack'd my Throat,
To please some Friend, with some fine Treble Note :
Chance does me then to you and others bring,
The second Compliment is—Pray Sir, Sing ;
I swear I can't, then Angry you retort,
All you good Singers are so hard to court :
To make Excuse, then modestly I tell
How hoarse I am, with what that Day befel ;
Yet all's in vain, you rail, I'm thought a Clown,
And (*Omnibus hoc vitium*) knocks me down :
   I often have, (I own) to Sing deny'd,
But not through resty Peevishness, nor Pride ;
But that perhaps I had been tir'd before,
Weary, or Ill, unable to Sing more :
Or that some Hour of Infelicity,
Had robb'd my Soul of usual Harmony ;
Yet all's the same, th' old Saw is still repeated,
You Singers, long to be so much Intreated :
Tho' at that time, to me no Joy could fall
Greater, than not to have been ask'd at all ;
   Th' Harmonious Soul, must have it's Humour free,
Consent of parts still crowns the Harmony :
We read the *Jewish* Captives could not Sing,
In a strange Land rul'd by a Foreign King ;
Contentment, the melodious Chord controuls,
And Tunes the *Diapazon* of our Souls :
What makes a Cobler chirp a pleasant Part,

At

At his hard Labour, but a merry Heart;
He Sings when ask'd, or bluntly else denys,
According to his share of Grief or Joys;
Thus the same Accidents to us befal,
And that which Tun'd the Cobler, tunes us all:
But if against our Will, we thrash out Songs,
For Singing then, is thrashing to the Lungs,
The blast of Airy Praise we dearer get,
Than Peasants do their Bread with toyl and sweat:
To Sleep at your command, is the same thing,
As when being Tir'd, or vex'd in Mind, to Sing:
And tho' Performance, ne'er so easie shew,
As it has Charms, it has Vexations too,
And the Singer's plague, 'tis none but Singers know.
How often have I heard th' unskilful say,
Had I a Voice, by Heaven I'd Sing all Day;
But with that Genius, had he been Endow'd,
And were to Sing when ask'd, or be thought Proud:
When weary, vex'd, or Ill, not to deny,
But at all Seasons, with all Friends comply,
He'd then blame *Horace*, full as much as I:
Whose want of Knowledge in the Vocal Art,
Made him lash all, for one Man's mean desert;
For had he the Fatigue of Singers known,
And judg'd their Inconvenience by his own;
Tigellius only had Correction met,
And *Omnibus hoc vitium* ne'er been writ.

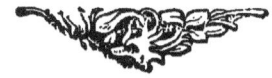

VERSES

Made in Honour of, and most humbly address'd to her Grace the DUTCHESS *of* SOMERSET, *as a grateful Acknowledgment of the Favour she did me to Her Majesty.*

AS when some mighty Monarch born to sway,
   Ready to fix his Coronation Day ;
Renown'd by Fame a Diamond has got,
Through distant Climes with Care and hazard brought :
Whilst skilful Artists all with Wonder gaze,
Sets it in his Imperial Crown to blaze ;
Which on the Day of Pomp he means to wear,
The Greatest, Noblest, and the Brightest there :
So Madam, shining in your Lofty place,
Replete with dazling Vertues is your Grace ;
So gaind our Soveraign *ANN*, the Jewel rare,
Which having purchas'd, she resolv'd to wear :
And in her Heart, as t'other in the Crown,
Inclose a Temper found so like her own ;
Grooms of the Stole, my Eyes have seen before,
But blind with Wealth, or else disguis'd with Pow'r :
Whose Opticks rais'd, nought but the Stars could see,
Too far aspiring to look down on me ;
But you, whose Clemency still cleers your sight,
Could know your Suppliant, even in shades of Night :
And in few Hours a noble Action do,
That might whole Years have tir'd me to pursue ;
Sacred Humility the Learn'd confess,
Beyond all Jems in a great Lay's Dress :
Small Merit Self-opinion still does guide,
The truly Great, are ever free from Pride ;
This last your Grace's Character is known,
Long may you Live then to exalt Renown :
From loud Applause, to reap your Yearly due,
You, in the Gracious Soveraign blest, the Soveraign
    blest in you.

Strat-

STRATFIELDSEA;

Or the CANAAN *of* HAMPSHIRE, *a* POEM: *Humbly addressd to the highly Honoured and worthy* GEORGE PITT, *Esq; and his good* LADY.

AS when repentant *Israel* once distrest,
    Reliev'd by a peculiar Grace from Heaven,
Was far beyond the Neighb'ring Nations blest,
    When *Canaan* was the happy Portion given.

Who through long tedious Years of toyl and care,
    Tho' toyl th' effect of erring Duty was;
At last, by Providence, was brought to share
    The darling Pleasures of that Blessed place.

The gay enamell'd Fields were gladly seen,
    Where plenteous Crops in fruitful Acres grow;
And lofty Trees were flourishing and Green,
    Where Fruit abounds, and chrystal Rivers flow.

So when the Genius of the *British* Land,
    First in our *Hampshire* Interest did appear;
It seem'd as Magisterial to Command,
    That *Stratfieldsea* should be the *Canaan* here.

On you, most worthy Sir, the Lot was thrown,
    A Guerdon for the Vertuous and the brave;
And in Felicity still equal known,
    With that blest Land that Milk and Honey gave.

Delicious Seat that treats the wond'ring Eye,
    With all that Nature for Delight can give;
And when Art therefore would new Methods try,
    Not Worthy, seems nor willing to receive.

The Park, that fam'd *Elizium* imitates,
    With spacious Arms expanding to your view;
As Heir to th' old brisk Fancy here creats,
    The beautiful resemblance of a New.

                          Here

Here happy herds of Dear we feasting see,
  That pass in joyful Peace succeeding Days;
Emblems of Innocence and Amity,
  All inwardly their great Creator praise.

Their Benefactor too that comes to view,
  They seem to bless with large uplifted Eyes;
No turns of State, or War, their fears renew,
  Nor sting of Conscience sprung from mortal Vice.

But well contented with what each enjoys,
  They waste the Year in that delightful place;
And now let the Viator turn his Eyes,
  And varying Pleasure, on the Garden gaze.

Here Nature's *Cornucopia* open shews,
  Repleat with Flowers and Fruits, for use of Man,
Here too a chrystal River sweetly flows,
  Just so through Paradise *Euphrates* ran.

The wanton Fish their choice Delights pursue,
  Themselves affording what all Sports excel;
From the cleer Stream uprais'd the Dome they view,
  Where second *Jacob* and *Rebecca* dwell.

Forgive me, Madam, if my grateful Soul,
  In worth applauding Rhimes, is here exprest;
Or tell my honour'd Patron 'mongst the whole
  Of his excelling Comforts, you are best.

Your Soul, where Vertue and Discretion joyn,
  Appearing still in both serenely great,
Thus makes in him the Joys of Life divine,
  And gives Perfection to the Wedlock state.

The beauteous Offspring too, that grace your Board,
  Like charming *Cupids* in a painted Heaven;
Amongst the rest Addition large affords,
  To all the Blessings plentifully given.

Oh

348   *Poems on several Occasions.*

Oh Happiness! too great for Verse to shew,
  And only in the joyful Parents breast;
Whose innate Comforts do from Nature flow,
  And from no artful Pen can be exprest.

Live then 'till Time grow old, as well as you,
  Whilst choice of Happiness each Year renews;
And whilst I Sing in tuneful Verse your due,
  Accept my Duty, and forgive my *Muse.*

A PROLOGUE,

For the first Part of DON QUIXOTE :
Spoken by Mr. BETTERTON.

IN hopes the Coming Scenes your Mirth will raise,
  To you, the Just Pretenders to the Bays,
The Poet humbly thus a Reverence pays.
And you, the Contraries, that hate the Pains,
Of Labour'd Sence, or of Improving Brains:
That feel the Lashes in a well-writ Play,
He bids perk up and smile, the Satyr sleeps to Day.
Our *Sancho* bears no Rods to make ye smart,
Proverbs, and merry Jokes, are all his Part.
The Modish Spark may Paint, and lie in Paste,
Wear a huge Steinkirk twisted to his Waste,
And not see here, how Foppish he is Dress'd.
The Country Captain, that to Town does come,
From his Militia Troop, and Spouse at home,
To beat a *London* Doxy's Kettle-Drum :
One, who not only th' whole Pit can prove,
That she for Brass Half-crown has barter'd Love,
But the Eighteen-penny Whore-masters above :
With his Broad Gold may treat his Pliant Dear,
Without being shown a Bubbled Coxcomb here.
                                                    Grave

Grave Dons of Bus'ness may be *Bulker's* Cullies,
And Crop-ear'd Prentices set up for Bullies,
And not one Horse-whip Lash here, flog their Follies;
Nay, our hot Blades, whose Honour was so small,
They'd not bear Arms, because not Col'nels all:
That wish the *French* may have a mighty Slaughter,
But wish it safely——On this side o'th' Water.
Yet when the King returns, are all prepar'd,
To beg Commissions in the Standing-Guard;
Even these, the Sons of Shame and Cowardice,
Will 'scape us now, tho' 'tis a cursed Vice.
Our Author has a famous Story chose,
Whose Comick Theme no Person does expose,
But the Knights-Errant; and pray where are those?
There was an Age, when Knights with Launce and
· Shield,
Would Right a Lady's Honour in the Field:
To punish Ravishers, to Death would run,
But those Romantick Days——Alas, are gone,
Some of our Knights now, rather would make one,
Who finding a young Virgin, by Disaster,
Ty'd to a Tree, would rather tie her faster.
Yet these must 'scape too, so indeed must all,
Court-Cuckold-makers now no Jest does maul,
Nor the horn'd Herd within yon City Wall.
The Orange-Miss, that here Cajoles the Duke,
May sell her Rotten Ware without rebuke.
The young Coquet, whose Cheats few Fools can dive at,
May Trade, and th' Old Tope Kniperkin in private;
The Atheist too, on Laws Divine may Trample,
And the Plump Jolly Priest get Drunk, for Church-Example.

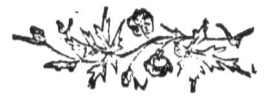

An

An EPILOGUE
To the first Part of DON QUIXOTE. By SANCHO, *Riding upon his Ass.*

'MONGST our Fore-fathers, that pure Wit profest,
There's an old Proverb, *That two Heads are best.*
Dapple and I have therefore jogg'd this way,
Through sheer good Nature, to defend this Play:
Tho' I've no Friends, yet he (as proof may shew)
May have Relations here for ought I know.
For in a Crowd, where various Heads are addle,
May many an Ass be, that ne'er wore a Saddle.
'Tis then for him that I this Speech intend,
Because I know he is the Poet's Friend;
And, as 'tis said, a parlous Ass once spoke,
When Crab-tree Cudgel did his Rage provoke;
So if ye are not civil, 'dsbud, I fear,
He'll speak again——
And tell the Ladies every *Dapple* here.
Take good Advice then, and with kindness win him,
Tho' he looks simply, you don't know what's in him:
He has shrewd Parts, and proper for his Place,
And yet no Plotter, you may see by's Face;
He tells no Lyes, nor does Sedition vent,
Nor ever Brays against the Government.
Then for his Garb he's like the *Spanish* Nation,
Still the old Mode, he never changes Fashion;
His sober Carriage too you've seen to Day,
But for's Religion, troth, I cannot say
Whether for *Mason, Burgis, Muggleton,*
The House with Steeple, or the House with none:
I rather think he's of your Pagan Crew,
For he ne'er goes to Church no more than you.
Some that would, by his Looks, guess his Opinion,
Say, he's a *Papish;* others, a *Socinian,*
But I believe him, if the Truth were known,
As th' rest of the Town-Asses are, of none;
          But

But for some other Gifts : Mind what'I say,
Never compare, each *Dapple* has his Day,
Nor anger him, but kindly use this Play :
For should you with him, conceal'd Parts disclose,
Lord ! how like Ninnies would look all the *Beaus*.

A PROLOGUE,
To the Massacre of PARIS: For Mr. BETTERTON.

BRAVE is that Poet that dares draw his Pen,
To expose the nauseous Crimes of guilty Men,
As once did our Immortal Patron, *Ben*.
And Wise are they that can with Patience bear,
And just Reflections moderately hear,
Unmov'd by Passion, as unsway'd by Fear :
These we present a Tragick piece to Night,
That has some Years been banish'd from the Light ;
Hush'd and imprison'd close, as in the *Tower*,
Half press'd to Death by a dispensing Power:
Rome's Friend, no doubt, suppos'd there might be
    shown,
Just such an Entertainment of their own,
The Plot, the Protestants, the Stage, the Town :
But no such Fears our *Hugenots* alarm'd,
True *English* Hearts are always better Arm'd ;
For if the Valiant in a little Town,
Batter'd and starving their brave Cause, durst own,
And now to take a Tryal for it's fact,
Is just come out by th' *Habeas Corpus* Act.
If Peasants scorning Death can guard their Walls,
And the mild Priesthood, turn to Generals ;
Britains look up, and this blest Country see,
In spite of byass'd Law serene and free,
Cleer'd from it's choaking Foggs of *Popery*.
No Massacres or Revolutions fear,
Affairs are strangely alter'd in one Year :

Lord

Lord what a Hurry was there here one Night,
The *Irish* come, they Burn, they're now in sight;
A city Taylor swore, with Fear grown Wild,
He saw a huge Tall *Teague* devour a Child;
We have no *Nuncio* in our Councils now,
Nor pamper'd *Jesuites* with our Heifers Plough:
Infallibility himself does run,
The Garden's Weeded, and the Moles are gone;
The barbarous *French* too that *Thuanus* quotes,
Of old so diligent in cutting Throats:
Which as Example to Posterity,
To Night you'll here this dreadful Mirrour see,
Must be remember'd in their Progeny:
A spurious Race now on our Seas are steering,
And beat us by the way of Buccaneering;
Not Gold to Lawyers, to th' Ambitious Power,
Not lusty *Switzer* to a lustful Whore:
To Gamesters Luck, to Beauty length of Days,
Nor to a wrincled wither'd Widow Praise;
Could give such Joy as to our Country-men,
To see great *Orange* seize his own again:
This glorious Chace, no doubt, you'll all pursue,
Mean while our Author begs a Favour too;
You that his Merit and Distress have known,
To guard him from the Criticks of the Town:
That this will be the *Poet's* Prophecy,
The *Poets* all were Voters formerly;
To incourage then give ours to Night his due,
His Tale is somewhat Bloody, but 'tis true,
A moral Truth shown to an honest End,
And can the Good or Wise of neither Sect offend:
Fancy and Stile far as the rest excel,
In our deliverance Year let no Tongue tell,
Poets the only Curst, on whom no *Manna* fell.
Plead therefore that they may by *Cæsar's* influence breath,
And mix a Lawrel with his Oaken Wreath;
So shall his Glory flourish to the height,
Then every Pen in leaves of Brass shall write:

This

This, this was he, that blest by sacred Power,
To England its Religion did Restore,
So firm, that *Rome* could never hurt it more.

An EPILOGUE.

For CRAB *and* GILLIAN: *In one of my Comedies.*

Crab. Come Spouse, to talk in Mode now like the Great,
We'll pack up Stuff, and home to our Estate:
But First, before we come to *Taunton* Steeple,
Prithee let's have one word, with these good People;
Thou know'st we've promis'd to befriend the Play,
Gill. Well, what of that, what would you have me say?
Crab. Why? set thy Face, and thy best Curchy make,
And then desire the Wits here for thy sake,
To spare the *Poet*, that his Whim may take.
Gill. Who I, Lord, Lord, d'ye think they'll do't for me,
No, no, dan't think zo Man,
Crab. Why not for thee? thou art a Woman;
Thou'rt of a Kind, that ne'er can fail to Please,
Gill. No zure, I am not vine enough for these:
My Vace is tann'd, and I've no White nor Red,
Nor e'er a ruffled Cap upon my Head;
I'm a loyn of Mutton plainly dress'd,
And these nice volk, love all their Mutton lac'd.
Besides yon Gentlewomen* that sit by,
That gave their twanking Cuffs on to, to vly,
Can do the Business better much than I.
Let them speak first,
Crab. Odrabit it, they Pay,
And all are Benefactors to the Play:

---

* *Pointing to some at the Play.*

No, we must do't, come, here's my Cap off taken,
Gill. My Curchy then as well as che can make one;
Crab. Be pleas'd good Sirs to praise what makes ye laugh?
Gill. And chear the *Poet* with a Smile and half
Crab. Crab then at Home with Stout shall make ye merry,
Gill. And *Gillian* bid ye welcome to her Dairy;
Crab. I'll grubble all my Jokes up to Delight ye,
Gill. And I'll divert ye with my Hoyty toyty;
With Fortune's choicest Blessings may regale ye,
And Wealth, and Wine, and Women, never fail ye.

A PROLOGUE.
To my Play, the French Coquet.

AS in Intrigues of Love we find it true,
Stale Faces pall, whilst we are charm'd with new
Our *Poet* thinking tho' some in Wit prevails,
Fearing to tire ye with more *English* Tales,
Has laid his Scene in the *French* Court *Versailes:*
Thus chang'd your Diet for Variety,
From Cheese and Butter of our dull degree,
To fragrant *Angelote,* and *cher fromage de Brie:*
He doubts not, many that sit here to Day,
That have observ'd the Title to his Play,
Suppose it for some Politick Essay.
'Gainst that he says a Proverb gives him Rules,
'Tis never safe to meddle with edg'd Tools;
For Railery, a Comick Theam is best,
War's but a Dull Occasion for a Jest:
And as in Cudgel Play, there comes no Joke,
From either Party when both Heads are broke;
But then perhaps it may expected be,
That he should fall upon *French* Foppery;
'Tis true, they have Fools, egad, and so have we.

In

In Apish Modes they naturally shine,
Which we Ape after them to make us fine,
The late Blue Feather was charmant divine;
Next then the slouching Sledo, and our huge Button,
And now our Coats, flanck broad, like Shoulder Mutton:
Fac'd with fine Colours, Scarlet, Green and Sky,
With Sleeves so large, they'll give us Wings to Fly;
Next Year I hope they'll cover Nails and all,
And every Button like a Tennis-Ball:
Nor on their Industry can he here reflect,
Cause, to our own there must be some respect,
Our Ills come by Misfortune, not Neglect;
And that they outwit us, we will ne'er agree,
Tho' they have damn'd Luck with our Ships at Sea:
How shall the Satyr then his Venom shed,
Their Heads are full of Air, and ours are full of Lead;
Their hot Brains make 'em swear in *Ela's* somes,
We in dull *Gamut* roar out Blood and Worms:
They to grow cool, from Herbs still seek Relief,
We to grow Hot, deboash our selves in Beef;
And for the Bone, when we to Battle run,
Priests of both kinds ne'er fail to Hiss us on:
To Trim the Matter, and use a Mean,
Our cautious Author in each coming Scene,
Resolv'd to baulk both sides, has us'd to Day,
No Plot, but Love Intrigues quite through his Play,
Yet that 'tis Good, I dare be bold to say:
The *Jacks* are fierce, and *Williamites* are flesh'd,
The *Poets* not so bold, but may be dash'd,
Wit has no Armour proof, 'gainst being thrash'd;
Therefore in Terror of the Warriours Trade,
Suspends all Satyr 'till the Peace me made.

An EPILOGUE.

AMONGST all Characters nearest Divine,
You that are Witty-men, should cry up mine;
And of all Bargains that are daily driven,
Ours is the most ingaging under Heaven:
Whose Souls in a Seraphick station move,
As all must do who Marry, Love for Love.
Sir *Sampson* here, a strange Old sordid Sot,
Meaning by Candle Inch to buy my Lot,
Would settle on me, Oh! the Lord knows what;
He for a Purchase the old way takes Care,
And like a Higler in a Country Fair
Bawls out aloud, take Money for your Mare:
Or Brother like Stockjobbing cheat would make,
My Friend so much you give, so much you take;
But *Valentine*, whose Person, Wit and Art,
Pleads fairer Title to a tender Heart;
With an endearing Claim, fine Words address,
A Graceful Person, and a taking Face:
A solid Judgment that can stand the test,
Trick humour gay——I fancy'd all the rest;
Compell'd my Love—The Passion strong did grow,
Whither all this, a Woman's Heart should bow,
Your Pardon Ladies, I am sure you know:
Besides by Subtilty I Tryal made,
Found out his Haunts, and Snares each way I laid;
Mark'd, tho' the frolick Widows——City Dames,
Inmates of *Leicester-field*, *Pall-Mall*, St. *James:*
The Tall, the Short the Freckl'd—Fair and Brown,
The straight-lac'd Maiden, and the Miss o'th' Town;
We're sure to work on in Adversity,
Yet still what Stock he had was kept for me:
And for such Love, if we should Love alow,
Your Pardon Ladies, I am sure you know;
I took Compassion on the Bankrupt Debtor,
He had no Money, But had something better:
Faith like a generous Girl, I paid his worth,
For I had Honour in me from my Birth;

I

I paid him well——A Wife that's Fair and Young,
Discreet and Kind, and Forty Thousand strong:
Is no bad Consolation sure——In Life.
How would some snigger here, for such a Wife;
Then if this part I Play be rare or no?
Your Pardon Gentlemen——You likewise know:
The Author of the Scenes appear to Day,
Draws every Figure justly through his Play;
Mind, Sence and generous Humour, seems to hit, }
Let Beauty grant him then superior Wit, }
Since by the Boxes it was chose and Writ. }

VERSES *Congratulatory*
To the Honourable William BROMLEY, *Esq.*

AS when *Hiperion* with Victorious Light,
Expels invading Powers of gloomy Night;
And vernal Nature youthful drest and gay,
Salutes the Conqueror that forms the Day:
The mounting Lark exalts her joyful Note,
And strains with Harmony her warbling Throat;
So now my *Muse* that hopes to see the Day, }
When clowdy Faction that does *Britain* sway, }
Shall be o'ercome by Reasons peircing Ray: }
Applauding Senates for their prudent choice,
The Will of Heaven, by the Peoples Voice;
First greets ye Sir, then gladly does prepare,
In tuneful Verse, your welcome to the Chair.
 Awful th' Assembly is, August the Queen,
In whose each Day of Life, are Wonders seen;
The Nation too, this greatest of all Years,
Who watch to see blest turns in their Affairs:
Slighting the *Hydra* on the *Gallick* shore,
Hope from the Senate much, but from you more;
Whose happy Temper Judgment cultivates,
And forms so fit to Aid our three Estates.

The

The change of Ministry late order'd here,
Was fated sure for this Auspicious Year;
That you Predestin'd at a glorious hour,
To be chief Judge of Legislative Power:
Might by your Skill that Royal right asserts,
Like Heaven reconcile the Jarring parts;
Nor shines your Influence Sir, here alone,
The Church must your unequal'd Prudence own,
Firm to support the Cause, but rough to none:
Eusebia's Sons in Law divine profest,
May learn from you, how Truth should be exprest;
Whither in Modest Terms, like Balm, to heal,
Or raving Notions falsly counted Zeal.
Oh sacred Gift in vulgar matters great,
But in Religious Tracts divinely sweet;
Which ancient *Bagington* can witness well,
And the rich Library before it fell:
Your Rural Hours amongst wise Authors past,
Your Soul with their unvalued Wealth possest;
And well may he to heights of Knowledge come,
Who learning *Pantheon*, always kept at home:
Thus once Sir you were blest, and sure the Fiend,
That first Intail'd a Curse on humankind;
A second Time a dire unequall'd Cross,
Design'd the Publick, by your private loss:
Oh who had seen that love to learning bore,
The Matchless Authors of the Days of Yore,
The Fathers, Prelates, Poets, Books where Arts
Renown'd, Explain'd the Men of rarest Parts:
Shrink'd up their shrivell'd Bindings, scorch their Names,
And yield Immortal worth to Temporary Flames:
That would not Sigh to see the Ruins there,
Or wish to quench them with a falling Tear:
   But as in Story where we Wonders view,
As there were Flames, there was a Phænix too;
An Excellence from the burnt Pile did rise,
That still atton'd for past Calamities:
So my Prophetick Genius—In its height,
Viewing your Merit, Sir, foretels your Fate;

Your

Poems on several Occasions. 359

Your valiant Ancestor that bravely fought,
And from the Foe, the Royal Standard got,
Which nobly now Adorns, your houshould Coat:
Denotes the Ancient Grandeur of you Race,
As present Worth, fits you for present Grace.
The Soveraign must Esteem, what all admire,
Bromley shall rise, and *Bagington* aspire.
Fate oft contrives Magnificence by Fire.

To his Grace the Duke of Bedford.
VERSES *Congratulatory, on the Birth of his Son the* Marquess *of* TAVISTOKE.

IN sweet Retirement, freed from anxious Care,
  From Court Delusions and the noisy War;
From business that disturb the tranquil State,
And palls the best Contentment of the Great:
From Town Disorders, and infectious Wine,
From Libertines who live by base Design;
Wisely your Grace, and worthy of best Praise,
Has chose to Consecrate your happy Days:
Oh lucky change, a Blessing only due,
By Heavens peculiar bounty, to a Few.
  Here in Ambrosial Bowers you entertain,
With varied Joys, the Body, and the Brain;
Sweet Contemplation gains the foremost place
Whilst Books Instructively do Science raise:
Sports too, for Relaxation of the Mind,
The Seasons fit, are proper in their kind;
Nor is the Blessing only on your part,
But shar'd by her, that wholly shares your Heart:
Your vertuous Consort of Elizium Dreams,
Here, Pregnant with Conubial love, she Teems;
And, that Concording Comfort may not fail,
T'inlarge your noble Race, brings forth a Male:
                                              Thus

Thus has Eternal Providence decreed,
To grant the only Blessing you could need.
　Take it my Lord, as 'tis divinely meant,
A Gift peculiar from Heaven sent;
A Sanction to promote your Happiness,
And crown your Solitude with lasting Bliss:
To please a Parent, Plants may kindly shoot,
But Children are the Quintiscential Fruit;
The charming Prattle, and the Tales they tell,
By Nature taught, all Musick far excel.
　May then, th' Illustrious Babe with speedy growth.
Stretch out his Infancy, and hast to Youth;
From Youth to Manhood, may his Years improve, ⎫
Blest with a Father's Joy, a Mother's Love, ⎬
And sacred Gifts descending from above. ⎭
Th' Eternal in your Favour does bestow,
A Comfort glittering Courts, but seldom know;
A quiet Life, from Proud Ambition free,
An Heir too, to support your Family:
Sent to Exalt, and make your Pleasures great,
In the calm *Halcyon* Days of your retreat.
　So in the *Roman* State, when Civil War,
Harrass'd the Natives, by Intestine Jarr;
When rage in Triumph rode through every Street,
And he whose Arm was strongest, had most Wit:
The noble * *Atticus* in Rural Bowers,
Past with selected Friends, and Books, his Hours;
Sometimes his beauteous Spouse too, would improve,
The Day, with Tales of Constancy and Love:
But yet no Males could bring, 'till *Juno* prone ⎫
To pity, summ'd at last all Joys in one, ⎬
Heard her devoted Prayers, ⎪
　　　　　　　And blest her with a Son. ⎭

---

* *Pomponius Atticus.*

FINIS.

www.ingramcontent.com/pod-product-compliance
Lightning Source LLC
Chambersburg PA
CBHW020305240426
43673CB00039B/704